Teaching Practice:
Problems and Perspectives

19 |7 .

Teaching Practice: Problems and Perspectives

A reappraisal of the practical professional element in teacher preparation

E. STONES & S. MORRIS

METHUEN & CO LTD
11 New Fetter Lane, London EC4

First published 1972 by Methuen & Co Ltd
11 New Fetter Lane, London EC4
© 1972 E. Stones and S. Morris
Printed in Great Britain by
Richard Clay (The Chaucer Press), Ltd,
Bungay, Suffolk

SBN (hardbound) 416 61120 6
SBN (paperback) 416 61140 0

Distributed in the U.S.A. by
HARPER & ROW PUBLISHERS INC.
BARNES & NOBLE IMPORT DIVISION

Contents

Acknowledgements

The authors and publishers wish to thank the following for permission to reprint the articles collected in Part 3 of this volume:

Rand McNally & Company for 'Model the master teacher or master the teaching model' by L. M. Stolurow; *The Journal of Teacher Education* for 'A conceptual model of instruction' by B. Strasser; the American Association of Colleges for Teacher Education for 'Teaching strategies for cognitive growth' by J. R. Verduin, and 'An approach to systematic training' by B. O. Smith; Addison-Wesley Publishing Company for 'Interaction analysis: recent developments' by E. Amidon and E. Hunter; *Theory Into Practice* and the authors for 'Microteaching' by D. W. Allen and A. W. Eve, and 'The model in use (microteaching)' by D. B. Young and D. A. Young; *Education* for 'The minicourse: a new tool for the education of teachers' by W. R. Borg, P. Langer and M. L. Kelley; the Office of Laboratory Experiences, College of Education, University of Maryland, for 'The teacher education centre: a unified approach to teacher education', edited by J. F. Collins; Stanford University for the Stanford Teacher Competence Appraisal Guide by the School of Education, Stanford University.

Permission from Paul S. Amidon & Associates Inc. to reprint the list of categories of verbal behaviour from *The Role of the Teacher in the Classroom* by E. J. Amidon and N. A. Flanders is also gratefully acknowledged.

Preface

This book tries to bring together information about some of the current new developments which are calling into question the fundamental assumptions of traditional methods of organizing teaching practice. We hope that supervisors will find the information useful and convincing enough to encourage them to scrutinize their current methods in the light of the very ample evidence which suggests that this scrutiny is long overdue. We believe that students will find in the book ideas and information about new approaches which will help them to understand the nature and function of professional practical work. We do not suggest that all we say is new, our major aim is making accessible what is scattered or in the process of development. We believe that any dispassionate survey of the field cannot help but persuade the investigator that something needs to be done. It persuaded us. That is why we wrote this book.

The plan of the book is as follows. Part 1 discusses the problems connected with current approaches to practical teaching as they are found in most teacher education institutions in Great Britain. Part 2 deals with some of the most promising innovations in the field and makes some suggestions for future lines of development. Part 3 brings together a selection of papers relating to the various themes discussed in Parts 1 and 2.

Additional note: The James report was published just as this book was going to press. We note with pleasure that it puts forward suggestions on teaching practice in line with some of our proposals and with those which we and a group of colleagues from colleges submitted in evidence to the James Committee. We feel, however, that the proposed arrangements for the second cycle provide for too short a time in the study of the theory and practice of education in the systematic way that we suggest. Nevertheless, the reader in search of further information about the suggestions made in the report should find it in sufficient detail to enable him to see their application to his own situation whether as teacher or learner.

Preface

Part 1 · Problems

1 · Concepts, approaches, objectives

SITTING WITH NELLIE

The underlying principles of current practices of student teaching are probably of extremely ancient lineage. Bruner (1966) discusses the way in which bushmen pass on adult skills to their children. There is very little explicit teaching, what the child knows he learns from direct imitative interaction with the adult community. These primitive practices are not dissimilar to those typifying our current approaches to student teaching. In other fields nearer to our own social situation we have the phenomenon of *Sitting with Nellie*. Nellie is the factory worker who has been doing the job for years to whom new recruits are attached while they learn the job. Sitting with Nellie has long been recognized by industry as an extremely inefficient method of job training and few teachers would consider the instructional methods of the bushmen as particularly efficacious. And yet it is only within the last few years that the approach has been questioned in teacher education. And in fact, at the moment of writing we are aware of several submissions to enquiries into teacher education which are pressing for an *increase* in the amount of time student teachers spend in schools watching other teachers and then trying their own hands as part of their initial training.

We believe that preoccupation with the need for this type of school experience reflects an attitude to the job of the teacher which is grossly at variance with some of the highfalutin language sometimes used about the profession. We profess to value the freedom of the teacher to develop his individual style, to be creative, to enthuse his pupils and, often less explicitly, to teach them some pretty complicated concepts. And yet we treat our aspirant paragons as if they were sitting at an assembly line learning which way to tighten a nut. Plaskow (1969) was justified when he said that it is extravagant and kinky to think that by putting students in schools for days and weeks they will somehow be trained to be teachers.

Kaltsounis and Nelson (1968) in more restrained language argue that the theoretical basis of student teaching is not tested, and that the conviction of academics, educationists, supervising teachers and students that student teaching is the best single factor for preparation to teach is based on legend rather than logic. They argue that our present system of student teaching is a conservative institution. It inspires conformity and tends to penalize innovation so that its products conform to a bureaucratically structured stereotype. Colleges do not encourage student evangelism, instead they dispatch their students to schools with such admonitions as 'Remember you are there to learn', 'Remember the class belongs to Miss So and So', 'Best observe for a week or two before starting'. When the student does get to school bearing in mind that he is a 'guest' and eventually stands in front of a class he is likely to model his behaviour on his memories of the teachers he had when he was a pupil, his college teaching and the example of the teachers he has observed. The teachers who taught him, and the teachers he is now observing, all in their time went through the same system so that all the pressures on the student are in the direction of conforming to the unadventurous stereotype.

But lack of evangelical fervour and innovatory zeal are not the only likely concomitants of present methods, there is a very real possibility that the job is learned ineffectively as well. A small scale study by Popham and Baker (1968) bears on this point. They found that thirteen teachers and thirteen non-teachers, given objectives of instruction and suggestions for pupil learning experiences over a four hour period of instruction in social science research methods, produced comparable learning in the pupils they were teaching. In other words housewives taught as effectively as trained teachers in this situation. Popham (1969) repeated the experiment with twenty-eight teachers and twenty-eight non-teachers of auto mechanics teaching more than 1200 pupils, and sixteen teachers and sixteen non-teachers of electronics teaching over 700 pupils. Again no significant difference was found between the performance of the different groups in the post test that followed the teaching. Popham's main comment on these results was that current teacher training programmes are essentially concerned with the instructional *means* employed by teachers rather than results of instruction. The sobering findings of these researches adumbrate our discussion of the main problems besetting the practical element in teacher education. In a way it is the crux of the problem: how to cope with it is a complex but crucial matter. We hope that some of the material that follows will help.

Industry's persuasion that sitting with Nellie is an inefficient method of training is based on the fact that when Nellie's work methods are examined they are usually found to be wasteful of time and effort. By careful analysis of the components of jobs in a wide variety of work situations it has been possible to devise more economical and more effective methods of operating. By using such job analyses it has been possible to train workers in more efficient methods of work using training schedules based on the analyses. Attempts have in fact been made to analyse the job of teaching, but in view of the tremendous complexity of the task progress has been necessarily slower than in other fields. Progress along these lines has also been impeded by the attitudes of many educationists who have resisted what they consider to be a most inappropriate approach to teacher training. The resistance is clearly expressed in the words of Jeffreys (1961) who declares: 'We think it is more important in training teachers, to produce well-educated people than to produce technically competent practitioners.' The disdain that drips from the last three words is at the root of the problem of providing meaningful practical experience for student teachers. We profoundly disagree with this statement. We deny the either/or implication, and we deny the suggestion that training for competency implies illiberality. We also wonder whether Jeffreys would be satisfied to apply the same criteria to the training of his doctor or dentist.

Morrison and McIntyre (1969) argue convincingly that the attitude expressed by Jeffreys has been responsible for a divorce between the theoretical elements of college courses and the practical work in the classroom. Whereas educational psychology could well be the key discipline to provide the theoretical insights to practical teaching, it has usually been taught as an academic discipline in a similar way to the way it would be taught in a course on general psychology in a university. Morrison and McIntyre also point out that the courses that are often mounted under the heading of *curriculum*, *method* or *professional* courses, and are intended to give the student a basic theoretical background to practical teaching, tend to take the form of a series of practical hints and suggestions which lack unifying concepts but are justified pragmatically.

The general drift of these criticisms of student teaching is reflected in research into the subject over the last decade. In a review of this research Davies (1969) points out that although the practical component in teacher education is considered of key importance it is attracting an increased amount of criticism in its present form. It has been considered largely ceremonial in its functions; its behavioural objectives, it is alleged, are seldom identified, and evaluation is suspect. The American National Council for Accreditation of Teacher Education in 1960 saw teaching practice as 'entangled in a mass of confusion, unmade decisions, and experiences . . . without a comprehensive definition and clear-cut statement of goals and purposes. . . .'

Davies's review, like the other critiques referred to earlier, also includes brief reference to developments that open up the possibility of a new approach to practice akin to the job analyses in industry which have to a great extent replaced sitting with Nellie as a method of training.

In the pages that follow we discuss developments in the analysis of teaching which should be of help to tutors wishing to help Nellie on her way.

The concept of teaching practice

Until quite recently the term *teaching practice* has been accepted almost universally and uncritically by all concerned with the preparation of teachers and its use has embraced all the learning experiences of student teachers in schools. The concept has been handed down from the earliest days of the development of training colleges in this country; it seemed such a 'commonsense' concept, completely accepted by the teachers, the college tutors and the students. Yet from the very earliest years of the training colleges there was tension between schools and colleges and this tension has centred on teaching practice. Students, while frequently preferring teaching practice to other elements of the college course, have yet been critical of their experiences in schools. The blame has often been put on the organization of the practice or on the attitudes of the participants. But the concept itself was rarely questioned. We now wish to question this concept since it appears to be both anachronistic and ambiguous.

AN ANACHRONISTIC CONCEPT

Historically the concept was based on craft apprenticeship. The pupil-teacher movement had at its core the initiation of the apprentice into the mysteries of the craft by processes of telling, demonstrating and imitating. The *master* teacher told the students what to do, showed them how to do it and the students imitated the master. This process depended for its success on certain prior conditions: the existence of an established body of subject matter, rules of thumb to be transmitted and the acceptance of the authority of the master by the student.

These conditions continued to hold good during the first decades of the present century. After the Second World War, however, the bases for their continued existence have been steadily undermined. The accepted body of knowledge appropriate for schools has been increasingly called into question by curriculum innovators led by Nuffield and Schools Council workers; the traditional teaching skills and techniques have been challenged as being inadequate for the new curricula; the exercise of critical faculties, which college staff were urging as one of the goals of education, has been taken to heart by the students and their willingness to submit to a master teacher's authority and to follow his techniques has been weakened. At the same time, partly as a result of the impact of the newly developing study of philosophy of education, the concept of *education* itself has been widely discussed. The recognition that the terms *education* and *training* denoted differences in aims, content and procedures led to the change in title from training colleges to colleges of education. But changing the name of the colleges did not transmute *teaching practice* into a more rigorous theory based activity. In our view the concept is now inappropriate and in need of reconsideration.

AN AMBIGUOUS CONCEPT

As currently used the term *teaching practice* has three major connotations: the practising of teaching skills and acquisition of the role of a teacher; the whole range of experiences that students go through in schools; and the practical aspects of the course, as distinct from theoretical studies. We presumably have in mind the first when we talk about a student's *teaching practice mark*; the second when we describe a student as being on *teaching practice*; and the third when we urge the need to integrate theory and practice in the education of teachers.

This ambiguity of meaning is not simply a philosophico-linguistic problem; it has practical implications. Which sort of activity do the participants in the practice have in mind on any given occasion? How can they be sure they are each talking about the same thing? When it comes to stating objectives and evaluating their fulfilment, may not serious difficulties arise if the participants have different sorts of activities in mind? In a practical field such as teacher preparation this ambiguity seems intolerable; therefore, as an attempt to resolve this ambiguity we suggest later (pp. 133 ff.) a unitary concept of teaching practice.

Current approaches to teaching practice

MODEL THE MASTER TEACHER

Just as there are diverse interpretations of the concept of teaching practice, so there are, among college tutors, teachers and students, varied approaches to teaching practice. These are subjective, often unconsciously adopted, seldom rigorously argued. The first, and most widely held, is linked to the craft apprenticeship concept mentioned above, referred to by Stolurow (1965) as the *model the master teacher* approach. The *master teacher* is the master craftsman and teaching practice is viewed as a process of initiation in which the master teacher's teaching skills, performance, personality and attitudes are acquired by the student through observation, imitation and practice. The arguments advanced in support of this approach stress its effectiveness, simplicity and commonsense. 'If you want to become an effective teacher, do what the effective teacher does.' Peters, who in general seems to support this approach, argues for it on more sophisticated grounds (Peters 1968). On the basis of an examination of the nature of teaching, he concludes that teaching is a highly personal business. The teacher cannot be expected to adopt and put into operation the findings of research couched in general terms as teaching principles since principles are impersonal. The teacher should model himself on a more skilled exemplar adapting what he sees to his personal use. The arguments against this approach are both theoretical and practical. A master teacher, however versatile, can offer a student only a limited set of skills, attitudes and personality traits. And the selection of skills and techniques is the master teacher's, reflecting the master teacher's values, experiences and personality. The student's values, experiences and personality will be at least marginally, and at most radically different from those of the master teacher. In its extreme form this approach denies the individuality of the student. In a moderate form it encourages the student to copy isolated bits of teaching behaviour, of attitudes and of relationships as being effective. But the effectiveness of these bits of behaviour may well hinge on their being a part of a *total* teaching behaviour; when fragmented and adopted by another, they may be ineffective or even harmful. Further, this approach is only superficially easy to follow. In essence it tells a student to adopt another person's teaching style which probably involves his changing his personality. If a student cannot do this, and the majority cannot, he can make little progress towards effective teaching. The student is advised to change his attitude or modify his personality traits, etc., advice that he does not know how to follow.

A further disadvantage of this approach is that it does not allow the student to go beyond the teaching that is observed. This teaching may be excellent but it is not exhaustively excellent; there will certainly be areas of teaching excellence that are not illustrated by any one master teacher and there may be other, more appropriate ways of doing things than those the master teacher employs. We, personally, have an even greater problem; we don't know what a master teacher looks like. We have some idea what he shouldn't look like but that is a different matter. This problem relates to the question of the identification of teacher effectiveness which we discuss later. Here we merely wish to say that there are no universally accepted criteria to help us to identify master teachers.

There is one further problem in the master teacher approach; there is a practical difficulty of finding sufficient master teachers in the right places to go round. Pedley (1969) calculates that statistically this is feasible; but clearly it will be quite impossible at certain times and in certain areas. An approach to teaching practice that is dependent for success on the chance distribution of master teachers must have serious disadvantages on practical grounds alone.

In sum, the *model the master teacher* approach, which seems to be the approach most widely favoured by teachers, results in a tendency to conservatism and traditionalism and operates against experiment and innovation. Ultimately it stands for imitation rather than analysis, and it puts obstacles in the way of understanding the processes of teaching.

MASTER THE TEACHING MODEL

There is some hope that this understanding may be achieved by students if their practical experience is based on mastering teaching models. The basic stages in developing a teaching model are: first, a theoretical analysis of teaching behaviour which takes into account the objectives of the teaching, the beginning knowledge and skills of the pupils, the processes by which the objectives are to be achieved, the variables likely to interact with these processes, the learning outcomes and feedback to the teacher; second, the building of a conceptual model which will make clear the relationship of these elements; third, the conversion of the model into lesson plans, or a series of plans by the incorporation of specific content and procedures; and fourth, the evaluation of the model in operation for its validity to describe and to predict processes and outcomes.

A number of models have already been elaborated applicable to some of the main areas of teaching and some have been widely tested and validated (Verduin 1967). Stolurow's own teaching model has been used for the development of programmed courses capable, when presented in conjunction with a computer, of providing for individualized learning (Stolurow and Davis 1965). Strasser's conceptual model of teaching was developed under the triple influence of Taba's concepts of the strategies and tactics of teaching, of Flanders's classroom interaction studies and of Smith's analysis of teaching (Strasser 1967, Taba and Elzey 1964, Flanders 1961, Smith 1963). Strasser follows Smith's (1963) approach: 'Everyone knows that the teacher not only influences student (pupil) behaviour but that he is also influenced by student behaviour. The teacher is constantly observing the student and modifying his own behaviour in terms of his observations. We may therefore say that instructional behaviour consists of a chain of three links – observing, diagnosing, acting.' Strasser identifies four aspects of instruction: teacher planning; teacher behaviour initiatory; teacher observation, interpretation and diagnosis of learner behaviour; teacher behaviour influencing/influenced. 'Instruction is regarded as a dynamic and, over a period of time, self-correcting, continually redirected, influenced/influencing interactive process' (Strasser 1967). Strasser's model may be seen on p. 177. Taba's model for teaching strategies for cognitive growth has been embodied in the *Teacher Handbook for Contra Costa Social Studies*. Taba taught student teachers the strategies in ten days using this model (Verduin 1967). Models of classroom interaction based on interaction analysis (discussed later) are now being used both in America and Britain to describe and predict verbal behaviour in the classroom.

The *master the teaching model* approach to practical experience makes possible, and necessary, the integration of theory and practice. This integration becomes not an abstract goal to be achieved only rarely, but a necessary, constant occurrence. Tutors and students together develop models out of their discussions of the theories of teaching and learning; the models are tested in teaching and learning situations and the results are evaluated. This approach necessitates precision and rigour. 'A model is a commitment to a position and can be tested if properly formulated. It is not a loosely assembled, unarticulated set of statements that some theorists can point at with pride in their eclecticism' (Stolurow 1965). Unlike the *model the master teacher* approach, this approach offers practical, usable help to all students irrespective of their personality traits, attitudes and abilities. A model is infinitely variable so that there is no contradiction between a student's following a theoretical model and his developing a personal teaching style.

TEACHING CAUGHT NOT TAUGHT

Akin to the *model the master teacher* approach is the view that it is impossible to teach anyone how to teach. Teaching is an art form akin to poetry or painting. The creative teaching act, like the act of writing poetry or painting a picture, can be facilitated by teaching but cannot, itself, be taught. Teaching ability is largely innate and the *born teacher, the natural*, owes little to training. Teaching performance is described in intuitive terms: the *born teacher knows* the *right* moment for the *right* activity. He is endowed with charismatic authority; the children never question his power; he is a *natural disciplinarian*. Teaching practice is viewed as providing the opportunities to display, recognize and refine the abilities that are latent in the student.

This approach, which depends on unexamined premises and half truths, is inimical to any rational understanding of the theory and practice of teaching and, therefore, to any rational approach to teaching practice. It assumes, in the first place, the existence of a *general teaching ability* operating in all teaching situations. The validity of this assumption is by no means established. On the contrary it seems likely that teaching behaviours are specific and closely related to given sets of conditions such as age, background and ability of children and type of school. A brilliant teacher in one environment may be a mediocre performer in another. In addition, as we have already intimated, *born teachers* are not so easily identifiable. Evidence is given below of the considerable difficulties involved in recognizing with certainty effective teaching (pp. 26 ff.); but here we have a claim of complete certainty. Further, not only is the effective teacher recognizable but his effectiveness is attributed largely to genetic endowment. In the light of the discussion over the last half century on the complexities involved in studying the genetic element in verbal intelligence, it would be a brave man who would maintain the genetic bases of so complex a set of abilities as those involved in teaching. Finally, this naive genetic argument is disproved by experience. Even though present methods of practical preparation of teachers are unsystematic and haphazard, some students, who begin their course with considerable disabilities of voice, stature, fluency and shyness still manage to overcome these disabilities.

TEACHING AS A SCIENCE

A quite contrary approach, and one closely related to the *master the teaching model* approach is adopted by those who regard teaching as a part of the behavioural sciences. Teaching is behaving in a social context and is therefore amenable to scientific observation and analysis. We discuss this at greater length later but here we may point out that teaching behaviour is modifiable by feeding back to the student teacher data about his ongoing behaviour in the classroom and the results of his teaching in terms of the children's behaviour and learning. Desired behaviour in the student, or approximations to it, is rewarded to ensure its persistence, a practice that is explicable with reference to learning theory. Similarly the student teacher's teaching is understandable and controllable only in terms of theories of teaching. Without a coherent theory of teaching, to which the student's teaching is linked, improvement in teaching is going to be a very haphazard affair.

Over the past twenty years theories of teaching have been proposed, particularly by American workers, embodying observation and analysis of current teaching, the development of conceptual models and feedback from field-testing of the models. As prerequisites for this work, instruments and techniques for the observation of teaching, methods of analysing and interpreting observational data and techniques of using computers for modelling have been developed. In addition a body of technical concepts and terms, a new scientific language relating to theories of teaching, has been elaborated so that discussion could take place without the crippling ambiguities of lay terminology. The five major areas in which contributions have been made to the theory of teaching need only be briefly mentioned here since we deal with the subject at greater length later.

First, educational goals and objectives have received wide attention and study. Empirical data and logical reasoning have led to the drawing up of taxonomies of educational objectives in the cognitive and effective areas (Bloom et al. 1956, Krathwohl et al. 1964). These have led on to the preparation of detailed objectives suitable for classroom fulfilment, and to a methodology for the preparation of objectives suitable for use by practising teachers and students (Mager 1962). In particular Stones (1972) has devised a model for the specification of objectives of general application, which has specific application to teacher preparation. The use of the model is exemplified by specified sets of objectives in educational psychology but a considerable proportion of the objectives produced are seen as having direct application to the classroom and in many cases they could be taken as objectives of practical teaching. Further reference is made to this approach later. Second, the teacher's and pupil's verbal behaviour in the classroom has been observed and analysed in considerable detail. The interaction between the teacher's and pupil's verbal behaviour has been studied and this behaviour has been related to the pupil's learning (Medley and Mitzel 1963a and 1963b, Bellack et al. 1966, Flanders 1961). Third, techniques and strategies for producing cognitive growth in pupils have been evolved and presented for teachers' use (Taba 1965). Fourth, the important area of classroom and group management has received detailed, empirical study and a body of theoretical and practical knowledge has been amassed which begins to put the problems of *discipline* on a scientific footing (Kounin 1970). Lastly, teachers' personality traits and their relation to both teachers' and pupils' behaviour have been the objects of considerable research (Getzels and Jackson 1963, Ryans 1960a). More recently studies of teachers' conceptions and performance of their roles have added to our knowledge of the ways in which teachers' personality traits, attitudes and values influence classroom climate and pupils' learning (Biddle and Thomas 1966, Walberg 1968, Amidon and Flanders 1967).

There is, then, a growing volume of material available on which to base a scientific approach to teaching. The implications of this for students' practical work are far-reaching. A new study of the goals and objectives of practical work in teacher preparation may now be undertaken and a beginning is made towards such a study in a later chapter. The student's own learning, before, during and after practical work, may now be approached in a scientific, objective fashion. In addition it is possible to conceive of the transformation of the 'mythology of student teaching' based on unscientific and mystical approaches into a scientific rationale of student teaching (Kaltsounis and Nelson 1968).

OBJECTIVES OF TEACHING PRACTICE

It is remarkable that no serious and detailed study of the objectives of teaching practice seems to have been carried out until quite recently. Presumably the objective has been taken as self-evident: 'to practise being a teacher'. This question-begging and largely meaningless statement corresponds to the undifferentiated concept of teaching practice discussed above. However, as the numbers of students have grown and more schools and teachers have become involved in teaching practice, so the weaknesses of the present system have become more apparent and criticism and dissatisfaction have been voiced. Some teachers want to know more precisely what their contribution in teaching practice should be. Some college tutors feel that, while they insist that their students have clear statements of lesson objectives, they themselves are not making clear to the students (and teachers) the objectives of the whole exercise. Some are also influenced, by pressures from various sources, to see a need to state their objectives in behavioural terms. It is particularly important for students to have a clear grasp of the objectives since it is for them primarily that teaching practice is organized and their future depends on their satisfactorily fulfilling the objectives.

THE BRISTOL STUDY

In response to such pressures, two studies of objectives have been recently undertaken, both as parts of larger studies but both undertaken in the awareness of the crucial importance of a study of objectives. In the Bristol study, Brimer and Cope analysed the objectives of teaching practice as perceived by students, staff and teachers in the practice schools of two colleges of education and were able to present a picture of the comparative importance attached to the various objectives by the three groups of participants (Cope 1971).

The first stage of the work consisted of assembling a body of objectives. Cope interviewed 109 teachers (78 primary, 31 secondary) in schools used by the two colleges for teaching practice, 72 students from the two colleges and 34 tutors (15 subject staff, 19 education), and drew from these discussions statements of objectives. She also obtained brief written statements. These were then analysed and grouped under seventeen headings. The next stage was to obtain the ratings by the three groups of the objectives and their ranking in order of importance. For this purpose questionnaires were answered by 109 teachers, 297 students and 71 college staff. The results were as follows:*

* Greater detail and extended discussion of these data are provided in Cope (1971) to which the reader is referred.

Objective	Rank		
	Students	Staff	Teachers
1 *To provide the student with an opportunity of establishing an appropriate teacher–pupil relationship with children.*	1	1	1

a) Students can get to know children as individuals.
b) Students can learn to communicate with children.
c) Students can get to know children in groups and classes.
d) Students can have the experience of working with children.
e) Students can develop with their pupils a reciprocal relationship of respect and liking.
f) Students can develop a working relationship with children of different temperaments and abilities.

Although all ranked this objective 1, in fact staff accorded it more importance than did students (difference significant at 0·01 level) and students more than teachers (sig. at 0·01 level).

2 *To provide the student with an opportunity for theory to be applied in the practical situation and to assist him, where necessary, to make the difficult discrimination between inappropriate theory and the inadequate implementing of sound theory.*	5	2	5

a) Students can try out apparatus based on theoretical approaches.
b) Students can try out ideas which they have evolved in college.
c) Students can attempt to relate theories of learning and child development in the classroom.
d) Students can test out in the school approaches suggested on the college courses.
e) Students can apply in the classroom the methodology of teaching basic skills and certain subject areas.
f) Students can relate their reading in education to what happens in the schools.

All differences significant at 0·05 level.

Objective	Rank		
	Students	Staff	Teachers
3 *To provide an opportunity for evaluating the student's potential as a teacher and suitability for the teaching profession.*	6	5	2

a) Students can discover if they experience satisfaction from teaching.

b) Students can find out if they are happy being with children.

c) Students can find out if they enjoy being in the school environment.

d) Students can find out if they are capable of promoting successful learning activities with pupils.

e) College and school staff can detect students unsuited to the teaching profession.

f) School and college staff can assess the students' potential as teachers and assign grades.

Difference students/staff significant at 0·05 level, other differences at 0·01 level.

---

4 *To provide the student with an experience of success in the teaching situation so that he acquires confidence.*	2	3	4

a) Students are enabled to gain confidence from perceiving evidence of learning by pupils.

b) Students are enabled to gain confidence from their satisfactory handling of school routine.

c) Students are enabled to gain confidence from the experience of talking effectively to individuals and a class.

d) Students are enabled to gain confidence from the approval of other adults in a professional situation.

e) Students are enabled to gain confidence from achieving in the classroom an atmosphere appropriate to the task.

f) Students are enabled to gain confidence from the pupils' enjoyment of an experience they have provided.

The significant difference (at 0·01 level) between students and others suggests that students on teaching practice feel insecure and need success.

	Students	Staff	Teachers

5 *To provide an opportunity in the practical teaching situation for the extension and deepening of the student's self-knowledge.*   3   6   7

  a) Students can discover from the intellectual challenge of their pupils the importance of extending their own knowledge.

  b) Students may discover if they sympathize with or are prejudiced against certain children and learn how to deal with their reactions.

  c) Students can learn to cope with the physical demands of teaching.

  d) Students can discover ways of responding to the demands imposed by their own expectations of themselves as teachers.

  e) Students can learn how to modify or utilize habits of voice, gesture or movement revealed in the classroom.

  f) Students can learn to accept responsibility for their actions in the classroom.

Staff/teachers' difference significant at 0·05 level; others at 0·01 level.

6 *To provide the student with practical experience in schools which will reveal some of the problems of discipline and enable him to develop personal methods of control.*   7   8   3

  a) Students can develop the ability to hold the pupils' attention for appropriate periods.

  b) Students can learn to contain the aggressive or destructive impulses of individual children or groups.

  c) Students can try to ensure that noise remains at an appropriate level.

  d) Students can learn to channel the energies of children constructively.

  e) Students can learn to retain ultimate control in the classroom while allowing appropriate initiative to pupils.

  f) Students can try out various procedures for engaging their pupils' cooperation.

A very marked emphasis on class control from the teachers. All differences significant at 0·01 level.

Objective	Rank		
	Students	Staff	Teachers

7 *To provide the student with opportunities for developing powers of organization.*   9   7   8

  a) Students can learn to take responsibility for the organization of equipment.
  b) Students can learn to organize subject matter so that it becomes significant to their pupils.
  c) Students can learn to organize their classes into appropriate working units.
  d) Students can learn to organize the keeping of notebooks and records.
  e) Students can learn to take part in organizing the smooth flow of daily events in school.
  f) Students can learn to organize extended sequences of work.

  All differences significant at 0·01 level.

8 *To provide an opportunity for the student to develop and display qualities of adaptability and sensitivity appropriate to the school situation.*   4   4   6

  a) Students can learn to adapt their procedures to the physical conditions of specific schools.
  b) Students can learn to improvise materials.
  c) Students can learn to show tact in relationships with teachers and supervisors
  d) Students can learn to show adaptability in response to unexpected situations.
  e) Students can show adaptability in varying their methods to the needs of different groups.
  f) Students can show adaptability in their treatment of pupils.

  Staff/teacher difference significant at 0·01 level; others at 0·05 level.

Objective	Rank		
	Students	Staff	Teachers

9 *To provide the student with an opportunity of becoming part of the school community, familiarizing himself with its practices and entering into appropriate professional relationships with its adult members, the most significant of which is his relationship with the class or subject teacher.* **8 9 9**

a) Students can familiarize themselves with the day to day routine in schools.

b) Students can enter into a professional relationship with practising teachers.

c) Students can experience the interplay of head, staff and pupils in the school community.

d) Students can become aware of the relationship of the school to associate groups – local education authority, parents.

e) Students can learn from the professional expertise of class and subject teachers.

f) Students can become aware of the professional responsibilities of teachers.

All differences significant at 0·05 level.

10 *To provide for the interchange of ideas and methods between schools and college by college staff and students perceiving new ideas, materials and equipment in use in schools, and by college staff and students introducing new ideas, materials and equipment into the schools.* **10 10 10**

a) Students can introduce new approaches to learning into schools.

b) Students can stimulate teachers to a reappraisal of their own procedures.

c) Students can introduce new material into schools.

d) Students can introduce new work situations into classes.

e) College and school staff and students can exchange ideas on teaching procedures.

f) Students can introduce new apparatus and techniques into schools.

All differences significant at 0·05 level.

The remaining seven of Cope's objectives refer mainly to the staff of colleges and teachers in schools. They are: that teaching practice allows college staff to develop contact with schools (11), to judge the student in schools (12), to keep in touch with schools (13), jointly with the student to develop learning situations based on teaching (14), to evaluate the effectiveness of college courses (15) and to evaluate the results of colleagues' work (16). It also allows class/subject teachers to have time free from classes (17).

Brimer and Cope draw two general conclusions from this analysis. First that students, college staff and teachers operate a closely similar system of values when considering the objectives of teaching practice. The pooled rank orders of objectives show correlations between the three groups in the region of 0·97, i.e. almost identity. Second that within the closely similar sets of values significant differences of emphasis exist between the three groups. However, a good deal of research evidence shows the existence of conflicting values between the three groups (Butcher 1965, Cohen 1965, 1969b, Sorenson and Halpert 1968, Shipman 1965, 1966 and 1967a, Griffiths and Moore 1967, Drabick 1967, Finlayson and Cohen 1967, McLeish 1970) and these conflicting general values might be expected to affect the attitudes of the three groups to the objectives of teaching practice.

THE BIRMINGHAM STUDY*

Stones and Morris (1972) conducted a survey of training institutions in England, Wales and Northern Ireland. Schedules were completed by 122 institutions of the 188 contacted. Part of the schedule asked questions about the criteria used in assessment, and respondents were invited to send copies of printed or duplicated sets of criteria or, if printed or duplicated material was not available, to indicate the criteria. Sixty-six sets of criteria were returned and from these it seems reasonable to draw a general picture of the objectives of teaching practice the respondents had in mind when putting forward their criteria for assessing students.

The objectives fall into six areas as follows (the number of mentions each received is given; the large numbers reflect the fact that most respondents mentioned different aspects of the same thing):

* See Part 3 (pp. 145–64) for the complete paper.

1 To provide opportunities for the student to acquire and improve teaching skills: 495
2 To enable the student effectively to plan and prepare lessons: 221
3 To help the student develop desirable traits, attitudes and abilities: 153
4 To enable the student to acquire the characteristics of a teacher and to display appropriate behaviour: 70
5 To allow the student to evaluate his own and his pupils' progress: 31
6 To enable the student to bring about learning in children: 14

The data show the major areas of concern of education staff in colleges. Although ranging over a narrower area than the Brimer and Cope survey, the Birmingham replies are more detailed and idiosyncratic, possibly because they were obtained in answer to open-ended questions and were wholly unstructured. The relatively slight attention paid to the actual learning that the pupils accomplish and its evaluation is shared by respondents in both studies. The almost total lack of reference in the Birmingham replies to the explicit relating of theory to practice, compared with the high place allotted to this objective in the Bristol research, is interesting. On the face of it one would have expected frequent and overt mention of criteria explicitly related to this objective from college lecturers in education. One possible answer may simply be that colleges do not pay as much attention to the relation of practice to theory as is commonly supposed, especially during teaching practice periods; and that out of consideration of the student's difficulties in fitting in with the practices of the host school, this objective does not figure prominently, at least as far as assessment is concerned.

OTHER STATEMENTS OF THE OBJECTIVES OF
TEACHING PRACTICE

Specific studies and discussions of the objectives of teaching practice are sparse. Morris (1969) has summarized in general terms commonly accepted objectives as he sees them and has examined the conflicts arising from their fulfilment. Davies (1969) reviews the scanty American research on the purposes of student teaching, gives a list of non-behavioural objectives culled from the American literature, talks of 'new concepts about the nature and purposes of student teaching that are developing . . . out of the research on teaching' and comments that 'despite the importance attached to it [student teaching], behavioural objectives are seldom identified'. One set of objectives was recently proposed by a conference of college staff, teachers and education officers (with college staff predominating) (University of Exeter Institute of Education 1969). The objectives proposed were:

1 To enable the students to acquire an understanding of the children in the classroom situation: to find out how their minds work and to learn how to make contact with them and to communicate with them.
2 To adjust their minds to the practical situation and to relate what they had learned in child development lectures to it. To learn to be clear about their own aims in a lesson or series of lessons.
3 To learn to be sensitive to the situation in the classroom and to learn how to structure it. To develop resourcefulness.
4 A major aim of *teaching* or *study* practice is to develop powers of observation.
5 Ability to make good relationships with children.
6 Interest in the learning process and ability to relate this to the learning situation.
7 An understanding of the need for organization and preparation in any situation, and the ability to analyse.
8 Personal maturity (e.g. social confidence).
9 To give a chance for students to assess themselves.
10 To give students the opportunity of becoming more a part of the normal teaching force as part of a teaching team.
11 To give the students awareness of and insights into the complex network of relationships involved in school and classroom, in particular recognizing and accepting that human relationships exist in depth.
12 Diagnosis. The first year's teaching practice is a contribution towards a diagnostic year.

The Plowden Report (Department of Education and Science 1967b) gives an unequivocal statement of the objectives of teaching practice: 'The purpose of teaching practice is to underpin and enliven theoretical studies in child development and education, and to

B

provide sources from which theory can be derived. Teaching practice must also familiarize students with the problems and the daily round that will await them when they qualify. Through it colleges and schools can learn about each other's new ideas' (Para. 985). 'Group practice (interacts) usefully with the more theoretical aspects of the education course (and provides) valuable occasions for experimental work in the schools and collaboration between schools and colleges' (Para. 988). Finally, two practical objectives are suggested. First, colleges should help meet the needs of the schools as well as those of their students 'especially in areas where there is a grave shortage of teachers'. 'The partnership between college and school and the close relationships often involved in group practice would be especially helpful to schools in under-privileged areas' (Para. 991). Second, students on final teaching practice can 'release teachers for periods of in-service training or experimental work' (Para. 991).

The National Union of Teachers. (1970) rejects the objectives of teaching practice as conceived in apprenticeship terms and endorses the objectives of longer periods of teaching practice as suggested by a conference of heads of comprehensive schools in 1964: 'To come to terms with realities of a teacher's duties, to see their way through complexities of an unfamiliar organization, to gain familiarity with routine tasks, to experience teaching as a continuous process rather than as a series of expository exercises and to find out something about their own strengths and weaknesses.'

WEAKNESSES IN CURRENT STATEMENTS OF OBJECTIVES

The first criticism that must be made of current statements of objectives is that with very few exceptions they are monolithic and undifferentiated and are seen as applying to teaching practice as a whole without regard to the stage of development of the student and to the school and child variables. While some objectives will be valid for all students at all times during their course, others will be specific. The objectives for students on their first term of *study practice* in a rural infants' school will clearly be to some extent different from those of a future specialist maths teacher on *block practice* in an urban secondary school.

Very often the objectives are only partial, stressing one set of outcomes rather than another to suit the subjective preferences of the writer, or to help support an argument. Clearly, in a learning situation of the complexity and wide span of time as is provided by teaching practice, it is desirable that outcomes should be systematically related to specific teaching activities. A statement of objectives will have to be comprehensive if it is to serve as a guide at each stage of the practice.

Not only do the statements lack comprehensiveness but, with the notable exception of Cope's objectives, they lack sufficient detail to be meaningful as guides to action. 'Developing powers of observation', 'acquiring an understanding of children', 'making good relationships with children', are examples of insufficiently developed objectives; they are of little practical value to the student as they stand.

This lack of detail is part of the general weakness of stating objectives in non-behavioural, or performance, terms. Most current statements do not state what the student will be *doing* when demonstrating his achievement of the objectives. The result is vague, subjective statements expressing some sort of feeling but lacking the objective clarity necessary for communication and discussion. 'To come to terms with the realities of a teacher's duties', for example, suggests that a teacher has some hard and rather unpleasant things to do and it is best if the student experiences them and swallows the pill sooner rather than later. But such a statement leaves both the student and the evaluator quite in the dark as to how to judge when this objective has been satisfactorily fulfilled.

Finally, the objectives as currently stated lack a taxonomical approach; that is, they are not arranged in any coherent system that shows the logical interdependence of the objectives.

2 · Grading and guiding

THE ASSESSMENT OF TEACHING PRACTICE

Despite increased interest in and research into the problem in recent years, the details of precisely how assessment is carried out by the colleges remain incomplete. The only recent comprehensive investigation into the problem is that by Stones and Morris (1972) which is reprinted in Part 3 of this book. This investigation focused on four main problems: the form of assessment used, the evidence used in assessment, the problem of criteria and the means of providing feedback to student teachers.

The findings of the investigation confirmed those of Anders-Richards (1969), in a survey of institutes of education, that the most popular means of grading was on a five-point scale. However, the Stones–Morris survey revealed a trend towards a less detailed rating scale which was not noticeable in the Anders-Richards investigation.

Stones and Morris also found that the large majority of assessments in training institutions are wholly impressionistic. The problems of this method of assessment are well researched. Shipman (1966) drew attention to the variables (such as size of classes, range of pupils' abilities, type of school and nature of teaching duties) that make such assessment hazardous. Lantz (1967) found a significant variation in the ratings by two sets of observers of the same student behaviour; Start (1968a) called attention to the effects of the rater's personality on his assessment; and Anderson and Hunka (1963) discussed research evidence showing the influence of an assessor's perceptual framework on his assessment. In the Stones and Morris enquiry the impressionistic basis of the assessment was confirmed by their failure to find out how much weight was given to the schools' report, the pupils' learning and the students' teaching notebooks.

The finding that almost a third of the respondents in this survey said they made allowance in their assessments for the student's likely development as distinct from his present performance adds further to the complexities of the assessment process. Of all the elements in this chancy business this seems the chanciest. Unforeseeable changes in the young teachers' private lives, in school organization, in subjects and age range of children they will teach, will all exercise unpredictable influences. For example, Start (1967b) found a surprisingly small percentage of teachers teaching the subjects they had been trained to teach five years after certification. Little wonder that whenever students are rated some years after qualification, the results of the various studies show no clear pattern. Some correlations between college final teaching marks and subsequent ratings are given in Table 1.

Table 1 Correlation between final teaching marks and subsequent ratings

Subsequent rater	Period	Correlation	Reference
H.M.I.s	6–12 yrs	0·81	Tudhope 1942 and 1943
Headteachers and trained raters (not tutors)	1 yr	0·276 on 'adaptability'; others 'negligible'	Bach 1952
Headteachers	3 yrs	0·077 (Primary) 0·566	Collins 1959
Headteachers	5 yrs	0·187	Rudd and Wiseman 1962
Headteachers	2 yrs	0·32	Clark and Nisbet 1963
Headteachers	5 yrs	0·335 (Grammar schools) 0·303 (Sec. Mods.)	Wiseman and Start 1965

It is difficult to see how an assessment could make allowance for the varied teaching conditions and teacher development that these correlations suggest. In only one study, that of Tudhope, is the correlation high. In this research the number of subjects was relatively small and the sample was to some extent self-selected rather than random since it was obtained from teachers who over six to twelve years had remained in the same post they had taken up on qualifying. Further the correlation coefficient masks not inconsiderable differences between the college final teaching mark and H.M.I.s' subsequent ratings. Thirty-eight per cent of the H.M.I.s' ratings showed a change from the college ratings, 22 per cent within a class (e.g. C to C+) and 16 per cent between classes (e.g. B to C).

A parallel problem faces the assessor in trying to allow for the 'difficulty' of the practice school. Collier (1959) quotes evidence of a top mark of B+ given in the more difficult schools, while in the remaining schools it was A. The mode in the more difficult schools was between C and C—; in the easier schools, between B— and C+. In a survey of 100 students over five years Shipman (1966) found that the school to which the student was assigned exerted an important influence on the final teaching mark. But when pressed for a specific statement of the weight of this factor, the respondents largely answered that it was taken into account.

Stones and Morris found that only half of the respondents to their questionnaire were prepared to divulge the criteria they used in assessment. The causes of this unwillingness on the part of heads of education departments can only be surmised. Perhaps they felt unable to speak for their colleagues in colleges where there was no standardization and no consensus; or did not believe in the specification of criteria; or were reluctant to embark on the troubled seas of teacher effectiveness knowing how many barks had foundered there.

If the last, it seems that there is confusion between three levels of discussion on teacher effectiveness. At the first level the discussion is simply concerned with the problems of judging whether a teacher (or student) has accomplished the goals he has set himself in a given lesson, series of lessons, course, etc. *Simply* is, of course, used in the sense of *only* for this is by no means a simple problem. It hinges on the adequacy of the statement of objectives, above all on the behavioural specification of the criteria by which the fulfilment of the objective will be judged. If a teacher fulfils his objectives he is being effective.

At the second level the discussion is concerned with making statements that describe effective teachers' behaviour. Connections are posited between teachers' behaviour and the observable behaviour of the pupils: their learning, attitudes, experience, activities, etc. Teachers' behaviour that produces desired effects in pupils is abstracted and generalized and built into definitions of effective teaching. At the third level the discussion is concerned with the investigation of the effective teacher's behaviour in terms of his personality and interaction with the pupils.

At the two last levels the discussion is complex and frequently leads to a reification of teacher effectiveness, endowing it with existence as an entity instead of seeing it as an abstraction or generalization. It is this attitude that seems to underlie Biddle and Ellena's oft-quoted statement: 'It is not an exaggeration to say that we do not today know how to select, train for, encourage or evaluate teacher effectiveness' (Biddle and Ellena 1964). This conclusion seems to arise from divorcing the discussion on teacher effectiveness from that on the aims of education and the objectives of teaching. If we adequately define objectives and criteria it seems possible to evaluate a teacher's effectiveness; and there is a growing body of data to enable us to explain this effectiveness in terms of the teacher's personal characteristics, skills and interaction with pupils (see pp. 13–14).

Whatever the reasons for the unwillingness of respondents in the Stones–Morris survey to give details of their criteria, sufficient were provided to allow reasonable conclusions about the general nature of criteria at present in use; and these conclusions are supported by the unstructured statements of tutors and teachers. When respondents are *presented* with a set of criteria and asked to rate them, we have different conditions: the criteria are not necessarily the respondents' but already have structure and, in some cases, precision given by the researcher, e.g. Poppleton (1968); whereas Stones and Morris found the criteria used to be varied, heterogeneous and idiosyncratic. There was evidence of attempts to standardize criteria in a small number of area training organizations but no group of criteria, however limited, was shared by all colleges. The presentation of the criteria generally lacked logical arrangement and structure; in only a handful of colleges was there evidence of a taxonomical approach. Nor was much attention paid to criteria relating to the ability of students to evaluate children's learning. While teaching performance in general is by far the most widely accepted criterion area, this crucial aspect of teaching performance, evaluation, is strangely neglected.

Discussions between tutors, joint assessment, participation with colleagues and external examiners, all exercise a normative influence and produce some degree of consensus on criteria. But this is often consensus about general, vague personality traits (*enthusiastic, sympathetic, committed,* etc.) and broad categories of teaching skills (*careful preparation, good class control,* etc.); and this consensus serves instead of any detailed approach to criteria.

Since 15 per cent of respondents in the Stones and Morris study did not communicate lesson assessments to students we assume that they do not seem to share the view that full and prompt feedback is highly important for effective learning. What seems to us even more serious, however, is that 22 per cent of respondents did not inform students of the criteria used by tutors. Again it seems that a proven factor in increasing learning, awareness by the learner of the learning objectives and criteria, is not being fully used.

Three major criticisms, then, may be levelled at current modes of assessing students' teaching. First, they make use of an extremely narrow range of assessment evidence and instruments. Twenty years ago Evans (1951) was discussing the potential value in assessment of pupil change, assessment by experts, rating scales and pupil assessment of teachers, but there is no evidence today to show that any considerable use is made of instruments other than rating scales. Second, the unstandardized, unsystematic nature of assessment evidenced by the wide diversity of assessment patterns among colleges, together with the variety and vagueness of the criteria and the idiosyncratic nature of their selection by colleges, suggest that different colleges and area training organizations are rewarding different student behaviours. The comparability of the practical teaching assessment element in the various area training organizations' certificates is, therefore, seriously in doubt. Third, assessment is of doubtful value in the preparation of teachers. The assessment role of the tutor very likely weakens his functions as adviser and helper. Assessment develops anxiety in the student which we think probably limits his willingness to risk experimentation. For practical purposes (as a guide to placement, promotion, etc.) assessment in its present form is almost useless. There seems, therefore, good reason to query its continuance as currently practised in teacher preparation.

Students in schools

SCHOOLS' VALUES AND ATTITUDES

When students go into schools for their first teaching practice they are not, of course, entering completely unknown territory. They take with them the knowledge and experience of schools they acquired as children: and these, as Maddox (1968) suggests, are one of their most important sources of educational ideas. But the new environment, which the student enters with high motivation, hopes and interest, will exercise a powerful influence on him; and the most significant element in the environment will be the teachers and headteacher. Does the student find the prevailing values and attitudes in schools similar to his own?

The evidence is conflicting and does not allow of generalization, which is not unexpected since teachers themselves do not share a homogeneous set of values. Brimer and Cope's (Cope 1971) study of objectives (see pp. 15–21) indicates that, when considering the objectives of teaching practice, teachers, college staff and students operate a closely similar system of values. However, when each objective is considered separately (see pp. 16–20), statistically significant differences appear between students and teachers. To take some of the major differences, teachers do not attach so much weight to teacher/pupil relationships as do students, nor to developing adaptability and sensitivity, but they attach more importance than do students to discipline, control and organizing the work.

Further evidence is provided by a study of 118 graduate students and 57 first year students in two colleges carried out by Butcher (1965). He tested the students and a sample of 300 teachers with the Oliver and Butcher attitude scales developed around three sets of values – *naturalism* (i.e. Rousseau/Dewey type approaches to children and teaching methods; child-centred), *radicalism* (as opposed to conservatism and traditionalism) and *tendermindedness*. The mean scores of the students were higher on all three sets of values. In naturalism and radicalism the students as a whole are significantly different from teachers; in tendermindedness the training college students scored lower than the teachers but not significantly so. Teachers were stricter than students on moral and disciplinary questions but slightly (not statistically significant) more *progressive* on questions of curriculum and teaching methods.

This difference in approach to discipline was brought out in Cohen's (1969b) research on students' views of the expectations held for them by teachers. As part of the research forty-three first year students were asked to give their views and the views they thought teachers held on eight items:

1 Cane the children who need it.
2 Punish the aggressive children for attacks on other children.
3 Start strict, then gradually relax.

4 Teach children to obey orders at once without question.
5 Give praise sparingly.
6 Turn a blind eye at times to infringements of school rules.
7 Allow children to confide in you with problems they would not wish to discuss with their parents.
8 Allow children to act on what you consider to be wrong at times.

On six out of the eight items there was a significant difference between students' own views and their conceptions of teachers' views, as shown in Table 2.

Table 2 Students' views on disciplinary matters correlated with their conceptions of teachers' views.

Item	Degree of significance of difference
I	0·001
2	0·001
3	0·05
4	0·001
5	0·01
8	0·05

Whatever the actual state of affairs, the students see themselves as having radically different values from the teachers.

Differences in four major fields of values and related role conceptions emerge from Finlayson and Cohen's (1967) research into the conceptions of the teacher's role as held by 268 teachers and 183 headteachers. In the field of children's behaviour, headteachers are significantly more in favour of teachers' interpreting right and wrong for children, making use of punishments, insisting on immediate obedience; significantly less in favour of children's learning from their own experience, formulating their own rules from activity and discussing personal difficulties with teachers. In this field headteachers differ significantly from students in the emphasis they put on good order, discipline and outward conformity. In the field of organization, headteachers are much more in favour of grouping children by attainment, and of teachers performing peripheral duties. In motivation, headteachers set greater store on the discipline of uninteresting work. They are more prepared than students to compare one child with another. In general aims, headteachers believe in more religious education and less sex education, and more rules on children's dress and speech, and they attach more importance to the three R's.

With regard to attitudes to educational theory, Griffiths and Moore's (1967) survey of twenty schools used for teaching practice showed that two-thirds of the headteachers believed that students' attempts to apply theory to practical teaching led to classroom difficulties, and twelve thought that theory produced unrealistic teaching methods. A recent analysis of graduate students' reactions to school practice, carried out by the students themselves at Birmingham University School of Education (1971), showed that the students believed that 27·2 per cent of the teachers in their practice schools had an unfavourable attitude to the students' work in educational theory at the University, 52·7 had a neutral attitude and 17·9 were favourable. Cope's (1968) survey showed that only 6 per cent of the students believed that teaching methods advocated by colleges had teachers' approval. However, when teachers themselves were asked, 20 per cent in fact approved of teaching methods supported by the colleges. Of the sixty-two graduate students interviewed by Maddox (Maddox 1968) thirty-four were critical of existing teaching methods in schools, twenty-three viewing them as too formal, involving too much dictation and lacking modern approaches, while eleven objected to the attitudes of teachers to children as seen in sarcasm, shouting and rejecting children's ideas. Students interviewed by Cope at Bristol (Cope 1969b) mentioned, as one of their major concerns, teachers' disapproval of teaching methods newly adopted by students from their colleges. American research, which should of course be applied with caution to the British scene, suggests a considerable difference between students and supervising teachers in methods. Sorenson and Halpert (1968) report that 60 per cent of the 248 student teachers in their study disagreed with the teachers at least part of the time on the handling of individual differences in children on the importance of record keeping and about the use of competition in the classroom.

COLLEGE STAFF

The college staff who supervise students in schools are, by and large, experienced schoolteachers. Taylor (1969a) found that 53 per cent had between seven to eighteen years' experience, 5 per cent had over nineteen years' experience, 33 per cent had between one to six years' and 9 per cent had no teaching experience. But their own teaching experience and subsequent college work led them to adopt theoretical and practical positions rather different from those of teachers and students. The picture that emerges from Brimer and Cope's survey is of an extremely child-centred orientation differing markedly from those of teachers and students (Cope 1971). College staff place a greater emphasis on the application of theory to practice than do teachers and students. They value assessment less than do teachers but more than students; they also attach considerably less importance to class control than teachers and students, and value more the organization of lessons. Significant differences in values were noted by Jervis and Congdon (1958) between staff and students, staff putting the major stress on the students' intellectual growth, students emphasizing the vocational value of their training. Pollock (1964) used Oliver and Butcher's attitude scale, in a study involving 168 science teachers and 41 college science lecturers and found the lecturers significantly more tenderminded than the teachers. Significant difference in attitudes to discipline and to children between college lecturers and teachers were observed by Shipman in his research with 159 teachers and 44 college lecturers (Shipman 1965). Similarly Cohen (1969b) found significant variations between college staff and students in their conceptions of the role of the teacher. In this study of a national sample of 158 education lecturers and 268 student teachers, significant differences in perceptions of desirable approaches to children were found in nine out of twelve items:

1 Alternate interesting with less interesting work.
2 Punish the aggressive child for his attacks on other children.
3 Put slow learners with slow learners for all academic work.
4 Interpret 'right' and 'wrong' for the children.
5 Never allow children to know how the teacher will react to classroom situations.
6 Start with strict discipline and gradually become 'approachable'.
7 Allow children to confide in the teacher about personal problems that they may not want to discuss with their parents.
8 Give praise sparingly.
9 Group friends together for Maths and English.

Are college lecturers eager for, and actively involved in bringing about innovations in curricula, teaching methods and the conditions of learning? Does the view commonly held by teachers, that colleges support new ideas and practices simply because they are new, correspond with reality? Taylor's (1971) research into the readiness of colleges to change suggests that this stereotype view needs to be modified somewhat. The information obtained showed lecturers' attitudes to educational change in general. The responses are given below:

Opinions of 137 members of staff of six colleges	Agree
a) There is too much educational change at present	20·6%
b) There is about the right amount of change in education	39·0%
c) There is too little change in education at present	37·5%
d) I have no views on the matter	2·9%

This suggests that the majority of lecturers (59·6 per cent) will either be positively opposed to further innovation, as far as their advice to students goes, or will be only moderately in favour. Women lecturers in the sample significantly favoured 'There is about the right amount of change' compared with men. The general lukewarmness of college staff to innovation is borne out by the relatively small part that they have played in developing new curricula and teaching methods either independently or in conjunction with agencies such as the Schools Council, Nuffield, etc.

College staff then seem to be child-centred, tenderminded and only moderately in favour of educational change. They believe above all in the value of the individual and of interpersonal relationships. They like efficient organization of learning but are not primarily interested in the pupils' learning. They value the personal growth of their students but are not too concerned with the relationship between this growth and the growth of the pupils. Taylor (1969a) argues that the values of the colleges are those of 'social and literary romanticism', marked by an anti-intellectualism, a 'stress upon the intuitive and the intangible, upon spontaneity and creativity . . . a hunger for the satisfactions of interpersonal life within the community and small groups, and a flight from rationality'. The research evidence quoted above tends to support this argument.

Given this set of values, conflicts in attitudes, practical advice and personal relationships between college staff and teachers are understandable. The student in school is faced with the problem of relating to both tutor and teacher, coping with the conflict between the two and at the same time endeavouring to teach his pupils.

STUDENT CHANGE

The picture that emerges as a result of recent enquiries and surveys shows the practice periods to be times of considerable stress and anxiety. Till fairly recently college staff on the whole regarded teaching practice as the one sure, satisfactory element in the whole course. The students were always happy to be in school and seemed to be making good progress towards becoming teachers. They were preparing their lessons, trying out new approaches, slipping into their new roles and vocations. They enjoyed reasonably harmonious relationships with teachers and pupils. The teaching practice periods were seen as times of maximum personal growth on the part of the students, growth in the direction hoped and planned for by the college tutors; of steady development in attitudes and skills towards the modern, enlightened standards set by college staff. This cosy picture, however, appears to bear little resemblance to the real state of affairs.

Shipman's work at Worcester College of Education provided the first major challenge to this picture (Shipman 1965, 1967a and 1967b). He tested successive intakes from 1961–5 and followed them through their courses, testing by interview, group discussion and questionnaire the changes in their attitudes to 'progressive' versus 'traditional' teaching methods, to restrictive discipline versus free activity and to child-centred versus subject-centred teaching. He found evidence that the students adopted the attitudes of college staff and used these attitudes in their contacts with the college, in college work, during discussions with visiting tutors and in answering questionnaires put out by the college; but that, in schools, in their contact with teachers and children they adopted and acted upon different attitudes. Discrepancies were found between students' answers to questionnaires and their statements in informal discussions and their observed practice. The students' answers to questionnaires were 'correct' (i.e. roughly in line with what they believed was expected of them) rather than 'true' (i.e. representing what they honestly felt). In informal discussions they appeared 'tougher, less progressive and more like teachers' (Shipman 1967b).

They came to college with attitudes already formed from their own school days and they changed little during teaching practice, and this little was in the direction of teachers' attitudes. This is further shown by the fact that after six months' teaching their attitudes approximate closely to those of the other staff in their schools. Shipman uses the term *impression management* for the process by which students handle the attitudes and expectations of cooperating teachers and supervising college staff. Cope (1969b) shows how students at the beginning of the course are rapidly 'converted' to the approaches and teaching methods advocated by colleges, show enthusiasm for them, identify with the children and anticipate their joy in operating the new methods. Gradually, from contact with the realities of school, these attitudes and the teaching approaches that flow from them are more or less reserved for the college supervisor. As one student remarked, 'If you know the supervisor wants projects, you give him a project'; and another, 'The file was to impress the supervisor'. Cope comments that quite a few students seemed to be able to 'manipulate the teaching practice situation in a fairly sophisticated way'.

Cohen's (1969b) research into the student's perceptions of the school practice period was limited to questionnaires, but since his aim was to ascertain how students saw the expectations of teachers and college staff, the element of impression management may not be a serious factor. The eight operational statements dealing with discipline and teacher/pupil relationships mentioned above (p. 34) were used and students were asked to state their own classroom practice in relation to each, and what they thought their cooperating teacher and college supervisor expected their behaviour to be. The results show a discrepancy between students, college supervisors and teachers and between supervisors and teachers. They also show a very close agreement between first and third year students' reports of their own classroom practices and their perceptions of tutors' and teachers' expectations, and students changed little over the three years of their course. Interestingly, in the one item in which there is a significant difference, third year students see their own behaviour as more authoritarian than do first year students. The prospective views which third year students were asked to supply confirm Shipman's findings. They were asked to 'think ahead to the time when you are a fully qualified practising teacher' and complete the questionnaire again. Significant differences were found on six of the eight items. As fully fledged teachers they would use the cane more, have greater recourse to punishment for aggression, be more strict, use praise more sparingly, counsel children less and give children fewer opportunities to learn from mistakes.

A change in attitude in the direction of the supervising teacher has been demonstrated by Johnson in America (Johnson 1968). His aim was to discover if any change in open- and closed-mindedness in student teachers was related to the degree of dogmatism of supervising teachers. Eighty student teachers were given Rockeach's Dogmatism Scale E at the beginning and end of a ten weeks' teaching practice, and their eighty supervising teachers were also given the test. The scores revealed two groups. In the first group, the students' preteaching practice scores were higher than the teachers' (i.e. they were more dogmatic); in the second, they were lower. In both groups there was a significant shift towards the dogmatism scores of the teachers. Group I's mean shift, in the direction of greater open-mindedness, of 5·34 points was significant at 0·05 level; group II's shift of 4·71 points in the direction of greater closed-mindedness was significant at the 0·01 level.

The attitudes, then, of students are ambivalent, and where there is change it is in the direction of the schools' attitudes. Does a parallel change occur in the classroom behaviour of students? Morgan and Woerdehoff (1969) observed the classroom behaviour of thirty-four American student teachers at the beginning and end of a teaching practice period, making use of the techniques of interaction analysis (see pp. 102 ff.). They found no significant change in the proportionate distribution of time devoted to the ten behavioural categories of the rating schedule. Of course this result may not hold good for the British situation and it measures the effects of only a six week period of teaching practice. But the generally held belief of important changes in the classroom behaviour of students is supported by no objective evidence, by the use of no reliable observation instruments, against few detailed statements of objectives and criteria (see pp. 26 ff.). What changes do take place seem to be in the direction of unadventurous, 'sound' practice of a 'competent' teacher. According to Maddox's (1968) interviews with sixty-four graduate student teachers, the students on teaching practice learned to secure the children's participation by arousing their interest in the topic (32 mentions), to prepare their lessons carefully with due regard to presentation, sequence of activities, appropriateness for the children's level of age, ability and language comprehension (27 mentions), not to lecture and to use summaries and short tests (26 mentions), to use visual aids where appropriate (13 mentions) and to begin strict and relax later (10 mentions).

The process whereby teachers influence students has not been studied as closely as it deserves. Cohen (1969a) examined the functional dependence of the student on the teacher, the services that the student could perform for the teacher in exchange for her help, and the power the teacher had to influence the student. The teacher in many ways holds the keys to the student's successful practice. The teacher controls the classroom setting and thus facilitates or hinders the student's teaching. The major exchange that the student can offer in return for the teacher's help is to effect a smooth transition in taking over the class, disturbing things as little as possible – i.e. carry on the teacher's ways of teaching, organizing and relating to the children. The class teacher has considerable power to influence the student: expert power (the power of her expertise), reward power (in assessment) and coercive power (the ability to withhold personal and technical help). The teacher's exercise of this power may contribute to the student's feeling of security. Compared with the teacher, the college supervisor is relatively powerless while the student is in school; his reward power (assessment) cannot provide the continuous influence that the teacher's powers do. Further, Cohen showed from role inventories completed by eighty-one students indicating the amount of help and encouragement accorded them by teachers and by supervisors that teachers make greater attempts to influence students than do college tutors; in particular (and in support of Johnson's findings above) teachers try to get students to approximate to their own level of authoritarianism. Shipman points out in his report of his survey of student teachers at Worcester College of Education that the value placed by students on the actual teaching situation tended to give disproportionate importance to instances arising from it. 'Hence pressures from schools could counter-balance theoretical educational influences even though exposure to schools was limited' (Shipman 1965).

The Birmingham students' survey asked the graduate student teachers to indicate the amount of assistance given them by teachers in five areas. The respondents ringed one of five levels of help given;

in Table 3 figures are given for those ringing the top two levels (i.e. very much help and much help). This indicates that a considerable amount of assistance is given.

Table 3 Amount of help given to students on teaching practice by teachers

	No. of students	%
Social help (i.e. in integrating with staff and school)	74	51·1
Specialist help (i.e. with presentation of subject)	85	58·6
Teaching help (i.e. with classroom teaching)	77	53·1
Administration (duties of form teacher, etc.)	48	33·2
Discipline	64	44·1

The mode of influence of students by teachers is not formalized and is probably more effective by being informal and highly personal. Students' observation of teachers' lessons (which is the most obviously institutionalized point of influence) is variable and haphazard. Of the Birmingham students 23·6 per cent did not observe at all while a further 24·3 per cent observed for one or two hours a week. In Maddox's survey all students were expected to carry out an initial observation period; in practice, 43·3 per cent observed for one day or less and a further 21 per cent observed for two to three days only; 8 per cent did no observation. Only 17·7 per cent had a continuing programme of observation after the initial period. Observation of students by staff seems open to even more vagaries. Forty-two per cent of staff according to Maddox sat in for at least some lessons and offered criticism; 24 per cent sat in but gave no comments; 34 per cent never sat in. In 33·3 per cent of the Birmingham schools a member of staff acts as a personal tutor to the students; of those students in schools where a personal tutor was not appointed, only 24·8 per cent said they would welcome such an arrangement.

But in general, though there are differences in initial values and attitudes between teachers and students, the students are received in a cooperative and business-like manner and it is in this atmosphere that the socialization of the student into the mores of the school takes place. Of the sixty-two students in Maddox's enquiry only three instances of intolerable behaviour by teachers (constant interruption to discipline the class and criticism of the student in front of the class) were reported. The Birmingham student survey found that the large majority of teachers (67·9 per cent) treated the students in a friendly and helpful way. Cope (1969b) found quite a few examples of strong support for the student from the teacher even to the extent of an alliance against the college supervisor, and, indeed, many supervisors have had experience of students' lessons more or less rigged by teacher and student for the benefit of the visiting tutor. The student is taken into the school community, the college tutor remains outside. Students and teachers combine during teaching practice to challenge, usually covertly but occasionally openly, the 'legitimacy of the professional authority of college staff' (Shipman 1967b).

The student's learning tasks in school are heavy. He has to learn basic teaching skills, how to relate to children and colleagues and the appropriate attitudes and behaviour of a teacher in a school community. For most of this learning he will have had little or no preparation of a theoretico-practical nature. He will normally have had little or no training in observing and analysing teaching behaviour (including his own). His observation of teachers will almost inevitably be unstructured and unsystematic so that he picks up in a random fashion bits of behaviour that seem to be effective. Discussion with teachers about methods and curricula is usually haphazard and unorganized. In the actual teaching situations in which the student finds himself almost from the beginning of the practice, the constant pressures of organizing and controlling the pupils, engaging them in learning activities, the immersion in a multitude of decisions and activities, provide obstacles to learning of any but the simplest kind. The feedback from teacher and tutor is irregular, relatively infrequent and often conflicting. Higher order learning under these conditions is generally impossible. The student learns either to apply simple rules learned without understanding such as 'start strict, relax later', 'use the blackboard a lot', or to operate tricks of the trade such as 'stand them all up at the beginning if they are noisy and don't go on till they are quiet', 'keep your eyes on the class while writing on the board'. Instead of providing a planned, sequential set of learning experiences to serve as a theoretico-practical framework for future development, teaching practice all too often consists in the *ad hoc* learning of routines for getting through the day (Sorenson 1967).

COLLEGE/SCHOOL RELATIONSHIPS

Although colleges depend on schools for teaching practice and schools depend on colleges for replenishing their staff, there is little evidence of an attitude of partnership between the two. There is, on the contrary, a fair degree of ignorance of each other's work. Griffiths and Moore (1967), in a survey of twenty schools cooperating in teaching practice, found that the schools did not possess syllabuses of the various college courses in educational theory and the colleges in the main kept no systematic records of recent developments in organization, curricula and methods in the schools. The purposes of the two institutions are viewed as wholly diverse. To the school, immersed in its teaching activities, the function of teacher preparation is a peripheral activity at the best to be tolerated as a regrettable necessity, at the worst to be rejected as harmful to its main function. To the college the school is an institution to be 'used' for teaching practice. The school does not participate in the college's internal work; the college seldom contributes directly to the work of the school. The schools seldom have the facilities for full participation in teacher preparation; often suitable members of staff are fully committed to teaching and administration. Very many teachers have neither the experience nor the supervisory expertise to help students. Above all school staff do not know what is expected of them in the supervision and evaluation of students. In sum, the relationship is ambiguous, unspecific and largely unformulated. The Department of Education and Science 1966) may well say 'The relations between colleges of education and the schools are a factor which decisively affects the quality of the training given to intending teachers.' But without fundamental changes, the present situation, in which the colleges have the responsibility for teaching practice without effective day-to-day control and the schools have control but no responsibility, will continue.

Part 2 · Innovations and perspectives

3 · Redirections

The general drift of our remarks so far has been to suggest a re-direction in teacher training from attempting to model the master teacher to one which stresses mastering the teaching model. We believe that teaching practice must move in this direction if student teachers are ever to derive enough from their practical experience to equip them to do better than the housewives in Popham's experiment (p. 4). We think there is little point in tinkering with the present system and we repudiate the suggestion made in some quarters (see p. 1) that the cure for present deficiencies is 'more of the same' and we would declare as our slogan 'Nellie must go'.

MASTERING THE TEACHING MODEL

It is one thing to analyse a job in a factory, perhaps an assembly skill or possibly a keyboard operation, it is another thing to analyse the job of the teacher. Human behaviour is far more complex than the operation of any machine or factory process, it is almost certainly one of the most complex phenomena in the universe. The modest vocation of the teacher is to change the behaviour of groups of humans in certain directions. The behaviour of one human being, that is, has to be so ordered that it influences the behaviour of others systematically. The complexity of this operation is so great that it is probably beyond our comprehension. Which is perhaps a good thing, otherwise we might never have tried. But it does present us with enormous problems when it comes to systematic analysis and experimentation in the field of teaching. It has been suggested (Ausubel 1968) that the 'flight from the classroom' of the experimental psychologists in the 1930s and 1940s was in no small measure a flight from the impossible complexities of the experimental milieu to the relatively uncomplicated world of the rat maze and the Skinner box. In view of the undoubted enormity of the problem, it is not surprising that efforts to analyse classroom transactions have made limited progress, nevertheless we believe that some current approaches show considerable promise and could be fruitfully employed to improve the teaching ability of student teachers.

An example of a step in this direction is the proposal of the Teacher Education Center in New York (Burkhart 1969). They have recommended that their current approach to teacher certification be abandoned as ineffective and inappropriate and that new programmes be designed whose criterion of effectiveness would be the teaching ability of their graduates. The assessment of effectiveness in this context was to be according to prespecified performance and criteria rather than the subjective views of supervisors, and they put forward a model for performance evaluation which draws on, among other things, different techniques of classroom observation.

The important point about this proposal is that it replaces the covert subjective criteria deployed by the supervisor sitting at the back of the class, by overt quasi-objective criteria which are prespecified and about whose validity there is some consensus of agreement. The application of this approach depends upon the use of different modes of classroom observation by observers using instruments that have been developed and validated over a number of years. These instruments for the observation of teacher activity come in different shapes and sizes but one of these, the Stanford Teacher Competence Appraisal Guide, may be taken as exemplifying one type of general approach. Such instruments are used to record teacher behaviour along certain prespecified dimensions and the rater evaluates the teacher along these dimensions awarding scores according to a standard form of rating.

THE STANFORD TEACHER COMPETENCE APPRAISAL GUIDE (see pp. 252–6)

Work on the Stanford Guide started in 1959 and since then it has gone through many revisions and a considerable amount of development work and evaluation has been carried out on it. The aim of the Guide was to serve as a structuring device to aid supervisors to focus upon important elements in the teaching act. At various stages of its development it comprised different numbers of items, starting with forty-three in the first draft but eventually reducing to thirteen items relating to classroom-based teacher characteristics and four relating to community and professional characteristics. The development work between these two versions has involved the removal of ambiguous items and the refining down of the scale to yield items that were productive of high levels of rater consistency. As it now stands the Guide comprises five sections. Section 1 deals with the aims of instruction, section 2 deals with the planning of the instruction, section 3 with the actual performance in the lesson, section 4 covers evaluation and section 5 is concerned with the teacher's relationships with the community and the profession at large.

Under each of the five general headings of the Guide are two or more subordinate, more specific items and these items in turn are expanded upon by way of guidance to the rater. Thus, for example, we have under *Aims* two items: 1 *Clarity of aims* and 2 *Appropriateness of aims*. The gloss on 2 reads 'The aims are neither too easy nor too difficult for the pupils. They are appropriate, and are accepted by the pupils.' Under the general heading of *Planning* are three items: number 5 is *Selection of materials* and the gloss for this item reads 'The specific instructional materials and human resources used are clearly related to the content of the lesson and complement the selected method of instruction.' Each of the seventeen items has to be graded by the rater on a seven point scale ranging from *Truly exceptional* to *Weak* with an additional category *Unable to observe*. To determine whether the student teaching programme is producing the desired effects according to the categories of the Guide, evidence is taken from experienced teachers, supervisors in schools, tutors in college or university, the student teacher himself and the pupils he teaches. The desirability of using the Guide to assist in a cooperative effort to assess and to improve levels of competence in teaching is stressed. The teacher/student himself is a key figure in this assessment, and self-appraisal and discussion of such appraisals with colleagues is an important aspect of the use of the Guide. Each use of the Guide should be followed by a conference of teachers and tutors in which 'the cooperative sharing of perceptions and ideas focuses on the target of improving teaching, supervising and learning' is emphasized. Clearly, such an exercise would not be possible without an instrument of this nature.

Readers will have noted the reference to the use of pupils as raters, possibly with some incredulity. In fact those involved at various times in the developing of the Guide capitalized on a rich and neglected body of research which recommended the use of the teacher's pupils as a primary source of evaluative perceptions. Following experiments using pupil ratings it was discovered that these ratings produced a strong composite of the more specialized raters (school supervisor, university supervisor and student teacher) and in fact yielded the best single criterion measure. In other words, if we are to rely on *one* rating alone, then we would be advised to use that of the pupils. Pupils' ratings have been used in this way and also to provide a preliminary picture which can be used by a student before a later rating by several professionals (including himself).

The Stanford Guide has been used in experimental situations by administering it before and after different treatments to assess the effects of various approaches to practical teaching, and it clearly offers a very useful tool in this field. It has, of course, been developed in an American context and may not be transferable to English conditions without some changes. However, it would clearly be pointless to start from scratch developing an English guide and we would urge that, as a first step at least, supervisors might start using the Stanford Guide to improve present practices. However, we do not feel that merely using the Guide in current conditions is the most desirable method of proceeding and we suggest the marrying of the use of the Guide to other techniques which we discuss later.

THE PROBLEM OF CRITERIA

There is a problem with such instruments as the Stanford Guide, however. Although few of us would disagree with the desirability for a teacher to have clear and appropriate lesson aims and well organized lessons with content appropriate to the aims (which are some of the dimensions of the Stanford Guide), one could still legitimately doubt that a teacher possessing these attributes and the others in the Guide was *ipso facto* a 'good' teacher. We are faced once more with the problem of the criterion of competence in teaching. It is, of course, possible, as we implied earlier, to make arbitrary definitions of teacher competence. However, in the development of the Stanford Guide the relationship between the teacher behaviours and pupils' learning was an important element in the selection of criterion categories. Items chosen were those most related to desirable pupil behaviour. With such an approach we can be more sure of the validity of our ratings. We cannot be entirely certain, however, since we are dependent upon the efficacy of the modes of assessment of pupil learning. The problem here is that unless we are quite certain that tests of pupil learning are valid we only remove the problem of teacher effectiveness one stage by using pupil learning as the criterion of competence. There is a further implication in this approach to teacher effectiveness. If we are to use pupil performance as our criterion, we are obliged to use criterion referenced instruments to assess their learning. That is, pupils' achievement must be assessed by the extent to which they have achieved the objectives set for them by the teacher rather than in relation to a distribution of class scores yielding average, below average and above average scores – that is, norm referenced tests. When we consider that classroom tests all too often transgress important principles of test construction, and that they are almost invariably norm referenced, we can see that the difficulties of getting a meaningful appraisal of the effectiveness of a teacher's performance may be compounded rather than solved by taking pupil performance as measured by most classroom assessment procedures as the criterion of effectiveness. Nevertheless it seems to us that this approach is the only reasonable one in present conditions. Being alive to the problems at least enables us to take avoiding action and at best to make some progress towards solving them.

THE QUESTION OF FEEDBACK

The Stanford Teacher Competence Appraisal Guide makes use of one of the key principles from the psychology of learning: the provision of feedback to the learner. Feedback from the conference that follows student teaching is multidimensional when the Guide is used. It is multidimensional in the sense that it covers several specific aspects of teaching behaviour and also in the sense that it emanates from different sources. The tutor, the pupils, the student teacher's peers, and the student teacher himself, all provide detailed comment about the student teacher's performance along a number of prespecified and fairly precisely delineated continua. Other instruments being developed and currently used in the training of student teachers all make use of this principle of feedback in different ways. Existing practices of the sitting with Nellie type lack this crucial element. It is true that the student gets feedback from his pupils who respond in different ways according to his own behaviour. But this sort of feedback tells him little if anything of an evaluative nature about his teaching which might be a useful guide of future activity.

The difference between the sort of feedback the student teacher gets from the Stanford Guide and from conventional teaching practice is that the latter is less specific than the former. However, techniques of observation are being developed which bring teaching transactions into still finer focus and increase greatly the possibilities of more precise and specific use of feedback. Some of these methods take as points of departure commonly accepted criteria of expertise in highly specific aspects of teaching (we leave on one side for the moment the validity of such criteria) and seek to arrange teaching situations that concentrate on these specifics. This makes it possible to isolate important elements of the teaching act which the student practises and then receives contingent feedback. Feedback is often enhanced by having the student's performance recorded on audio or video tape for the student himself to examine and discuss with his supervisor or other observers of his lesson. We discuss two of the most important training procedures that make use of these techniques when we discuss microteaching and interaction analysis later, but at this juncture we should stress that the feedback provided by the hardware is efficacious only to the extent to which the concepts, relating to the skills being practised, are meaningful, relevant and identifiable. These concepts are often embodied in instruments such as the Stanford Teacher Competence Appraisal Guide and such instruments are of key importance in ensuring that the concepts involved have the attributes mentioned. The development of the techniques of microteaching has led to the devising of evaluatory instruments of more specific application than the Stanford Guide. Such instruments are related to individual teaching skills identified by the supervisory staff and are likely in the long run to prove more useful than the more global scales such as the Stanford Guide. This is because the instruments related to specific teaching skills focus on a much narrower field and hence make for greater precision in evaluation. In addition, because of their close links with specific molecular teacher activity, the possibilities of reciprocal development of the instruments and our perceptions of optimum teacher behaviour are enhanced. Thus the evaluatory instruments sharpen up the picture we have of the teaching skill and the consequent changes in our approach to teaching and learning the skill in turn make demands for further development of the instrument. This type of cyclical development is much more difficult with more global instruments geared to complete lessons with their very great complexity and looser structure than teaching episodes concerned with specific skills.

Undoubtedly future developments in our understanding and control of teaching processes depend very much on the development of much more sophisticated instruments than we presently possess. The ones we do have at the moment are probably rightly considered as fairly crude but in our view they are much more valuable and show considerably more promise than those discussed in our account of current evaluation techniques in teacher preparation.

EFFECTIVENESS

Most of the developments referred to above reflect a shift in attitude with regard to the assessment of teacher effectiveness. Flanders (1969) hopefully sees this as a movement towards more objective approaches. He quotes Anderson and Hunka (1963) who concluded from a review of studies that attempts to base research in the field on predictor variables have come to a dead end. They argue that attempts to build a theory of teaching from a statistical description of what is happening fail to prescribe what should be happening. This is the question of sitting with Nellie once again. More promising, however, are some of the findings coming from research using some of the recently developed approaches to the study of teaching processes such as interaction analysis and microteaching. What is emerging is not spectacular and may do little more than illustrate the undeveloped state of knowledge in the field but it is an encouraging augury for the future. For the first time it is becoming possible to identify certain teaching activities and say with confidence that these activities have a direct influence on pupil achievement and attitude. Examples of such activities are the teacher's making use of the ideas and opinions of pupils in his own statements, or the avoidance of punishing comments and use of positive reinforcers. It is developments like these that are likely to prove the growth points in our understanding of teaching phenomena and help us to etch out the beginnings of a theory of teaching.

4 · Theory of teaching

It is a revealing fact that only in the last few years has there been any sustained and serious discussion about the possible nature of a theory of teaching. Teaching, as we have seen in our animadversions on sitting with Nellie, has been regarded essentially as a practical skill and undoubtedly a very large majority of practising teachers would not only be unable to identify the possible elements in such a theory, but would be sceptical of its existence and doubt its utility even if it did exist. And yet more than ever before the times demand and are ripe for the first growths of this theory. The times demand such growth because snowballing developments in all sectors of education such as educational technology, curriculum theory, the 'new' approaches to teaching half a dozen subjects, are inchoate and sorely in need of a body of concepts and principles of explanatory and predictive validity. As often occurs, the problems that demand the new thinking are the most likely instruments to bring it forth and it is the many small innovations in a variety of fields that, taken together, promise to change our thinking about the larger problems and hopefully descry some solutions.

CONCEPTIONS OF TEACHING

Possibly one of the obstacles to the earlier speculations about the theoretical bases of teaching was the widely held stereotype of the didactic authoritarian dispensing instant learning. The reaction against the stereotype led to a de-emphasis of the importance of the teacher's contribution to the child's learning and to a stress instead on the importance of independent learning. This view had its most extreme exponents among some of the advocates of discovery learning who saw the teacher more as an observer than a participant in the transactions of the classroom. A view of teaching such as this in effect needs no theory other than that of theory related to human learning. Given the approach to teaching implied in the more extreme non-interventionist approaches, any theory of teaching would be isomorphic with a theory of human learning. That is, it would be a descriptive theory. We take the view that this is not enough and that there is a need for a theory or theories of teaching different from theories of learning in at least one attribute, that such a theory or theories would be prescriptive. In other words, our view of teaching is not non-interventionist and there is more to it than children learning.

We are in good company. A distinguished writer in the field, B. O. Smith (1961), put it like this: 'Learning does not necessarily issue from teaching, that teaching is one thing and learning is quite another, is significant for pedagogical research. It enables us to analyse the concept of teaching without becoming entangled in the web of arguments about the processes and conditions of learning: in short to carry on investigation of teaching in its own right. What is needed for scientific enquiry is a concept which recognizes teaching as a distinctive phenomenon general enough to embrace normative definitions as well as special cases.' Smith suggests as a definition 'Teaching is a system of actions intended to produce learning'. Clarke (1970), reviewing the literature on the subject, refers to other writers who take this view and considers the views of teaching upon which the positions of various authorities are based. From this he derives and expounds a view of teaching, which, while being broad and general, does make a distinction between learning and teaching. Learning is often defined as a *relatively permanent change in behaviour*; this is usually qualified to exclude the influences of growth or lesion. Clarke suggests as a definition of teaching *activities that are designed and performed to produce change in student (pupil) behaviour*. He goes on to instance some of these activities: lecture, question and answer session, discussion, discovery, individual assignments. He thinks that activities can be at different levels as exemplified in the Bloom taxonomy (Bloom *et al.* 1956) and also of a cognitive, affective or psychomotor nature. He also refers to Komisar's (1966) suggestions for more specific activities. These include introducing, demonstrating, citing, hypothesizing, reporting, conjecturing, confirming, contrasting, explaining, proving, justifying, explicating, defining, rating, appraising, amplifying, vindicating, interpreting, questioning, elaborating, identifying, designating, comparing. The point about this list is that they are all constituent skills of teaching according to the view we have taken and they are all engaged in with the intention of getting the pupil to learn. They are all interventionist and reflect the difference between the definitions of teaching given above. While we would want to qualify Smith's position of 1961 and that proposed by Clarke, we nevertheless consider that both are useful approaches which we make use of later in suggesting our own views.

Although the claims made by some of the authorities referred to above may give the impression that learning and teaching are quite independent this is not really the burden of their argument. The word 'distinctive' is the key word. Learning can be distinguished from teaching but we imagine that few would claim that teaching could proceed without taking cognizance of what is known about the optimum conditions for learning. Gage (1967) considers that the processes of teaching and learning must be adapted to each other so as to make whatever combination of procedures pays off best. 'We need not consider learning to be an immutable, fixed, given process to which teaching must be adapted. Instead we should conceive of a teaching–learning process, both of whose parts can be changed to make learning more effective.' Gage believes that teaching should be made a central concern for the discipline of educational psychology, which seems a reasonable proposition in view of the concern of educational psychology with the question of learning. He makes a similar distinction in his definitions of learning and teaching to the one we have already made. He considers that teaching should be viewed as the 'exercise of psychological force'. This psychological force is exerted to bring about changes in behaviour of the taught of a fairly stable kind; this is learning. Gage proposes that there are three kinds of psychological force in teaching which make use of our knowledge about different types of learning. These are: conditioning, in which the teacher makes use of knowledge of conditioning procedures to bring about learning; modelling, in which the teacher provides models of behaviour he wants the learner to acquire through imitation; and cognitive force, through which the teacher makes use of techniques calculated to get the learner to form concepts, principles and relationships. Each of the three types of psychological force will be used by the teacher in the situation to which it is most appropriate. Thus, for example, conditioning is likely to be most used for affective behaviours, modelling for behaviours that have no logical structure but might be too complex to teach economically by conditioning, and cognitive force for learning characterized by identifiable cognitive structure. The last of these three is, of course, the content or substance of 'subject' teaching.

It is clear that a view of teaching such as that expounded by Gage is a far cry both from that which regards it as a craft to be learned on the job and from the non-interventionist approach. It is a prescriptive and theoretical approach which will not appeal to those who view teaching as an art to be caught not taught but which seems to us to offer great prospect of interesting and valuable developments in the field which will probably become the applied science of teaching.

ASPECTS OF THEORY

For the multitude of empiricists that man the nation's chalkboards, theory is all right for the theorists but in the meantime they have to get on with the job. One cannot help but sympathize with this attitude in view of the past contribution of theorists in the field. Not that the theorists themselves are particularly culpable since, as we have seen, it was long denied that there could be such a thing as a theory of teaching, and consequently the material subvention to make theorizing practicable has always been hard to come by so that theorists in this field are somewhat thin on the ground. Which is a pity and a disadvantage both to the theorists and to the teachers. Popper (1959) provides an appropriate gloss on this comment when he says: 'Theories are nets cast to catch what we call "the world": to rationalize, to explain, and to master it. We endeavour to make the mesh ever finer and finer.' The mesh of our theory of teaching is enormously wide at the moment but the teacher in the classroom will not be helped by our throwing the net away.

Dubin (1969) describes a theory as a model of some segment of the observable world. 'Such a model describes the face appearance of the phenomenon in such terms as structures, textures, forms and operations. In order that such a model be considered dynamic, it also describes how the phenomenon works, how it functions.' Kerlinger (1965) proposes a definition with similar attributes. 'A theory is a set of interrelated constructs, definitions, and propositions which presents a systematic view of phenomena by specifying relations among variables, with the purpose of explaining and predicting

C

phenomena.' The common theme of all these definitions is the deeper understanding of phenomena which will enable us better to predict the consequences of the interrelated operations of the elements of the phenomena. These, in the case of teaching, would be the variables in the teaching situation which a theoretical insight would enable us to control along dimensions calculated to achieve the objectives we set in our teaching.

A THEORY OF TEACHING

The characteristics a theory of teaching would ideally possess may be deduced from our discussions on the nature of theory and ideas about teaching. As Bruner (1964) and Gage (1967), among others, have argued, such a theory would be of general application. It should not 'specify in an *ad hoc* fashion the conditions for efficient learning of third-grade arithmetic. Rather such conditions should be derivable from a more general view of mathematics learning' (Bruner). It should be concerned with the 'general methodology of teaching, general in the sense of transcending the special requirements of any given subject matter or grade-level' (Gage). Gage is here talking about courses in educational psychology but in this context they are being considered essentially as being concerned with the conceptions, theories and methods of teaching. Smith (1963) spells it out in a little more detail. 'A theory of teaching will consist of (*a*) a statement of the variables comprising teaching behaviour, (*b*) formulation of the possible relations among these variables, (*c*) hypotheses about the relations between the variables comprising teaching behaviour and the variables descriptive of the psychological and social conditions within which teaching behaviour occurs.' Additional detail is provided by the (American) Commission on Instructional Theory (Gordon 1968). They consider that a theory of instruction should:

1 Include a set of postulates and definitions of terms involved in these postulates.
2 Should make explicit the boundaries of its concern and the limitations under which it is proposed.
3 Must have internal consistency; a logical set of relationships.
4 Should be congruent with empirical data.
5 Must be capable of generating hypotheses.

6 Must contain generalizations which go beyond the data.
7 Must be verifiable.
8 Must be stated in such a way that it is possible to collect data to disprove it.
9 Must not only explain past events but must also be capable of predicting future events.
10 At the present time, instructional theories may be expected to represent qualitative synthesis.

This information is clearly useful as a set of guidelines or a check list against which to measure our current state of development in this field. There is an implication, however, which not everyone will accept, the implication that there is one grand theory that will explain all teaching activities. As we have seen from Gage's arguments, there may be a good case for concentrating on what he calls paradigms of teaching which will test more specific theories relating to such things as teaching by conditioning or modelling and so on. At the same time, it must be admitted that, even taking the list and applying it in less general approaches, our knowledge is still at a pretty primitive level. Nevertheless we have some empirical data largely culled from learning research which can undoubtedly make a contribution to some of the categories suggested. If as a start we merely collate these data and systematize them as suggested in item 10, according to the criteria referred to earlier, we shall be making a contribution to the practical professional training of teachers far more useful than that provided by the wisest of conventional wisdom; a contribution that really offers the possibility of being prescriptive in the sense of suggesting the appropriate teaching behaviours to produce specific types of learning. This is not to say that the theory is itself specific, but that specific teaching activities may be derived from a body of general principles. It is the fact that theory is not situational-specific that leads most critics of theory in teaching to deny its use in the practical teaching situation. B. O. Smith (1969) provides a cogent answer to this criticism when he says: 'One of the chief differences between a teacher who is theoretically trained and one who is not, is that the theoretically trained teacher will perform with a set of sophisticated concepts taken from the underlying disciplines of pedagogy as well as from the pedagogical field itself. The teacher who is not theoretically trained will interpret events and objects in terms of common sense concepts that have come from the experience of the race permeated with outmoded ideas about human behaviour.'

An approach such as this poses sharply the question of the relationship between theory and practice. Stones (1972) argues that the acid test of a student's competence in the field of educational psychology (which he takes to be, ideally, akin to a theory of teaching) is his ability to make use of the principles in the actual teaching situation. Taba's work on teaching for cognitive growth exemplifies this approach (Taba 1965). In discussing teaching for conceptual learning she makes use of the generalizations from the psychology of learning on the nature of concept learning. On this basis she develops teaching strategies which direct the children into the necessary activity through the use of structured questioning. We thus have a teaching paradigm which starts with the concepts of learning theory (which is descriptive and non-interventionist); to this are added concepts from the field of teaching (which is prescriptive and interventionist); the teaching is then evaluated by the extent to which the children's behaviour has been modified by the teacher's activity. Applying a similar approach to teacher training we need to add another stage. We would then use the concepts of learning theory to devise teaching activities intended to bring about changes in students' teaching behaviour which would be evaluated proximally by determining the extent to which their teaching behaviour had changed, and distally (and more importantly) by the degree of the *pupils'* learning.

Many leading writers in the field of educational psychology are currently associated with positions like the one related to the paradigm we have just discussed. Bruner (1966) considers that learning theory as studied as a branch of educational psychology has been '. . . distilled from descriptions of behaviour in situations where the environment has been arranged either for the convenience of observing learning behaviour or out of a theoretical interest in some special aspect of learning – reinforcement, cue distinctiveness, or whatever.' But in his view '. . . a theory of instruction, which must be at the heart of educational psychology, is principally concerned with how to arrange environments to optimize learning according to various criteria – to optimize transfer or retrievability of information for example.' Anderson *et al.* (1969) stress the centrality of learning and teaching in educational psychology and consider that its main tasks should be directed towards answering two questions: Under what conditions is pupil learning maximized? And what features of instructional materials and teaching procedures facilitate pupil learning? Similarly there was a fair degree of agreement among a group of leading educational psychologists at a recent symposium in Ottawa that the pressing concern of educational psychology was to say something useful about how best to bring about pupil learning (Herbert and Ausubel 1969). The American psychologist Ausubel (1969) declares that educational psychology should be concerned with the significant variables that make for school learning; especially should we be concerned with the influence of the variables that are manipulable by the teacher and other educationists.

The paradigm we sketched in connection with Taba's work and the proposals made by the other writers suggest that we should look to educational psychology in the first instance for some indication of the important variables and constructs in our preliminary outline of a theoretical approach to the problems of teaching. B. O. Smith (1969) follows a critique of existing teacher education programmes by arguing that the theoretical content of a trainee teacher's course should mainly comprise concepts from the realm of educational psychology. 'What should be the theoretical content of an introductory programme of teacher education? To answer this is to identify concepts such as motivation, feedback and explanation, which are needed to interpret situations the teacher most frequently encounters.' He later proposes that the cognitive and affective processes of learning and feeling should form an important part of the course. But none of these subjects should be considered as elements of a curriculum to be studied in academic isolation or as providing the groundwork for further study, they should all be studied as part of the practical professional work of the student teacher. They should be related to the analysis of actual teaching situations and be part and parcel of what Smith calls the situationally-oriented part of the (teacher education) programme.

Smith's statement seems to offer great promise for the future development of a theory of teaching. The meshes of the net of our theory may be pretty wide at the moment but it is likely that concepts taken from learning theory supported by some of the ideas current in curriculum development and aspects of philosophy of education will help to make the net finer. But the existence of a body of knowledge about and a commitment to the study of learning processes are likely to produce more concepts relevant to the development of a theory of teaching than are other disciplines.

VARIABLES IN TEACHING

From a general discussion we now turn to the finer grain of the possible theoretical studies related to the practice of teaching. The identification of key variables here will be an important element in helping the student teacher to perceive the outlines of a teaching model. Subsequent study of methods of controlling the variables will directly influence his classroom practice.

Central to any consideration of the variables in a teaching situation is the question of teaching objectives. It may be that such objectives are considered essentially to be the province of curriculum designers; nevertheless, if we hope to develop a consistent theoretical position *vis-à-vis* the practice of the teacher in the classroom the objectives specified must be possible of achievement and evaluation in terms of teaching activities without further interpretation. This is not to suggest that such objectives need be spelled out precisely for the teacher to operate with. Curricular aims are likely to be stated in fairly global terms; the teacher will have to derive from these objectives more specific ones for his own guidance. If the curricular objectives are not amenable to this sort of treatment, i.e. if they need translation, it seems to us they are inappropriately specified.

If a teacher is to be able to derive objectives that are to be useful for him in the classroom from generally stated curriculum objectives, the objectives must be interrelated in such a way as to permit or facilitate such an operation. This implies a taxonomic arrangement in which the logic of the taxonomy guides the teacher in the derivation of the objectives appropriate to the task in hand. In addition to helping the teacher derive his teaching objectives, a taxonomic approach helps guard against the production of a multitude of atomistic objectives. Stones (1972) has outlined such an approach. In this scheme global objectives are analysed to reveal the implied subordinate skills to be acquired by a student and the concepts subordinate to the overall content which students are expected to acquire. The product of an analysis of this nature is a network of objectives related hierarchically along two main dimensions. A teacher using a heuristic device such as this will not only be helped in producing useful sets of integrated objectives but will be more consciously attending to the theoretical aspect of his work and the interrelationship of teaching variables. Stating his objectives in behavioural terms, as we believe is desirable, will sharpen his perceptions of the way in which the variables are likely to apply in specific practical situations.

It is possible to classify the variables relating to teaching in three important groups; the first group may usefully be considered as belonging to a diagnostic phase; the second as belonging to a prescriptive or 'treatment' phase; and a third as belonging to an evaluation phase. All three phases are related to the central objectives in different ways. Phase one is related to the objectives in the way that the teacher makes decisions about the prerequisite skills and knowledge that the children need before embarking upon teaching aimed at achieving the objectives. In phase two decisions are made about the interrelationships of the variables deemed appropriate to the achieving of the objectives, and phase three is concerned with evaluating the efficacy of phase two in achieving the objectives, and this should involve an examination of the way in which the variables have interacted in phase two. The purpose of phase three should not merely be to produce a global assessment of the efficacy of teaching and learning but to give diagnostic information to pupil and teacher. On the basis of this information the teacher will be able to make recommendations about the next stage in the pupil's learning programme and to feed back into the teaching system information that will help to correct any shortcomings in phase two.

Phase one, what we have called the diagnostic phase, involves the teacher in the analysis of the teaching problem before teaching takes place. This analysis requires that the teacher should have a competence in the evaluation of pupil attainment and other factors relating to individual differences that may influence the course of the child's learning. The teacher should also have expertise in the skills of task analysis. The variables to be considered here are of two main types. On the one hand there is the analysis of the content of teaching and on the other there is the analysis of the nature of the learning which is planned. Content analysis will seek to expose the conceptual framework of the teaching task. It will identify the main concepts, rules and principles involved and seek to discern their interconnections. Analysing a teaching task in terms of the types of learning involved, such as, for example, concept formation, simple response learning, and stimulus discrimination, will help the teacher to plan the manipulation of the variables that influence them in order to enhance learning of the types identified.

In phase two the teacher deploys the skills necessary to put into practice the planned manipulation of the variables decided upon in phase one. We discuss some of these specific skills in more detail below but some examples would be the presenting of exemplars of a concept in a controlled way in order for the children to learn the concept most economically or the arranging for feedback to a child learning a discrimination, say in learning to read. Although the decision about which exemplars to use or how to provide feedback had been made in phase one, implementing the decisions demands a different sort of skill, the sort of skill in fact which most studies of teaching concentrate on but which nevertheless depends on phase one to an extent that is becoming increasingly recognized but is by no means universally accepted at the moment.

Phase three demands a knowledge of the theory of testing. Unfortunately until quite recently there has been a gap between the test theorists and learning theorists which has tended to keep them apart to the detriment of both. Only recently have questions of a fundamental nature such as the debate on the merits of criterion referenced tests (Glaser 1963, Stones 1970a) been raised. We would argue that the teacher needs the expertise of test construction to develop effective methods of evaluating his teaching so as to optimize the feedback from the pupils informing him of the strengths and weaknesses of his teaching. Such tests would need to be measures of the pupils' learning according to a predetermined criterion of competence rather than indicators of the merits of a child's attainment in comparison with the other children. They would, in fact, in most circumstances be criterion referenced tests. A teacher devising tests of this nature would be able to 'key' sections of the tests to the various elements in his teaching so that weaknesses in any of these sections, exposed by unsatisfactory results by a large number of the pupils taking the course, would readily be related to the section of the course that was working unsatisfactorily. This would constitute the diagnostic feedback referred to earlier and would enable the teacher to correct his teaching accordingly.

It is, we think, important to view the problems of classroom performance by a teacher or student teacher in the context of the three phases in teaching outlined above. Although we are here mainly concerned with phase two we firmly believe that the three phases should be regarded as different elements in the one process and not three different types of activity. Nor should it be overlooked that the activities are more likely to be cyclic or simultaneous in their occurrence than linear. Strasser (1967) suggests a conceptual model which depicts various teaching activities in this light and considers teaching as '. . . a dynamic, and, over a period of time, self correcting, continually redirected, influenced/influencing, interactive process' (see Part 3, pp. 172–86). With these monitions we now turn to a consideration of some specific variables in the teaching situation.

THE TEACHER'S PERSONALITY

Clearly the teacher's personality is one of the key global variables in the teaching situation. It is the basis of much of the argument that teachers are born and not made. Coupled with the craft view of teaching it justifies a non-interventionist approach to teacher training and reduces the problem to merely picking the winners. The problem with picking the winners has been spelled out in our discussions on teacher effectiveness. In addition, it seems extremely doubtful that enough teachers are likely to be born to meet the demand in what is now the largest profession. It thus seems desirable that any approach to a theory of teaching must say something about the personality characteristics of the teacher.

In line with our stance earlier, we do not suggest that a theory of teaching should *describe* the way in which personality characteristics influence teaching. Rather, we look for proposals that will help teachers to develop their personalities along lines calculated to improve their teaching. The implication is that teacher trainers are not only concerned with the cognitive development of their students but also with changing their personalities. Many will react against this suggestion, as they have in the past when it has been suggested that the job of the teacher is to change children. In both cases the objectors have been unperturbed so long as the influences changing children or students are fortuitous and covert. Making the processes overt and planned is what raises the anxiety levels of the objectors. We would associate ourselves with Smith (1969) when he says: 'The prospective teacher's attitudes and feelings are too important to leave the shaping of them to the accidents of human association or to the interests of individual instructors. A definite plan for identifying personality problems and attitudes should be developed in every programme of teacher education. These problems and attitudes should be identified in the early stages of each trainee's preparation. And a systematic programme of remedial situations should be worked out and followed through.'

Some of the problems that such a programme could be designed to cope with might be helping a withdrawn teacher to be more outgoing; to train a teacher to be more sensitive towards the children's affective behaviour, to be less authoritarian and more receptive of pupils' contributions. Attitudes such as racial prejudice, favouring individual pupils because they come from socially privileged homes or because they are conformist, or having low expectations from pupils from deprived backgrounds could be given greater emphasis by teacher trainers. Smith discusses methods of changing a student's personality characteristics mainly of the affective type, such as allowing a child to draw instead of doing arithmetic because he likes the child and wants to please him, although the child may need the practice in arithmetic, and suggests methods of counselling. Attitudes that have a greater cognitive content (for example, attitudes towards an issue in which a teachers' strike is involved) can be tackled by an analytic approach in which a group of student teachers analyse and discuss the pros and cons of different arguments underlying such attitudes and examine them for validity and consider their implications for teaching. It is true that assumptions are being made by the counsellor or tutor when he raises issues such as those outlined: assumptions of an evaluative nature in preferring this kind of attitude to that. Some of these assumptions have a basis in empirical findings, others are less soundly based but would be likely to obtain acceptance from a large majority of teacher trainers. Further evidence is needed concerning the effect of the various personality characteristics on pupil learning, but, working with the information we have, a theory of teaching such as we are considering would provide guidelines for making decisions about desirable personality traits such as openness to change and critical ability and how best to develop them in student teachers.

Before leaving this subject we should perhaps stress that deliberately setting out to modify a student teacher's personality characteristics does not imply that we are solely interested in a standardized product. Each student will maintain his essentially unique personality and some will be stronger on certain traits than others. But all will be aware of the effects of different personality characteristics on pupils' learning and will be helped to modify any factors that will be deleterious to that end.

PEDAGOGICAL FACTORS

It is impossible, of course, to separate affective and cognitive factors in teaching. Pedagogic considerations refer pre-eminently to the planned deployment of teaching skills according to a body of scientific principles. But these skills are deployed by real teachers with all the confounding effects of personality variables, some of which we have alluded to. But on the other hand the acquisition of many of these pedagogical skills will itself contribute to the development of more desirable personality traits. For example, a teacher who is naturally prone to be assertive and given to holding the floor in debate and yet is intellectually convinced that pupils learn better by being involved more in class decisions is likely to attempt to modify his personality so as to be less assertive and more encouraging of pupil participation. It thus seems to us desirable to focus upon the important specific pedagogical factors in our search for a viable body of general principles.

Studies in many fields have focused on the verbal behaviour of teacher and pupils when studying variables in teaching. Interaction analysis, which we discuss later, has been given particular attention (Amidon 1968, Amidon and Powell 1966, Barnes et al. 1969, Wragg 1971) but workers in other fields have subjected it to scrutiny. For example, Smith (1964, Smith and Meux 1962) has studied the logical aspects of teaching through the language of the teacher, and Taba (Taba and Elzey 1964) has focused on language in the development of concepts. Among the skills that have received attention have been such things as questioning, explaining, eliciting responses, defining, describing, comparing and contrasting, stating, confirming, justifying, amplifying, rating, appraising and interpreting. This list does not purport to be exhaustive but it is probably comprehensive enough to provide an indication of the level of generality of the teaching behaviours under consideration and so suggest to the reader possible lines of extension.

As an example of the application of systematic principles in this field we may consider the work of Taba. She used such skills as enumeration, listing and grouping in training for concept formation. She evolved specific strategies of questioning to get children to carry out operations calculated to enhance concept formation. These questions are arranged sequentially in order of cognitive complexity so that in the case of concept formation she would ask questions calculated initially to focus on the enumeration of criterial qualities of the concept, followed by questions to encourage grouping by identifying common properties, and finally to ask questions which make overt the labelling and categorizing of items according to hierarchical principles.

Although many of the examples of teacher skills referred to above focus on the teacher's own verbal activity, many of the items depend on, or are intended to elicit, pupil responses. Much of the work on interaction analysis stresses the benefits to be obtained from the teacher's taking a more indirect role than is normally the case and using his classroom techniques to produce more pupil involvement. Hill and Medley (1969) report some interesting work which illustrates how pupil involvement and learning are correlated and also gives us some specific information about the effects of different types of teacher verbal behaviour. In a small scale clinical type experiment they investigated the behaviour of four junior school teachers for four days of teaching. Their teaching was recorded and analysed using the OScAR 5V recording schedule. The OScAr 5V (Observation Schedule and Record 5 Verbal) is a recording schedule designed specifically to record information relevant to the affective and interpersonal interaction between teacher and pupil. The schedule was based on the approaches to the analysis of classroom interaction discussed in Chapter 7. It has eighteen separate categories: four for pupil utterances and fourteen for teacher utterances. However, these categories may be subdivided and sometimes combined so that the instrument makes possible the recording of up to sixty-eight different classroom events, thirteen kinds of statements and fifty-five kinds of interchanges. The record of these events forms the basis of inference about classroom environment. Hill and Medley used the instrument to record teacher social–emotional interaction and in addition took measures of pupil gain and measures of content coverage. When the results were analysed it was found that one teacher's pupils learned substantially more than the pupils of other teachers. This was particularly the case when the efficacy of teaching for the application of principles was being considered, but it also applied in the learning of facts. This teacher also covered more ground than the other teachers who did less well in the teaching for application. This in itself is an interesting finding since often teachers excuse cramming on the grounds that it is the only way of covering the syllabus and this teacher was doing the reverse of cramming. However, the main thing of interest to our present discussion is the comparison of the attributes of the worst and the best teacher in their deployment of classroom skills. When teaching to the goal of application of principles, the following teaching behaviours were seen to characterize the two teachers:

The best teacher (in terms of pupil gains) scored highest on	*The worst teacher scored highest on*
informing statements	directing statements
pupil non-substantive statement: approved	rebuking statements
pupil questions: not evaluated	non-substantive statements (i.e. statements not about subject matter)
pupil questions: approved	pupil responses: not evaluated
pupil statements: approved	problem structuring statements
pupil responses: acknowledged	convergent interchanges: not evaluated
convergent interchanges: supported	convergent interchanges: neutrally rejected
elaborating questions: not answered	

It is not difficult to relate most of the above categories to existing knowledge about learning and it is particularly interesting to note the affective element in teaching which results in pupils' achieving mastery in cognitive skills.

A similar study, which suggests possible lines of investigating the relationships between theoretical principles and actual practice, has been reported by Baker (1969). In this experiment thirty-eight Peace Corps trainees were given instruction in the use of theoretically based learning principles. Observers were concurrently trained to record teachers' use of the principles. The trainees were then required to teach high school pupils in lessons which were recorded on video tape. Each trainee was assigned a behavioural objective to achieve and the pupils were pre-tested and post-tested on items measuring the objectives. Positive relationships were found between pupil achievement and the trainees' use of certain learning principles. The principles investigated comprised appropriate practice, perceived purpose, individual differentiation, knowledge of results and graded sequencing. The experimental method was correlational and other aspects of the procedure incline us to caution in considering this investigation; nevertheless we suggest that it illustrates very well an extremely useful way of proceeding in this field.

Since the bulk of a teacher's work consists of helping pupils to form bodies of concepts it is inevitable that his verbal activities will be predominant. Non-verbal behaviour should not, however, be overlooked. In fact one of the weaknesses of audio taping classroom interactions is that the non-verbal element is lost. When we discuss microteaching we shall consider the methods that have been used to modify non-verbal behaviour. Some of the aspects of non-verbal behaviour that have been investigated are such things as facial expression, approaching a pupil to encourage him, the effect of movement about the classroom and methods of focusing attention upon individual children. Concluding this section we should like to make reference to some of the points made by Clarke (1970) which seem to us to pinpoint some of the key issues in this field. He presents his suggestions in the form of prescriptions and under each prescription spells out the teaching behaviours that are likely to contribute to the fulfilment of the prescription. We give here only the headings of the prescriptions which may provide a framework for the reader to construct his own model. He proposes that teaching prescriptions should be classified under three headings. At level 1 he considers that teaching must:

1 Provide for communication between the pupil and teacher and among students.
2 Develop teacher–pupil interpersonal relationships conducive to student learning.
3 When groups of pupils are involved, develop and maintain a social order conducive to pupil learning.
4 Ensure that pupils are motivated to learn.
5 Ensure that pupils are active.

At level 2:

6 Employ strategies that produce minimum interference with other objectives and that are appropriate to (*a*) the character-

istics of the learner, (*b*) how pupils learn, (*c*) the specific curricular objectives.

At level 3:

7 Appraise student progress towards curricular objectives with a view to reteaching, revising teaching strategies, revising curricular objectives, or a combination of these.
8 Provide a minimum level of performance in each (preceding) prescription.

We have not attempted in this section to develop our own prescriptions or, indeed, to report other people's prescriptions on how best to train student teachers in the behaviours discussed. This is, of course, not unconnected with the fact that, in our present state of knowledge, this would be a most difficult enterprise. However, we feel that we shall have achieved our objectives if we have alerted the reader to some of the possibilities and problems inherent in the very difficult undertaking of sketching out the outlines of a theory (or theories) of teaching.

5 · Simulation

Theories do not spring fully grown from the heads of theorists in teaching any more than in other fields. Thus the inductive nature of the scientific method is likely to be as appropriately applied in the field of pedagogy as elsewhere. It seems to us, therefore, to be entirely reasonable to hope that empirical observations of teaching procedures involved in the working out of teaching prescriptions, such as those outlined in the previous chapter, will not only provide useful guidelines for teachers but will also add to the data from which we may eventually be able to abstract principles relevant to a body of theory. Thus the scrutiny of some of the more promising developments in the manipulation of variables related to teaching in the training situation, which we now take up, should have an eye to their possible contribution to theory as well as to their more obvious practical utility.

In this section we take up briefly the general question of the simulation of the practical teaching situation. Some of the methods are by no means new although it is probably true to say that they have been undervalued and underused as adjuncts to practical professional work in teacher education. Thus, for example, the ideas of role playing have been around for a long time and have, in fact, been employed in teacher training. Student teachers have taught their peers in simulated classroom encounters and followed up by discussion and lesson critique.

Simulation is by definition 'artificial' and some people are inclined to dismiss it because of that and prefer instead the 'real' situation of the student teacher in the classroom. On the other hand, telling the students in lectures how to cope with various classroom situations is quite common. Simulation techniques, for all their artificiality, can often be preferable to putting students into the classroom to learn on their own or to lecturing to them about the classroom. In other spheres pilots train in the 'artificial' circumstances of the link trainer, driving schools have their traffic simulators and medical students their cadavers. And this is eminently sensible. By the same token classroom simulation removes the risk from the first steps of the neophyte and enables him to come to terms with the demands of a complex skill learning without the stress of the real situation. At the same time it is to be preferred to merely 'telling' the student, for much the same reasons as it is better to allow the beginning pilot to practise operating the dummy controls rather than telling him how to do it when he finds himself in the air.

Apart from the most important aspect of simulation in introducing the student to teaching in non-stressful conditions, we would remind the reader about other important features already referred to when considering the problems of mastering the teaching model. Simulation gives us greater control over the teaching variables. We can arrange for the student to have experience of situations which he might well not otherwise get if he were entirely dependent upon the fortuitous circumstances of the classroom. We are trying to build up concepts about teaching in the student and the best way to do this is to present exemplars of the concepts, i.e. concrete examples of teaching problems and activities, in a structured way so that the student is able to abstract the common general features from the specific particular examples. Leaving this process entirely to the chance configurations of classroom interactions is likely to give a student only a partial picture. On the other hand, although it is possible to present a wide variety of specific instances of classroom situations verbally, this won't do either. The reason for this is that the verbal examples depend for their efficacy on a knowledge of the real situation. The words of the tutor are only useful to the extent to which they are relatable by the student to concepts he already has. If he has had no sensory experience in the field he will have no concepts to relate to the tutor's words so the most that can be hoped for is the rote learning of the tutor's precepts. It might be argued that the crucial concepts can be learned vicariously since anyway any student will have had experience of classroom situations as a pupil, but this is an argument that cannot really be taken seriously in view of the very different relationship of the student as pupil and the student as teacher to the classroom environment.

If, then, we accept the argument that there is some merit in the 'artificiality' of simulation as a means of introducing the student to the teaching situation, what approaches seem to offer most promise for practical teacher training? The answer seems to be that there are two main areas that are relevant: those that relate to activities within the actual teaching situation, and those relating to activities outside the teaching situation. The former refers to what we called earlier the *prescription* phase of teaching, the latter to what we called the *diagnostic* and *evaluation* phases of teaching. It is also possible to conceive of another dimension of simulation which relates to the degree of structuring in the simulated situation, ranging from the completely unconstrained play acting of sociodrama to the highly structured game type activity of *in basket* techniques.

Sociodrama is very much related to the practice, referred to above, of role playing by student teachers. The accent is upon the spontaneous interaction of the group, it is the unstructured simulation situation *par excellence*; it might, in fact, be denied the title of simulation (Tansey and Unwin 1969). When a degree of structure is introduced we get the situation more typical of student teacher role playing. Students in this situation are usually given some indication as to subject, method, level of pupil competence and so on. Sometimes the group of students that normally constitutes the class is briefed as to the type of pupil behaviours to manifest.

Much more sophisticated approaches using the so-called *in basket* techniques provide the student with a great many more data and increase the degree of structure. Cruickshank (1968) has developed a teacher training system which can present the student with up to thirty-one different simulated problems related to teaching. The aim of his 'Teaching Problems Laboratory' is for the participant to assume the role of the teacher and to practise solving the critical teaching problems he has identified. The participant is introduced into the situation as if he were a new teacher in a school, Longacre, in a fictitious town, Madison. He is provided with information and opportunities to solve the problems of a beginning teacher by exposure to a variety of potential solutions to particular problems and given the opportunity of observing the results of his chosen line of action. He is introduced to the situation by film strips on the town and its schools and Longacre school in particular. He is also given the materials that a teacher going to the school would actually receive: such things as the school rules and regulations, curriculum handbook and record cards on thirty-one children, together with sociograms and samples of the children's work. The student is then presented with thirty-one problems, ten on film and others in role playing situations, written incidents or combinations. After the presentation of each problem the student responds to an Incident Response Sheet which demands that he identify the problem, identify the factors influencing the problem, locate the relevant information, suggest appropriate alternative courses of action, communicate and implement a decision. Small group discussion now follows which considers the analysis and action taken and this is followed by larger group discussion. The objective of the discussions is not to come up with the 'right' answer but to push the analysis of the teaching problem and attempted solution as far as possible. Cruickshank considers that his scheme provides the student with simulated laboratory experiences. Among these experiences are such things as the preparation and teaching of meaningful lessons, the construction of a classroom test, the holding of parent conferences, locating instructional materials, developing a reading programme, learning to use records, considering motivational techniques, preparing behavioural objectives for learning, and providing for individual differences in learning. Cruickshank found as a result of two field tests that student teachers were very favourably disposed to his system and considered it much more helpful than lectures and more valuable to them than the two weeks of teaching practice that it replaced. He suggests a number of advantages for simulation techniques which crop up repeatedly when we discuss other alternatives for student teaching practice, some of which we have already considered. The common thread is the fact that in using these techniques we are forging close links between theory and practice. Among the advantages claimed are that students are given intensive focused opportunities to study and analyse critical teaching problems that may not recur in other pre-school activities; situations are also created which permit of group discussions of teaching problems which bring those problems out into the open and 'objectify' them so that questions of censure or failure on the part of individual students do not arise; possibilities are also opened up for classroom teachers to analyse their own classroom behaviour. Cruickshank considers that much more work needs to be done to develop the techniques of simulation as he conceives them, both into their efficacy and into their best mode of use. We would hope that colleges and university departments in Britain will be parties to such experimentation since there seems little doubt that there are some very interesting possibilities in the techniques for effecting considerable improvements in the various practical skills of student teachers.

The reader will have noted that the work outlined by Cruickshank embraces all three elements in the teaching paradigm of diagnosis, prescription and evaluation which we discussed earlier. First steps in the application of simulation techniques could well be taken in the diagnostic and evaluation fields. Such exercises as the preparation of a classroom test or the designing of a reading course are obvious examples of work that would not be too difficult a first step (and in fact some colleges already do this sort of thing). Any extra-classroom activity connected with the work of the teacher could be simulated in this way and in many cases such work can very closely approximate to the real thing if students are able to relate the products of exercises to actual teaching situations, for example by trying out tests or teaching programmes.

An example of simulated extra-classroom activity, but in a slightly different field, is that used by workers at Worcester College of Education (Checketts *et al.* 1970). They used simulation techniques as a method of assessing students in the final year of the college course. Their approach employed similar techniques to those of Cruickshank and made use extensively of dossier material. Students were presented with dossiers providing information about the borough of Kingswick, about its schools, about specific classes and children, and were then presented with problems which asked them to make judgements about courses of action related to a school, a class, or individual children. While this operation was not a part of teaching practice or its assessment, it exemplifies an approach that could be used with little modification in that connection.

Role playing before classes of fellow students takes the participant into the classroom situation. Providing the type of structuring that Cruickshank suggests gives the exercise more rigour than the unstructured sociodrama. Along somewhat different lines Kersh (1962) has provided a particularly sophisticated example of structuring the role playing exercise. He simulated classroom situations by the use of films and printed materials. The student responds to the simulated classroom problems presented on film by deploying certain teaching skills. The object of the exercise is to help the student to acquire the ability to detect, diagnose and learn how to deal with such problems as confusion, inattention and distraction in the children. As in all approaches to simulation the supervising tutor is in the position of being able to give the student immediate feedback related to the action he takes.

A recent development in the field of simulation which connects with other new developments in teacher training is the use of micro-teaching methods in simulation situations. We discuss the micro-teaching approach in detail later; at this stage we give an outline of the method as it relates to simulation.

Essentially the method employs a scaled down teaching act in-volving role playing student teachers as pupils. The teaching act is scaled down in terms of length and size of class and in general four or five students make up the microclass. The trainee teacher pre-pares a short lesson to last only six to eight minutes but the lesson should be self-contained and not merely the introduction to a longer lesson. It is possible to do this by concentrating on single concepts. The trainee then teaches his microclass and the lesson is recorded on video tape. The student teacher's supervisor is present and sometimes another member of the education department or other trained helper. At the end of the lesson the supervisor, the other observer(s), the microclass and often the student teacher him-self complete an evaluation form which appraises the lesson. A dis-cussion then takes place among the observers, the microclass and the student teacher on the strengths and weaknesses of the lesson within a positive general atmosphere. Suggestions as to key points in the lesson are made and the video tape played back for the student teacher to observe his performance in the light of the discussion. It is desirable and customary then for the trainee to modify his lesson plan and reteach it to a new group of students and even to repeat this process. However, simulation of this type has been used without the reteach cycle with apparently satisfactory results and with very positive acceptance by students (Webb et al. 1968). In their evalua-tion of the effectiveness of a large scale simulation at Brigham Young University involving over 700 students in the initial course in teacher training, 88 per cent of a random sample of eighty-one students considered that the simulation exercise very definitely indicated to them areas in which they could improve their teaching. In another random sample (N = 41) 87 per cent rated the micro-teaching exercise as excellent, compared with 37 per cent rating the next most popular learning activity on the course (writing behavioural objectives) excellent. The evaluators who observed the lessons and advised the students were also very positively inclined towards it and thought that the time, effort and expense necessary to provide each student with one microteaching experience was justified. They all considered, however, that it would be better to provide more than one experience.

This positive acceptance by students of simulation has been found generally in studies of its use. As we have already said, students thought the experience more useful than two weeks' practice in school or lectures. They also found it very enjoyable, realistic and helpful. The experimenters concluded that simulation techniques were an unqualified success. They concluded that simulation motivates and involves students and that it was at least as effective as the same amount of teaching practice and they confidently expected that it could be improved with more development. This seems a very reasonable conclusion since there is no reason to doubt that what has been found useful in other spheres of training would be useful in student teaching.

Simulation procedures are not without their problems, of course. Rowell (1968) gives an interesting account of the difficulties encountered when the techniques were used to simulate the teaching of fifth grade (American) pupils. The student teachers were inducted through the use of simulated experiences employing film, filmstrip, records, cumulative record folders, written teaching problems and role playing cards. Students had to carry out all the functions of real teaching such as getting to know the children, teaching daily lessons, planning the curriculum, conducting parent meetings, studying children and gathering teaching materials. Problems encountered by Rowell related to most of these activities and clearly indicate areas for investigation by other workers who wish to make use of the techniques. One problem was that of deciding on the optimum amount of preparation to be given to the simulation exercise. Clearly there are basic concepts that are prerequisite to tackling the exercise and yet if too much information is given about the actual task before the event it may vitiate the effect of the exercise itself. In the actual practice of role playing of teaching lessons, some students were reluctant to assume the roles and it seems necessary to make clear to students that the assumption of the role in the simulation situation provides a realistic induction to real classroom problems. If the simulated lesson lacks a clearly articulated overt relationship with real teaching problems some students will not be persuaded of the value of the exercise and may well be reluctant as in the case of Rowell's students. It should not be thought, however, that all students disliked role playing. On the contrary; along with film viewing this was the best liked of all the simulation exercises. And this presented problems of its own. It is necessary, but not always easy, to distinguish between positive student attitudes towards an exercise and student progress. As Rowell points out, this emphasizes the need to have an objectives-based approach to help to get one's criterion of efficacy clear. A similar problem arose with regard to the selection of teaching material: students had a tendency to choose material according to personal preference rather than for its relevance to the problem under consideration. Other difficulties were those of getting students to take an analytical approach to the solving of problems, the identification of professional materials relating to simulated incidents and providing suitable follow up material related to simulated incidents. (A cited example of the latter problem was the student who could cope with the immediate problem of handling a disturbing child but who would benefit from an examination into the possible causes of the disturbing behaviour.) One other possible pitfall could flow from the desirability to keep fairly detailed records of the various teaching incidents. The problem here lies in the fact that record keeping might become an end in itself. Finally there is the overriding problem, not peculiar to simulation exercises, of providing efficacious methods of evaluation. And the answer to this as to all methods of providing vicarious experience of the classroom must be in the final ability to read the classroom situation as effectively as he reads the vicarious experience.

The simulation of experiences related to the job of the teacher including, but not wholly concerned with, actual classroom encounters thus seems to us to present interesting perspectives for the future development of techniques that actually involve students in the business of teaching before they are faced with the situation itself. We see no reason why the problems involved should be impossible of solution and think the positive student reactions are encouraging signs. Indeed, it seems highly likely that simulation techniques could form a valuable element in the practical professional work of student teachers. However, we should be disappointed if such work were to be entirely of an *ad hoc* nature. We would urge that the teaching problems chosen for attention should be related to some hypotheses or established principles wherever possible so that experience in the use of the techniques will have the potentiality of adding to our information about the teaching model and not merely solving a specific teaching problem in isolation.

6 · Microteaching

Simulation techniques provide a means of student teacher induction through the medium of experiences demanding skills that closely approximate to those appropriate to real situations. In this section we consider techniques that involve the use of real teaching situations, but situations that are not normally found in a teacher's day-to-day activities. They are simplified teaching situations which allow of a greater degree of control than that normally found in classroom teaching and enable provision to be made for feedback to student teachers far more effectively than in the practice lesson with complete classes which is currently the staple of teacher training procedures. These are the techniques of microteaching.

Microteaching

Microteaching is one of the most important developments in the field of teaching practice. It originated in Stanford University in 1963. Workers in the Center for Research and Development in Teaching evolved an approach to practical teacher training, which owed something to already existing techniques such as group practice but which transcended them by introducing tighter control, more analytical methods and a completely new approach to the providing of feedback. Since then there has been an explosion in the use of these techniques in the U.S.A. and a very rapidly developing interest in Great Britain. The new methods go under the generic title of *Microteaching* and we are convinced (along with an increasingly large number of teacher educators) that these methods hold very great promise for the future of teacher preparation.

The basic principles of microteaching are simple. A student teacher teaches a short lesson of about five minutes' duration to a small number of pupils. At the end of the lesson the pupils leave and the student discusses the lesson with his supervisor. After a short break the student repeats the lesson with a different group of pupils making use of the feedback from the supervisor to attempt to improve on his previous lesson.

This basic format is in fact rarely employed. Normally the micro-lesson, while aimed at teaching the pupils genuine subject content, focuses upon a specific teaching skill decided upon beforehand. In addition, feedback to the student is enhanced by the use of a video tape recording of the lesson and by the use of instruments such as the Stanford Teacher Competence Appraisal Guide. Allen and Ryan (1969) in the currently most comprehensive book on the subject give the following as the main propositions of microteaching:

First, microteaching is real teaching. Although the teaching situation is a constructed one in the sense that the teacher and students (pupils) work together in a practice situation, neverthe-less bona fide teaching does take place.

Second, microteaching lessens the complexities of normal class-room teaching. Class size, scope of content, and time are all reduced.

Third, microteaching focuses on training for the accomplish-ment of specific tasks. These tasks may be the practice of in-structional skills, the practice of techniques of teaching, the mastery of certain curricular materials, or the demonstration of teaching methods.

Fourth, microteaching allows for the increased control of practice. In the practice setting of microteaching, the rituals of time, students (pupils), methods of feedback and supervision, and many other factors can be manipulated. As a result, a high degree of control can be built into the training program.

Fifth, microteaching greatly expands the normal knowledge-of-results or feedback dimension in teaching. Immediately after teaching a brief microlesson, the trainee engages in a critique of his performance. To give him a maximum insight into his per-formance, several sources of feedback are at his disposal. With the guidance of a supervisor or colleague, he analyses aspects of his own performance in light of his goals. The trainee and the super-visor go over student (pupil) response forms that are designed to elicit students' (pupils') reactions to specific aspects of his teach-ing. When the supervisor has video tape available, he can use video tape playbacks to help show the teacher how he performs and how he can improve. All this feedback can be immediately translated into practice when the trainee reteaches shortly after the critique conference.

Belt (1967) reports a particularly interesting approach to the evaluation session which involved asking the high school pupils to participate along with the supervisor, the student's colleagues and the trainee himself. Often the pupils' comments were thought to be most beneficial by the student teachers.

Microteaching goes a fair way to solving some of the problems involved in student teaching practice. One of the most obvious is that the student is phased into real teaching gradually instead of being dropped in at the deep end as is the case in most existing situations. Apart from the benefits that accrue to the student from this approach, there is the added consideration that the pupils are less 'at risk' than in conventional student teaching practice. The fact that microteaching focuses upon specific teaching skills enables supervisor and student to approach the job in the spirit of mastering the teaching model, rather than trying to imitate the practised (but not necessarily perfect) performance of a 'master' teacher. One other important feature of microteaching which is reported by various practitioners is that the conflict between the student teacher's view of the supervisor as guide and mentor and his view of him as assessor is reduced. The fact that the student himself is involved in the appraisal of his microlesson is clearly important in producing this different attitude, while the use of the video tape recorder and the involvement of pupils and peers as well as the tutor in appraisal sessions may well contribute in an important way to making appraisal more objective in the student's eyes.

THE VIDEO RECORDING

It is generally considered by practitioners of microteaching that video recording is not essential to the exercise. Microteaching can be carried on using supervisor and peer group notes and comments coupled with the completion of evaluative instruments by supervisor, other student teacher observers and the pupils at the end of the microlesson. The discussion session after the microlesson is perfectly viable even in the absence of the video recording. Audio recordings are possible substitutes for video recordings and some of the microteaching packages known as 'minicourses' make use of audio recordings as an alternative to video recordings. It is generally agreed, however, that the availability of video recording enhances the effectiveness and flexibility of microteaching (Pinney and Miltz n.d., Goodkind 1968, Voth 1968, Kallenbach 1969). McDonald and Allen (1967) found that student self-viewing of a video recording with prompting by a supervisor was the single most effective variable in an experiment on the acquisition of a teaching skill, while Wragg (1971) suggests that video recording and interaction analysis (discussed below) in combination can effect substantial changes in teaching behaviour.

Some of the obvious advantages of using video recordings flow from the fact that they can be used to reinstate teaching activities after the event in the post-teaching discussion. In this situation the supervisor can comment on quite specific teaching acts and direct attention to the strengths and weaknesses of a lesson. Often in the early stages of microteaching with inexperienced students a good deal of the comment by the supervisor is supportive and as much intended to reinforce as to inform, but even at this stage when the overall effect is of global encouragement it is possible to be more specific than is the case when a supervisor discusses a lesson after observing a student teacher in the normal school practice situation.

One interesting finding, which makes for increased flexibility in the practical professional work of student teachers, is the fact that feedback and reinforcement from supervisor to student are effective even if the critique session follows the microlesson at an interval of several days. Principles from learning theories are generally agreed that it is important to reinforce behaviour or to provide knowledge of results (feedback) almost immediately after the behaviour has occurred. This new finding from empirical studies thus has import for the general principles of teaching. In addition to the need to discover what are the optimum methods of using recordings there is the further interesting and important area of investigation to attempt to identify the parameters of the teaching and learning process that enable us to dispense with the immediacy of feedback hitherto considered essential. McDonald and Allen (1967) 'explain' the phenomenon by saying that it may be that the video recording reinstates the trainee's performance for him in a way that is quite different from having another person tell him about it. This unexceptional statement may be considered a first general comment on the question; what is needed is much more analytical study analogous to the studies of reinforcement carried out in classical learning experiments.

Other questions concerned with the use of video recording are of a more practical nature. The reaction of most supervisors and teachers on first becoming acquainted with the ideas of micro-teaching is to enquire whether the hardware is so obtrusive as to transform the lesson completely. They think it likely that the teacher and children will be so conscious of the television camera that the lesson will bear little resemblance to real teaching. The answer to this misgiving seems to be quite universally that once the novelty has worn off teacher and pupils seem to forget that the equipment is there. This familiarization takes place very quickly, so much so that it seems to be hardly a problem at all. The student teacher's reaction on viewing himself for the first time after a microlesson is also a form of familiarization. The reaction seems to be similar to that which most people experience on first hearing their voice on audio tape, except that instead of comments such as 'I didn't know I had such a pronounced accent' the students' remarks are likely to be of the nature of 'I didn't know I paced around the room so much'. The experience of workers at Stanford shows that these reactions, which they refer to as 'cosmetic' considerations, soon give way to matters of relevance to the actual teaching when the student has his second session of microteaching.

Here we think it important to make reference to comments made by Pinney and Miltz regarding the optimum use of television in teacher education. They make the point that some of the most obvious ways of incorporating television into teacher training do not fully capitalize on the resources it offers:

For example, using television as a labour saving device and in an observation program that is merely a replica of what has been done traditionally is an enormous waste of technological resources. Such an application of television would be analogous to using sophisticated computer facilities to schedule a student (pupil) body in a school where the curriculum has not been revised for twenty-five years and which maintains the traditional 'lock-step' schedule. In both instances a powerful new tool is applied to an outworn model. The obvious alternative is to examine the new resources and ask how they would allow for the revitalization of the old model or the creation of a completely new one.

This comment is very much in line, of course, with our arguments on the need to master the teaching model.

Video recordings offer interesting possibilities in remote supervision. The idea here is that student teachers, teachers on in-service courses, or teachers wanting to consult staff in training institutions would send in video recordings of microlessons. These recordings would be reviewed by the member of staff concerned who would add a commentary on the second sound track of the video tape so that the teacher would be able to play it back when it was returned to him and have the benefit of the supervisor's comments. A development of this envisages a series of microlessons recorded over a period of time so that a supervisor would be able to comment on progress. Using techniques like these could effect enormous savings in supervisor time, not to mention supervisor wear and tear travelling from school to school.

One further use of video recording to which Pinney and Miltz make reference is to bring supervisors from schools and colleges and universities together to view examples of teaching so that problems of interpretation and evaluation of teaching performance can be squarely faced with a view to arriving at some form of consensus on criteria of evaluation.

EVALUATIVE INSTRUMENTS

We have already referred to one evaluative instrument, the Stanford Teacher Competence Appraisal Guide. This has been widely used both at Stanford and elsewhere in connection with microteaching (Kallenbach 1967, Fortune et al. 1967, Wragg 1971). Clearly the quality of the evaluative instrument is a crucial factor in any scheme of training and all the elaborate arrangements one might make come to nothing if feedback to the student teacher is based on a crude or faulty diagnostic tool, and to a great extent the Stanford Guide avoids these failings. A range of other instruments with a similar rationale has been developed, but one of their shortcomings is their non-specific nature. That is, they tend to focus rather generally upon the global activity in the classroom, whereas the developing techniques of microteaching tend to focus on particular aspects of teaching: what we discuss below under the heading of *constituent skills*. Instruments of this type are related to quite specific teaching skills and although most of them have relatively few categories as compared with, say, the S.T.C.A.G. they each produce a 'microprofile' of teacher performance in that specific skill. Taking a number of such profiles together would give a more detailed overall profile than is provided by the more global instruments. Microprofiles have an important advantage over the global instruments through their very specificity. Since the profiles focus on short teaching encounters related to clearly defined teaching skills, it is possible to gear the categories of the profiles to particular teaching objectives. Experience has shown that inter-supervisor reliability can be raised to reasonably high levels with training (Berliner 1969, Young and Young 1969). Whether or not the scales are valid is a matter for consensus of experts, as is almost universally the case in attempts to assess the validity of evaluative instruments in the field of complex human learning. The advantage of the microteaching profile over the teaching assessment mark discussed in Chapter 2 is that it is amenable to consensus agreement because it is analytical, because it is of limited scope, and because it is related to clearly specified student teacher activities which can be recorded and discussed after the event. This is not to suggest that there is no problem of evaluation. Clearly these first generation instruments will be subject to scrutiny and development as knowledge and experience of their use in connection with microteaching expands.

To give the reader an idea of the type of instrument currently in use we may refer to the evaluation sheet for the skill of reinforcement used at Stanford University (Allen and Ryan 1969). This evaluation sheet is completed by pupils, supervisors and teachers. It has four dimensions.

1 When a student (pupil) answered a question correctly or asked a good question, did the teacher reward him with such words as 'Fine', 'Good', 'Excellent', etc.?
   List the words he used and the number of times he used each.
2 What non-verbal cues (e.g. a smile or a nod of the head) did the teacher use to encourage his students?
3 When a student (pupil) gave an answer that was only partly correct, did the teacher give him credit for the correct part?

4 Did the teacher ever refer to the positive aspects of a student's previous response?

The number of categories in the different instruments will depend upon the number of identifiable major teacher behaviours related to the achievement of the objectives of the microteaching lesson. Often the categories are assessed on scales ranging from three to seven points. In some cases it is possible to make quantitative measures of teacher behaviour related to the objectives. For example, when training student teachers to ask more higher order questions (discussed below), it is possible to check the records of lessons to see if in fact the number of such questions increases with training.

COMPONENT SKILLS TRAINING

Our discussion of evaluative instruments has referred to the merits of focusing upon specific teaching skills rather than having a global approach. This aspect of microteaching offers particular promise for the development of a useful teaching model. An attempt is made to identify the component skills of teaching and to apply what is known about the optimum conditions for human learning to encourage their development in student teachers. Training is given to help the students to develop skills related to the instructional concepts involved and to practise them with a small group of pupils in a microlesson. We give here a brief résumé of some of the skills that have been included in work at Stanford (Allen and Ryan 1969).

Stimulus variation Training in the skills of stimulus variation is aimed at helping student teachers to avoid teaching styles likely to induce boredom in their pupils. A stimulus situation that changes in different ways is one of the most powerful influences in maintaining orienting activity by the pupils. Carefully structured teaching material and approaches to the subject can have an important effect here, but so can the way a teacher conducts his lesson. Stimulus variation, in the Stanford sense, focuses mainly on the latter. Some of the things the student teacher is trained in are the use of movement in a systematic way and the avoidance of teaching from one spot, the use of gestures, the development of verbal and non-verbal methods of focusing children's attention, the development of teaching methods other than the teacher monologue by encouraging pupil participation, the systematic use of pauses, and the controlled use of different sensory channels by switching primary modes of communication: going, for example, from the oral to the visual.

Set induction This skill is concerned with methods of preparing classes for a lesson: that is, pre-instructional orientation. Students practise methods of starting lessons.

Closure This is the obverse of set induction. It involves training in different methods of concluding a lesson with the student taking steps to ensure that the pupils have understood and are able to see the connections with other phenomena.

Silence and non-verbal cues Most teachers talk too much. Training in the use of silence and non-verbal cues is aimed at remedying this state of affairs. But it is not just a negative thing. Silence can have a powerful effect if used insightfully and non-verbal cues can very often be more effective than verbal ones.

Reinforcement skills Reinforcement is one of the most widely known principles of successful learning and probably one of the most widely transgressed against by practising teachers. Training in the skills of reinforcement involves the development of discriminating methods of rewarding and encouraging pupil's efforts and of avoiding the often unconscious punishing comments on a child's work.

Other skills that have been taught through the component skills approach are such things as fluency in asking questions, asking probing questions, higher order questioning, asking divergent questions, recognizing attending behaviour, illustrating and use of examples, lecturing, planned repetition, completeness of communication.

A report by B. E. Ward (1970) on 141 teacher training institutions in America using microteaching showed that they considered the five most important technical skills of teaching to be: probing questions, reinforcement, asking questions, higher order questions, establishing set, in that order. The five technical skills most frequently used in the teach–reteach cycle were: asking questions, establishing set, reinforcement, use of examples, varying the stimulus, in that order. Ward also found that, although technical skills are regarded as an important element in microteaching, there seemed to be a lack of knowledge about them in view of the fact that only a third of the programmes reported had written rationale or video taped or filmed

D

models of the skills. This deficiency is probably a function of the fact that most of the institutions reporting had only recently started to use microteaching.

MODELLING

One other important element in current approaches to microteaching is the use of filmed or video taped models of teaching behaviour. This apparent regression to the model the master teacher approach is, in fact, more apparent than real. Far from reverting to the un-controlled complexities of orthodox classroom observation, model-ling in the microteaching context is highly structured and tightly controlled. It is an important adjunct to the specific skills approach. Instead of explaining to a student how to exercise a specific skill or how to improve his own performance of the skill, he is shown a short example of the skill on tape or film. These models are not sub-stitutes for the other methods of training but complement them. They focus on specific skills and present short examples of the skills modelled by teachers to bring out their essential features. In some cases the model exaggerates the key aspects of the skill being modelled. In addition, the models are carefully prepared and vali-dated on student populations and revised until they are functioning satisfactorily. Once prepared, of course, they can be viewed by any student a number of times, unlike the ephemeral incoherence of the typical classroom transaction.

The rationale of modelling is derived from theories of imitative learning such as those proposed by Bandura and Walters (1963). In general it is considered that modelled behaviour which is rein-forced will be learned. Applied to the teaching situation, imitated behaviour that produces increased pupil learning, attention or motivation will be acquired. Since the models provided are designed to do just those things it seems reasonable to expect that students will imitate the behaviours exemplified by the models. There is ample evidence, in fact, that different types of models do produce student learning but it is by no means clearly established that alternative approaches might not be successful in certain circumstances.

Young (1969), Claus (1969), McDonald and Allen (1967) and Koran et al. (1969) all produce evidence of student learning through the use of models, and all raise issues that relate not to the efficacy of modelling, but to questions concerned with the best types of model for different types of skill training and possibly for use with different students. Such things as the use of visual or symbolic models, the relative efficacy of audio and video recordings, and the role of the supervisor, have all been the subject of investigation. James (1970) used film models of teaching behaviour showing direct and indirect teaching strategies in comparison with video recordings of students' own teaching as adjuncts to traditional teaching supervision. She found that there was no difference in performance after supervision between the group that had the filmed model and the normally supervised group, whereas there was a difference between the group that viewed video recordings of their own performance and the traditionally supervised group. The point about this finding is not that filmed models are ineffective but that students probably need guidance when viewing models and in fact other investigations suggest that focusing methods used by supervisors either in the critique of the microlesson or on the second sound track of the video recording of the student's own teaching are important elements in the student's learning from models (Young 1968, Young and Young 1969, Claus 1969).

One of the problems in this field is that there seems to be some confusion as to what constitutes a model. Berliner (1969), for example, reports an investigation which demonstrated that a perceptual model of higher order questioning behaviour was no more effective in producing student learning than a symbolic model. The symbolic model for Berliner was a printed transcript of a lesson given by an experienced teacher: it was, in fact, an actual example of higher order questioning. On the other hand some authors use the term *symbolic modelling* to describe such things as written instructions on how to perform certain skills (Borg et al. 1969). In our view the latter use is erroneous. If students treated a set of instructions as a model they would imitate them presumably by producing another set of instructions! We do not think this is splitting hairs – on the contrary, we think it essential to strive for optimum clarity in a field in such an early state of development. If we do not make explicit distinctions we shall not only muddy the conceptual waters in our search for a body of theoretical principles, but we could also make faulty judgements in our attempts to provide optimum learning situations even within our present state of knowledge.

It seems likely that skills that are less dependent upon verbal interaction may be best modelled perceptually, and of course in our definition of the terms it would not be possible to provide a symbolic model of non-verbal teaching behaviour. Precisely what are the most effective and economical types of model is still an open question, and in addition to the problem of video recording versus symbolic modelling there are such possibilities as the use of film, slides, audio tape or combinations of these. Other problems of modelling relate to such things as the optimum degree of exaggeration of the skill being modelled (or, indeed, whether there should be any exaggeration at all) and to questions about the conceptual level of the content of the lesson, and the most appropriate place for the presentation of such models in the microteaching cycle. At the present moment, then, the place of modelling in the microteaching cycle is very much a research question. What is not in doubt, however, is that models of different types do, in fact, help to bring about changes in student behaviour along prespecified and specific dimensions of teaching skills.

THEORY AND PRACTICE

The use of models raises interesting questions of the relationship between principles from learning theory and practice in the class-room. It would be generally agreed that it is necessary when developing new skills or concepts for the learner to have experience of a variety of exemplars of the skill or concept to be learned. The point of this is that the learner builds up patterns of behaviour based on the essential elements of the skill or concept (the criterial attributes) and ignores the non-essential aspects. If the supervisor is using models this would suggest that a number of models exemplifying the essential elements in a specific skill would be necessary to produce effective learning of the skill. There is currently no clear understanding of the optimum number or most appropriate types of exemplars, but it seems likely that the controlled presentation of models exemplifying in turn different key aspects of the skills to be learned, and probably introducing some models that are non-exemplars, will be more effective than an unprogrammed approach.

An approach such as this has an interesting side effect. If it is successful the student teachers will be acquiring the basic important elements of the skills that are not particular to any one 'master teacher'. Each student will have his own style dependent upon his personality but in the context of his idiosyncratic approach he will deploy the essential elements, as currently perceived, of those skills. The bogy of standardized products sometimes raised in objection to systematic approaches to changing human behaviour in this field is laid if we have such considerations in mind. We do not look for the production of teachers cast in the same mould but the production of teachers who will make effective use of certain fundamentals of a repertoire of specific skills expressed in personal and individual ways.

Models may be used in a different way which raises other questions of the relationship of theory to practice. B. O. Smith (1969) suggests that models of various kinds be used not merely to provide exemplars in the process of skill acquisition or concept learning, but in problem situations to engage the students in the analysis of teaching activities by using the principles relating to teaching that they have acquired in the training situation. Smith uses the term 'protocol' when he refers to this material and this term provides a useful distinction between the approach he proposes and the one we have discussed in modelling proper which involves imitation rather than analysis. Smith argues that protocol materials should not be used '. . . merely to illustrate points in education courses. The whole procedure should be turned about so that the principles of the psychological, sociological and philosophical studies as well as those of pedagogy, are brought to the analysis of protocol materials, not the other way around. These materials suggest the knowledge that is relevant to the teacher's work.' Analysing teaching acts in this way seems to us to offer possibilities of bringing together theory and practice in a common focus not hitherto achieved.

THE SUPERVISOR

The supervisor in microteaching classes plays a more active part in the student's training than normally happens in traditional methods of school visiting. Although in many cases of traditional supervision the teaching practice is prepared for and lessons discussed with the supervisor, any connection between the pre-practice discussion and the actual teaching that goes on in the classroom is more likely to be coincidental than the result of deliberate planning. Post-lesson discussions will range over a variety of teaching activities, but, given the complexity of the situation, it will be very difficult for the supervisor to give detailed and specific reference to individual teaching skills. While the lesson is in progress the supervisor may be observing but will not be able to comment until the end of the lesson or until the children are working on their own. For 90 per cent of the time, of course, the supervisor will not be there at all. In the microteaching situation the supervisor is himself in a *teaching* situation which involves his deliberate intervention throughout the teaching exercise. In the planning of the micro-lessons he must decide on the specific skills to focus on and then carry out analyses of the teaching tasks involved in order to arrange for the optimum presentation of models, protocols and critique sessions, and the optimum sequencing of microlessons and reteach sessions. He is also present during the microteaching lesson, completes the evaluation schedule and arranges discussion critiques with other student teachers if necessary. During the critique session he has the key task of interpreting the events recorded on the video tape to the students.

According to a survey of student opinions conducted by Johnson and Knaupp (1970) students expect two main things of a microteaching supervisor. They expect him to give them expert guidance in planning for, conducting and evaluating their teaching and also they think he should give them unhampered opportunity for them to find their own teaching styles. They look for self-guided professional development which provides them with opportunities to practise and share experiences with their peers, the supervisor acting as a standby while they do their own thing. Fair enough, but the freedom to do one's own thing is enlarged by the supervisor's early planning taking into account factors that the students are unlikely to apprehend. Essentially, of course, the main aim of the supervisor's work is precisely that: to cut the umbilical link as soon as possible without cutting off the student's pedagogical nourishment prematurely.

One function the microteaching supervisor can fulfil much better than the supervisor in the traditional classroom set-up is that of supporter of student morale in the early stages of practice. Whereas in school practice the student can go disastrously astray and suffer considerable loss of morale unnoticed and unsuccoured, in the microteaching situation the supervisor can give support in the early lessons and build up the student's confidence.

Since the functions of the microteaching supervisor are so different from the traditional ones it is necessary for anyone changing from one method to the other to appraise the situation, note the differences in the two approaches and attempt to acquire the appropriate skills. Reference is made in the literature (Berliner 1969, Allen and Ryan 1969, McAleese and Unwin 1971, for example) to typical difficulties experienced by neophyte micro supervisors. Some of the things mentioned are the supervisor's playing back the whole of the video recording of a microlesson instead of selecting important elements in it and focusing discussion in the critique session on those; the supervisor's talking the whole of the time the recording is being replayed; and the supervisor's thinking that he *must* make use of the video tape or he is neglecting his duty.

Some experimentation has been carried out which reduced the role of the supervisor in the actual teaching situation and placed the onus more on the student and his peers. The work of the supervisor in the planning and preparation, however, still goes on but the movement is towards methods of self-instruction in the microteaching format and we discuss these methods below. Whether we can still legitimately use the term supervisor for a person in such a role may be debated.

A most interesting byproduct of the introduction of microteaching into teacher training has been the effect on the supervisors themselves. In the survey of microteaching in American teacher training institutes referred to earlier, Ward found that out of the 141 respondent institutions 35 indicated that they increased their focus of attention and teaching on specific teaching behaviours, 31 reported that they became a better model of good teaching as they had to practise what they preached, 23 felt they became more objective towards teaching and more practical than theoretical, 21 placed more emphasis on student participation and less on lecture and 18 reported an increase in self-evaluation of their own teaching behaviours.

THE EFFECTIVENESS OF MICROTEACHING

Allen and Ryan (1969) make the point that the general question of how effective is microteaching is really not relevant. Effective for what, we might ask, and under what conditions? When it comes to making comparisons with traditional methods we have further problems, as we have seen in our earlier discussion of the criteria of effectiveness in the assessing of teaching practice. The lack of agreed criteria, the difficulty of disentangling the various elements in the customary observation of complete lessons and the lack of explicitly stated objectives really rule out the possibility of meaningful comparisons using present approaches to teaching practice. To make meaningful comparisons would involve making much more specific and explicit the variables being considered. It would involve concentrating on specific skills rather than on vaguely specified global performance.

There is, however, considerable evidence that microteaching 'works' in the sense that it consistently achieves its proximate objectives as discussed on p. 58: that is, it is effective in changing teacher behaviour in the classroom (Berliner 1969, Young and Young 1969, Kallenbach 1967, Goodkind 1968, Wragg 1971). Borg *et al.* (1970) provide a list of behavioural changes brought about by microteaching among which, for example, are decreasing the amount of teacher talk in class discussions, increasing the number of times the teacher uses redirection, increasing the number of times the teacher uses prompting and increasing the percentage of total questions that call for higher order pupil cognitive responses. Some objectives were not achieved at statistically significant levels. For example there was very little change in the frequency of punitive teacher reactions to incorrect pupil responses, although in fact the number of such reactions was low in any case. An important point, however, is that the strengths and weaknesses of a teacher's performance are identifiable in the specific skills training approach. Information about effectiveness can be fed back into the system and help to correct it so that the possibility of eventually achieving all the objectives is a real one.

Despite the evidence of success in achieving the proximate objectives in microteaching, there still remains the problem of the distal objectives: that is, the degree of pupil change. It is true, of course, that the two can be considered separately and the degree of correlation between certain types of teaching behaviour and pupil achievement can be a matter for empirical research apart from questions of teacher training. It is also true that this criterion of effectiveness has been considered only very rarely in any assessment of teacher training methods and, as we reported in Chapter 2, only a tiny proportion of English colleges mentioned pupil learning as a criterion in student teacher assessment. It is thus clear that at this moment of time proximate criteria are the ones that are operative. We consider it important that progress be made as quickly as possible to investigate the causative links between the achievement of proximate and distal objectives.

STUDENT ATTITUDES

As was instanced by the report on the simulation exercises at Brigham Young University (p. 75), student acceptance of microteaching approaches is very positive. Students felt that even a limited experience was more valuable than traditional methods of teaching practice. B. E. Ward (1970), reporting a survey of American institutions using microteaching, also found positive attitudes. The 141 respondents reported the changes in student attitudes as shown in the table below. Turney (1970) gives an interesting account of student reactions. He reports how Sydney University introduced microteaching into its teacher training courses and found very

Rank order	Times mentioned
1 Greater understanding of the teaching process as a complex challenging profession.	41
2 Greater interest and enthusiasm towards education.	36
3 Increased self confidence.	35
4 Greater concern for self-improvement and self-evaluation.	28
5 Greater awareness of teaching image.	20
6 Greater awareness of specific skills in teaching.	18
7 Feel better prepared for teaching.	17
8 Healthier attitude towards criticism.	16
9 Feel that microteaching is most relevant.	15
10 Greater enjoyment in education.	14
11 Greater awareness of verbal and non-verbal communication.	12
12 Decreased anxiety.	11
13 Greater awareness of importance of objectives and planning.	5
14 Greater awareness of individual differences.	4
15 More tolerant of others' errors.	3
16 Greater humility.	2
17 Feel that the microteaching setting is phoney.	1

positive student reaction. Comments made were of the nature of 'I learned more in the first two or three sessions than in four weeks practice teaching'. The students valued the opportunities provided for concentrating on the development of one particular skill or technique and the ability of the method to provide insights into significant aspects of teacher–pupil relationships. They also valued the participation of their colleagues in the critique sessions run in conjunction with the microteaching video recording. Perrott and Duthie (1970) report that students at Stirling University respond very positively to microteaching and perceive the technique as helpful. It is not known to what extent student attitudes and student teacher performance are related, but we consider, in the absence of evidence that positive student attitudes are deleterious to student performance, that student acceptance of training methods is greatly to be desired and we think it most encouraging that student teachers do not just accept microteaching but embrace it with enthusiasm.

MINICOURSES

The basic concepts of microteaching have been extended by Borg and his colleagues at the Far West Laboratory for Educational Research and Development to provide microteaching in in-service courses, dubbed *minicourses*. Minicourses are packages of materials produced by the research centre and sent out to cooperating educational authorities. The materials include instructional and model video tapes, teachers' handbooks, self-rating forms and instructions to teachers on ways of improving their teaching without the aid of a supervisor. The materials are produced and then validated in schools, generally going through several revisions.

The first draft of a minicourse is prepared by the staff of the Teaching Laboratory and then subjected to a preliminary field test. This field test is mainly concerned with the qualitative evaluation of the course and involves the workers from the laboratory and a small group of teachers. No attempt is made at this stage to assess the efficacy of the minicourse in achieving the objectives set. The main field test, which follows, is concerned with assessing the degree to which the objectives have been achieved. At this stage the course is used by thirty or more teachers and in order to assess effectiveness, video recordings are made of teacher performance before and after the course. Follow-up recordings are carried out six months later to assess the degree of permanence of any behavioural changes. Analysis of behavioural changes on the video tape recordings between pre- and post-tests provides the main evidence for determining whether the course objectives are being achieved. In addition, questionnaire and interview information is gathered to guide the course designers in any revision that might be called for as a result of this field test. If the results of this field test indicate that the objectives are not being achieved the course is revised and a second main field test is carried out. This procedure could in theory be continued until the behavioural objectives set for the course are being achieved; in practice should the second field trial not produce satisfactory learning the course is likely to be abandoned.

The final field test is the operational field test. At this stage the course is tried out in normal operating conditions. All the materials will have been thoroughly tested and the total course package is handed over to the teachers in the schools. Staff of the Laboratory interview the teachers and questionnaires are completed to provide further information about the course, this time in relation to its functioning as is intended in independent in-service courses for teachers. After this operational field test any necessary revisions are carried out and the final course package results. Monitoring of the final minicourse is carried out by the Laboratory's maintaining contact with teachers using the materials.

The contrast between the thoroughness with which the preparation of minicourses are developed, and the *ad hoc* intuitive nature of traditional approaches to the providing of practical professional work, is the obvious external manifestation of the fact that we have here not a variation on an old theme, but a completely different thing. Borg (Borg *et al.* 1970) points out another crucial difference between minicourses and other methods of training in his preface to the teacher's handbook to various minicourses. Minicourses are skill-oriented rather than content-oriented. In his words to the teacher: 'You will find no lengthy textbook to read, no lists of "main points" to memorize, no lectures to take notes on, and no final examination. All the skills in this minicourse could be presented in a single lecture, but hearing that lecture would not make you a better teacher. There is a great difference between *knowing about* a teaching skill and *being able to use* that skill effectively in a classroom. In most courses on teaching methods you learn how to answer multiple choice questions about teaching – in the minicourse you learn how to teach!' Borg also goes on to point out that probably the most important single fact about the minicourse is that it works; that teachers do in fact change their teaching behaviour as a result of taking the minicourse.

Minicourses have been developed for in-service teachers but there seems no reason to us why they should not be used in pre-service training. The effectiveness of minicourses has in fact been assessed in an experiment by Kallenbach (1969) where he found that experienced teachers made similar gains to student teachers, the implication being that the former needed the experience as much as the latter! McAleese and Unwin (1971) report that some students in in-service training were quite capable of good self-evaluation in microteaching situations. Given the exhaustive preparation and validation of the minicourses it would seem highly likely that the technique would be effective. There is no doubt that such developments could have enormous implications logistically apart from any educational considerations.

MICROTEACHING IN USE

Reference has already been made to the report by B. E. Ward (1970) of American institutions using microteaching. We now present briefly some of the findings of this survey to indicate the way microteaching is developing in teacher training in the U.S.A. Ward found that out of 442 colleges and universities accredited for teacher training 176 used microteaching in their secondary teacher education programmes; of these 141 replied to the survey. 104 (73 per cent) of these institutions had been using microteaching for two years or less at the time of the survey (1968–9). The following are the main findings of the report.

> About two-thirds of the microteaching programmes involved a relatively small number of students (150 or less); most of these provided students with only six or fewer microteaching encounters. A few of the programmes, however, provided many teaching encounters.
>
> Most microteaching programmes were conducted in the education and audiovisual departments using 'peer' (college) students for pupils of the microclass. However, some institutions con-

ducted their microteaching programmes in the campus school or public schools, using 'real' pupils for the microclass.

Many of the larger, more mature programmes used the complete teach-critique, reteach-critique sequence of microteaching during all or part of the programme. Most of the programmes used six or fewer pupils for the microclass. In the majority of the institutions, the college student, the supervising professor and the pupils of the microclass were active in the critique.

Fifty-four institutions reported contributing directly to the use of microteaching in the in-service education of the state in which they are located.

Ward comments that Stanford experience suggests to him that an optimum programme of microteaching should involve all education students in a minimum of twenty initial teach encounters and twenty reteach encounters during their course. This criterion would suggest that a large proportion of the institutions are not providing the most adequate experiences for their students. Similarly the large number of institutions using simulation techniques (the use of peers in the microclasses) rather than microteaching with pupils is perhaps unsatisfactory (Stanford uses 'real' pupils throughout). As in the case of the shortcomings in the use of technical skills (pp. 87–8) it seems likely that many of the unsatisfactory features of some of the programmes are attributable to their very recent introduction and the lack of experience in the use of the techniques.

Ward reports one further use of microteaching which is of interest for its somewhat unusual approach. At Stout State University student teachers are required to participate in microteaching each semester until they complete the terminal objectives. The criterion was successful attainment of the objectives and not a specified period of time. The students could elect to take the length of time they preferred (from one to six or seven semesters). The objectives of the course were that each student would be able to:

1 Develop behavioural objectives for each microlesson.
2 Develop a well structured lesson plan for each microlesson.
3 Develop a course outline that encompasses the microlesson.
4 Demonstrate successful performance in each technical skill of teaching.
5 Develop a minimum of two behavioural objectives for each

level of the cognitive domain of Bloom's Taxonomy of Educational Objectives.

The students were given course options as follows per semester:

1 Sixteen 5-minute lessons.
2 Eight 10-minute lessons.
3 Six 20-minute lessons.
4 Four 30-minute lessons.

In the view of the University staff, distributing the microteaching experience over the entire programme provided realistic integration of theoretical and practical work for student teachers.

Work at the University of Stirling (Perrott and Duthie 1970) exemplifies very well the utilization of microteaching in an integrated teaching system in a way that seems to us to avoid the weaknesses of some of the institutions reported on by Ward. At Stirling a considerable effort went into ensuring integration of theory and practice in the education courses. Thus, '. . . instead of the usual course in educational psychology almost totally divorced from the business of learning to teach, psychology is seen as providing a relevant conceptual framework and rationale for the skills to be practised in microteaching. The skill of varying the stimulus is introduced to the students in terms of an exposition of the relevant theoretical and experimental work in perception and attention. The skill of explaining is prefaced by a description of theoretical and experimental work in concept formation and concept attainment.' At Stirling the student teachers practise five teaching skills in the course of twelve weeks, so they do, in fact, receive a reasonable amount of microteaching experience and all the work is with secondary children so it is real teaching and not simulation.

The teacher training programme of the New University of Ulster has a similar approach (Unwin and McAleese 1971). Students are inducted into teaching in the second year of their course through twenty microteaching experiences followed by longer sessions with larger groups of children later. The children are 9–13 years old from local schools, so we have 'real' microteaching and not simulation. The microteaching work is integrated with the education courses and the specific skills are introduced by lectures in the educational psychology course and are then applied to the teaching situation.

It seems to us that these two examples of the use of microteaching are admirable illustrations of an approach to practical professional work in teacher preparation worthy of emulation.

PUTTING THE TEACHER TOGETHER AGAIN

Borg's point (pp. 97–8) that microteaching is skill-oriented rather than content-oriented may be looked at more broadly. It is skill-oriented in contrast to content-oriented and skill-oriented in that it teaches specific skills and not broad and imprecise patterns of behaviour. The minicourse approach also teaches these specific skills but takes steps to relate them to each other. Thus the course on effective questioning covers sixteen skills including such things as the handling of pupil responses, the increasing of pupil participation, prompting, refocusing, seeking further clarification from the pupil and asking questions calling for answers demanding higher cognitive processes. There is thus in the minicourse a clear emphasis that the skills are not to be seen in isolation from each other. Snow at Stanford (*Teaching*, No. 1, 1970) and his colleagues are working on methods of improving the teacher's ability to use his theoretical knowledge and grasp of specific skills to deliberately monitor classroom transactions and take appropriate actions to regulate the teaching/learning situation most effectively to achieve his objectives. The conception of teaching that is emerging from studies of this kind is of 'a complex information processing activity, perhaps better described as an orchestration of skills'.

Work such as this will no doubt add further skills to the existing repertoire but increasingly microteaching is likely to be not so much a collection of discrete skill acquisition experiences but more a 'systematically arranged programme where individual skills might be practised both separately and in exercises designed specifically for particular combinations of complementary skills. In other words, training may start with isolated elemental skills, but it must also put the teacher back together again.'

7 · Interaction Analysis

The 'compleat' teacher in the classroom will be practising a complex repertoire of skills orchestrated as we have suggested. Using the techniques of microteaching and the minicourse he will be able to analyse and evaluate his own performance in the execution of the individual skills with the assistance of peers or supervisors in the interpretation of the feedback from recordings of his classroom performance. There is likely to be a common feature to most of the behaviours he is attempting to evaluate; they are likely to involve talk between pupils and the teacher.

Teacher talk/pupil talk is not just one of the constituent skills of teaching in the sense we used it in the previous chapter, it slices across nearly all the activities that take place in the classroom and its analysis can add another dimension to our understanding of what goes on when a teacher teaches and thus help us to guide students more insightfully in their classroom practice.

A considerable amount of work has gone on in the last decade in defining and developing methods of analysing classroom talk and at the present moment there are probably well over a hundred systems. We propose here to consider the general ideas of the subject, usually referred to as *interaction analysis*, and to give examples from the more well-known approaches. We shall also give some attention to the question of non-verbal interaction and consider some of the more interesting proposals for extension or modification of current approaches.

INTERACTION ANALYSIS

Interaction analysis is closely associated with the name of Flanders who developed the system originally as part of a research into teacher influence and pupil attitudes and achievement. The Flanders system is concerned only with verbal behaviour in the classroom but makes the assumption that verbal behaviour is an adequate sample of a person's total behaviour; it does not overlook the fact that other behaviour might be important.

The Flanders system attempts to categorize all the verbal behaviour to be found in the classroom. It thus has as its two main categories, teacher talk and pupil talk. A third category covers other verbal behaviour. The first main category is subdivided into two, direct and indirect teacher talk. Indirect influence is then subdivided into the more specific categories of (1) accepting feeling, (2) praising or encouraging, (3) accepting ideas, (4) asking questions. Direct influence is divided into three categories: (5) lecturing, (6) giving directions, and (7) criticizing or justifying authority. Pupil talk is divided into two categories: (8) responding to teacher, and (9) initiatory talk. Category 10 is usually referred to as silence or confusion. All categories are mutually exclusive but subsume all types of verbal behaviour. The categories are now detailed below.*

Teacher talk

Indirect teacher bchaviour

Category 1: Acceptance of feeling The teacher accepts feelings when he says he understands how the children feel, that they have the right to have these feelings, and that he will not punish the children for their feelings. These kinds of statements often communicate to children both acceptance and clarification of the feeling.

Also included in this category are statements that recall past feeling, refer to enjoyable or uncomfortable feelings that are present, or predict happy or sad events that will occur in the future. In our society people often react to expressions of negative feelings by offering negative feelings in return. Acceptance of these emotions in the classroom is quite rare; probably because teachers find it difficult to accept negative emotional behaviour. However, it may be just as difficult for them to accept positive feelings. Feelings expressed by pupils may also be ignored by the teacher if he considers the classroom to be a place where people are concerned primarily with ideas rather than feelings.

Category 2: Praise or encouragement Included in this category are jokes that release tension, but not those that threaten pupils or are made at the expense of individual pupils. Often praise is a single

---

* Taken from Amidon and Flanders (1967).

word: 'good', 'fine' or 'right'. Sometimes the teacher simply says, 'I like what you are doing'. Encouragement is slightly different and includes statements such as, 'Continue', 'Go ahead with what you are saying', 'Uh huh; go on; tell us more about your idea'.

Category 3: Accepting ideas This category is quite similar to category 1; however, it includes only acceptance of student ideas, not acceptance of expressed emotion. When a student makes a suggestion, the teacher may paraphrase the student's statement, restate the idea more simply, or summarize what the student has said. The teacher may also say, 'Well that's an interesting point of view. I see what you mean.' Statements belonging to category 3 are particularly difficult to recognize; often the teacher will shift from using the student's idea to stating the teacher's own idea.

Statements belonging to category 3 can be identified by asking the question: 'Is the idea that the teacher is now stating the pupil's or is it the teacher's?' If it is the pupil's idea, then this category is used; if it is the teacher's another category must be employed.

Category 4: Asking questions This category includes only questions to which the teacher expects an answer from the pupils. If a teacher asks a question and then follows it immediately with a statement of opinion, or if he begins lecturing, obviously the question was not meant to be answered. A rhetorical question is not categorized as a question. An example of another kind of question that should not be classified in category 4 is the following: 'What in the world do you think you are doing out of your seat, John?' With proper intonation the question is designed to get John back in his seat; if such is the case, it must be categorized as criticism of the pupil's behaviour (category 7).

Questions that are meant to be answered are of several kinds. There are questions that direct in the sense that there is a right and wrong answer. The question, 'What are 2 and 2?' is a question that limits the pupil to some extent. Although he can refuse to answer, give the wrong answer, or make a statement of another kind, in general this kind of question focuses the pupil's answer more than does a question such as 'What do you think we ought to do now?' Questions, then, can be either narrow and restrict the pupil in his answer, or they can be very broad and give the pupil a great deal of freedom in answering. All questions, however broad or narrow, which require answers and are not commands or criticisms, fall into category 4.

Direct teacher behaviour

Category 5: Lecture Lecture is the form of verbal interaction that is used to give information, facts, opinions or ideas to children. The presentation of material may be used to introduce, review or focus the attention of the class on an important topic. Usually information in the form of lecture is given in fairly extended time periods, but it may be interspersed with the children's comments, questions and encouraging praise.

Whenever the teacher is explaining, discussing, giving opinion or giving facts or information, category 5 is used. Rhetorical questions are also included in this category. Category 5 is the one most frequently used in classroom observation.

Category 6: Giving directions The decision about whether or not to classify the statement as a direction or command must be based on the degree of freedom that the pupil has in response to teacher direction. When the teacher says, 'Will all of you stand up and stretch?' he is obviously giving a direction. If he says, 'John, go to the board and write your name', he is obviously giving a direction or a command. When he says, 'John, I want you to tell me what you have done with your reader', he is still giving a direction.

Category 7: Criticizing or justifying authority A statement of criticism is one that is designed to change student behaviour from non-acceptable to acceptable. The teacher is saying, in effect, 'I don't like what you are doing. Do something else.' Another group of statements included in this category are those that might be called statements of defence or self-justification. These statements are particularly difficult to detect when a teacher appears to be explaining a lesson or the reasons for doing a lesson to the class. If the teacher is explaining himself or his authority, defending himself against the pupil, or justifying himself, the statement falls into this category. Other kinds of statements that fall into this category are those of extreme self-reference or those in which a teacher is constantly asking the children to do something as a special favour to the teacher.

All statements made by the teacher must be categorized into one of the categories detailed above. If the observer decides that with a given statement he is restricting the freedom of children, the statement is tallied in categories 5, 6 or 7. If, on the other hand, the observer decides that the teacher is expanding the freedom of the children, the category to be used is 1, 2, 3 or 4.

TEACHER TALK	Indirect influence	1 *ACCEPTS FEELING: accepts and clarifies the feeling tone of the pupils in a non-threatening manner. Feelings may be positive or negative. Predicting and recalling feelings are included.
		2 *PRAISES OR ENCOURAGES: praises or encourages pupil action or behaviour. Jokes that release tension, not at the expense of another individual, nodding head or saying 'uh huh?' or 'go on' are included.
		3 *ACCEPTS OR USES IDEAS OF PUPILS: clarifying, building or developing ideas or suggestions by a pupil. As teacher brings more of his own ideas into play, shift into category five.
		4 *ASKS QUESTIONS: asking a question about content or procedure with the intent that a student answer.
	Direct influence	5 *LECTURES: giving facts or opinions about content or procedures; expressing his own ideas; asking rhetorical questions.
		6 *GIVES DIRECTIONS: directions, commands or orders with which a student is expected to comply.
		7 *CRITICIZES OR JUSTIFIES AUTHORITY: statements intended to change pupil behaviour from non-acceptable to acceptable pattern; bawling someone out; stating why the teacher is doing what he is doing, extreme self-reference.
PUPIL TALK		8 *PUPIL TALK-RESPONSE: talk by pupils in response to teacher. Teacher initiates the contact or solicits pupil statement.
		9 *PUPIL TALK-INITIATION: talk by students which they initiate. If 'calling on' student is only to indicate who may talk next, observer must decide whether pupil wanted to talk. If he did, use this category.
		10 *SILENCE OR CONFUSION: pauses, short periods of silence and periods of confusion in which communication cannot be understood by the observer.

* No scale is implied by these numbers. Each number is classificatory; it designates a particular kind of communication event. To write these numbers down during observation is to enumerate, not to judge, a position on a scale.

Pupil talk

Category 8: Pupil talk-response This category is used when the teacher has initiated the contact or has solicited pupil statements, when the pupil answers a question asked by the teacher or when he responds verbally to a direction the teacher has given. Anything that the pupil says that is clearly in response to initiation by the teacher belongs in category 8.

Category 9: Pupil talk initiation In general, if the pupil raises his hand to make a statement or to ask a question when he has not been prompted to do so by the teacher, the appropriate category is 9.

Distinguishing between categories 8 and 9 is often difficult. Predicting the general kind of answer that the student will give in response to a question from the teacher is important in making this distinction. If the answer is one that is of a type predicted by the observer (as well as the teacher of the class), then the statement comes under category 8. When in response to a teacher question the student gives an answer different from that which is expected for that particular question, then the statement is categorized as 9.

Other events

Category 10: Silence or confusion This category includes anything else not included in the other categories. Periods of confusion in communication when it is difficult to determine who is talking, are classified in this category.

A summary of these categories, with brief definitions for use of the observer is set out opposite.

CATEGORIZING PROCEDURES

The classification of the various interactions is carried out either by an observer in the classroom, or from a tape of a lesson. In the case of the latter it is possible for a student or teacher to record and analyse his own lesson with a view to obtaining an insight into his own activities. In the case of the observer in the classroom, it is desirable to take five or ten minutes to become acclimatized to the classroom situation and then start recording. This is done by noting every three seconds the type of interaction that is taking place. The activity is recorded by writing down the number of the category to which it belongs. Clearly the ability to do this is dependent upon training and recorders do need about eight hours' training.

In the process of recording the observer notes the verbal events in sequence and if one kind of interaction persists he notes the number repeatedly until there is a change. Should there be a complete change in the type of classroom activity the observer stops recording until a pattern is re-established. By considering the sequence of numbers on his record sheet the observer can discern the ebb and flow of different patterns of verbal behaviour. By entering up the numbers in an interaction matrix the observer is able to get a picture not only of the number of interactions falling in each category, but also the way in which categories tended to follow each other. Thus he might notice that praise followed student response about 10 per cent of the total lesson time. By going to the raw data he would be able to discover when during the course of the lesson these particular interactions took place.

Constructing an interaction matrix from raw data is relatively straightforward. A ten by ten matrix (for the ten categories of interaction) is prepared and the category numbers entered up in sequence pairs in such a way that each number is entered twice, once as the first and once as the second number in each pair. The rows of the matrix represent the first number in the pair and the columns represent the second. For example, the category numbers in sequence 10, 6, 10, 7, 6, 1 would be entered as follows: the first sequence pair, 10–6 would be tallied in the cell that is located at the intersection of row 10 and column 6; the next pair is entered in cell 6–10, the third pair in 10–7, the fourth in 7–6 and the fifth in cell 6–1. The location of these tallies is shown in the matrix.

Once the data are systematized in a matrix it is possible to carry out various types of analyses. An obvious and interesting first step is to compute the percentage of tallies in each of the columns. This gives the proportion of the total interaction in the observed classroom situation found in each category. Similarly, the amount of teacher talk in each category expressed as a percentage of total teacher talk can be calculated. Another key calculation is the amount of teacher talk that takes place as a proportion of the total interaction. This is ascertained by dividing the total number of tallies in the teacher talk section by the total number of tallies in the whole matrix. A closer scrutiny of the teacher talk columns will reveal the relative emphasis on direct and indirect talk. This is done by dividing the number of tallies in the indirect influence columns (1, 2, 3 and 4) by the total number of tallies in all the teacher talk columns (1–7). The ratio which this operation produces is usually referred to as the I/D ratio or the ratio of indirect to direct teacher

Table 4 Sample interaction matrix

	1	2	3	4	5	6	7	8	9	10
1										
2										
3										
4										
5										
6	1									1
7						1				
8										
9										
10						1	1			
Total	1					2	1			1
%										

(Naturally matrices normally contain many more entries than this example which is merely designed to illustrate the method of entering up the tallies.)

statements. An I/D ratio of 0·5 means that for every direct statement there was one indirect statement; and an I/D ratio of 0·67 means that for every two indirect statements there was only one direct statement and so on.

Further more specific analyses may be made, which shed interesting light on the type of teaching style a teacher uses. For example, a heavy loading on both the 4 and 5 rows and columns indicates emphasis on content, because the cells consist primarily of lectures, statements of opinion and teacher questions about information and content. Viewed on a matrix this pattern of tallies tends to form a cross along the 4 and 5 rows and columns; this Amidon and Flanders refer to as the 'content cross'. Amidon and Flanders (1967) give examples of other commonly occurring matrix patterns which may be interpreted as indicating specific types of classroom inter-action. They refer to one pattern where the teacher gives a direction to a pupil but the direction is not followed. The teacher criticizes and repeats the direction. If the direction is not followed on this second occasion criticism again ensues. This cycle is shown in the pattern 6–6, 6–7, 7–6, 7–7 and often indicates discipline problems or problems of pupil rejection of teacher influence. It is probably true that when serious problems of discipline occur, the teacher or observer is unlikely to need an interaction matrix to tell him. Nevertheless, the analysis will analyse the situation to some extent and make apparent the main contributory factors to the problem. Other matrix patterns may reveal aspects of teaching style not otherwise readily noticeable. A concentration of tallies in the cells represented by rows and columns 1, 2 and 3 will reveal the use of extended indirect teacher influence, with the teacher using pupils' ideas and accepting pupils' feelings.

These examples of types of identifiable patterns of interaction provide only a few instances of the range of interpretations that can be made by analysis of matrices. Clearly the method offers con-siderable scope for the analytical appraisal of the teacher's classroom behaviour even if he does only focus on very broad aspects of verbal behaviour. Certainly, it seems to us, that if supervisors could acquire the ability to analyse student teachers' classroom activities along these lines they would be adding a new and valuable dimension to their supervision.

Apart from the addition to the armamentarium of the supervisor, the techniques of interaction analysis lend themselves to general use in the preparation of student teachers. Instruction in the techniques and the analysis of sample lessons recorded on audio tape can develop insights into the nature of the teaching process not other-wise attainable. In addition, the student or in-service teacher can record his own lessons and then analyse them in terms of the categories we have discussed above. Amidon and Flanders (1967) have produced a training kit for teaching interaction analysis. The kit comprises a handbook, training tapes, training tapes manual, tally sheets and matrix forms. This kit can be used by a teacher or student to acquire the skills of interaction analysis and then apply them to his own teaching. He could thus embark upon interaction analysis as a piece of self-instruction and subsequent self-analysis.

OTHER APPROACHES

The Flanders approach is not the only approach. In fact, one of the problems of those interested in the field is that of keeping track of new observation instruments as they appear. There is, in addition, a propensity for research workers in the field to feel dissatisfied with existing instruments for some reason or other and to produce their own. This is understandable since very often such people have specific problems in mind which need instruments with differential emphasis suited to the problem they are investigating. Such instruments are often not suitable for use in teacher training because of the fact that they were designed for a different purpose.

One instrument designed for research work which has a lot to offer to the trainee teacher but which is difficult to use in a practical teaching situation is that devised by Bellack and associates (Bellack et al. 1966). This instrument focuses on the pedagogical significance of the verbal interaction between teacher and pupils. It considers that each utterance in the classroom situation has a number of important functions. For example, it could launch a new topic, ask a question or reply to a question at the same time as making reference to the substance of the topic under consideration and involving the interactors in activities at different cognitive levels.

Since the various functions of each utterance are considered important they are categorized simultaneously. This procedure clearly creates problems, which puts the technique more or less out of court for the individual teacher interested in self-improvement since it is necessary to transcribe recordings of lessons in order to carry out the analysis. It is also unlikely that colleges or university departments will have the facilities for this sort of operation on a scale sufficiently extensive to analyse student teachers' lessons as they go through the course, as can be done in the case of taped interaction analyses of the Flanders type or microteaching recordings. However, transcripts of lessons could undoubtedly be used in the training of teachers to bring out the kind of language categories that are to be found in classroom transactions.

The Bellack system categorizes six sets of items:

1 *Speaker*, i.e. source of the utterance.
2 *Pedagogical move*, i.e. function of the verbal interaction.
3 *Substantive meaning*, i.e. the subject matter being studied.
4 *Substantive–logical meaning*, i.e. verification process used with 3 above.
5 *Instructional meaning*, i.e. the social and managerial aspects of teacher–pupil interaction.
6 *Instructional–logical meaning*, i.e. verification process used with 5 above.

These six categories comprise sets of specific items as follows.*

1 *Speaker*
  A *Teacher*
  B *Pupil*
  C *Audiovisual device*
2 *Pedagogical move*
  A *Structuring* moves 'serve the pedagogical function of setting the context for subsequent behaviour by launching or halting-excluding interaction between pupils and teachers and by indicating the nature of the interaction.'
  B *Soliciting* moves 'are designed to elicit a verbal response, encourage persons addressed to attend to something or elicit a physical response. All questions are solicitations, as are commands, imperatives and requests.'
  C *Responding* moves 'bear a reciprocal relationship to soliciting moves and occur in relation to them. Their pedagogical function is to fulfil the expectation of soliciting moves.'
  D *Reacting* moves 'are occasioned by a structuring, soliciting, responding, or another reacting move, but are not directly elicited by them. Pedagogically, these moves serve to modify (by clarifying, synthesizing or expanding) and/or to rate (positively or negatively) what has been said previously.'
  E *Not codable* – function uncertain because interaction inaudible.
3 *Substantive meaning*. This category is concerned with the

* The description that follows is taken from Bellack *et al.* 1966.

content of the lesson and will vary from subject to subject. An analysis of this item would involve a conceptual analysis of the field of study.

4 *Substantive–logical meaning* (reference to cognitive processes used in dealing with subject matter)
 A *Analytic process*
  (1) Defining
  (2) Interpreting
 B *Empirical process*
  (1) Fact stating
  (2) Explaining
 C *Evaluative process*
  (1) Opining
  (2) Justifying
 D *Logical process not clear*
5 *Instructional meaning* (factors related to classroom management)
 A *Assignment*
 B *Material*
 C *Person*
 D *Procedure*
 E *Statement*
 F *Logical process*
 G *Action – general*
 H *Action – vocal*
 I *Action – physical*
 J *Action – cognitive*
 K *Action – emotional*
 L *Language mechanics*
6 *Instructional – logical meaning* (cognitive processes related to teacher's didactic verbal moves)
 A *Analytical process*
  (1) Defining
  (2) Interpreting
 B *Empirical process*
  (1) Fact – stating
  (2) Explaining
 C *Evaluative process*
  (1) Opining
  (2) Justifying
  (3) Rating

　　　　　a positive
　　　　　b admitting
　　　　　c repeating
　　　　　d qualifying
　　　　　e not admitting
　　　　　f negative
　　　　　g positive/negative
　　　　　h admitting/not admitting
　　D *Extralogical process* (when physical response is elicited, or
　　　　logic of verbal response cannot be determined)
　　　　(1) Performing
　　　　(2) Directing
　　　　(3) Extralogical process not clear

The observer using this system of analysis listens to a tape recording of the lesson and reads a typed transcription. He categorizes the verbal interaction in each of the six categories every time there is a change of speaker and/or pedagogical move. He writes the chosen categories on the typescript as well as the number of lines used in transcribing the interaction so that he obtains a quantitative as well as a functional measure of the interaction (Hyman 1970).

By analysing the data from the different pedagogical moves Bellack discerned patterns which he called teaching cycles. A cycle begins with either a structuring or soliciting move which Bellack called an initiatory manoeuvre. These moves elicit what Bellack calls reflexive manoeuvres and include the responding and reacting moves and thus complete the teaching cycle. Bellack's approach can be used to illuminate the nature of the relationship between the teacher, the pupil and the subject matter by an examination of lessons using this approach. One of the important elements in classroom discourse, which can be scrutinized using this instrument, is the question. Students could examine a record of a lesson for the kind of questions to ask, the kinds of responses required, the cognitive level of the questions and so on. Other classroom phenomena could, of course, be scrutinized in the same way.

We have considered at some length two systems of classroom observation attempting to do rather different jobs, but both bringing to bear an analytical approach to understanding what in fact goes on in the classroom. To the convinced opponent of such analytical approaches probably neither will cut any ice. But we hope that, for those who see some utility in this approach, we have provided two instances of a general approach to examining the processes of teaching and learning in the fairly traditional classroom situation. Both approaches, we feel, have significance as they stand for teacher training in the practical situation, the Flanders approach being the more useful from the point of view of direct practical instruction and self-instruction in classroom techniques, but the Bellack approach with its emphasis on the pedagogical substantive aspects being extremely useful in bringing some important elements in teaching into more detailed focus. However, the two exemplars of the general approach which we have discussed could provide ideas for other different instruments designed to do specific jobs different from those for which the Flanders and Bellack instruments were designed.

INTERACTION ANALYSIS IN USE

Amidon (1966) has provided an interesting example of the use of different approaches to interaction analysis in teacher preparation. Interaction analysis was introduced into the student teacher programme at Temple University as part of a project to test the hypothesis that student teachers who received behavioural training in interaction analysis would demonstrate different student teaching patterns from students receiving conventional training in learning theory.

The experiment was mounted partly because of dissatisfaction with traditional methods of preparation for practical teaching, dissatisfaction based on similar grounds to those we have outlined in earlier sections of this book. Central to their approach was the concept of the key objective of student teaching as being to provide a laboratory in which the student teacher has the opportunity to experiment with, practice and learn new teaching behaviours.

The programme that was mounted to test the hypothesis comprised three basic courses: a lecture course, a workshop and a student teaching seminar. In these lectures the students are introduced to the Flanders system of analysis, four categories for classifying thinking developed by Gallagher and Aschner (1963), Hughes's (1963) teaching functions, Bellack's (Bellack *et al.* 1963) moves and teaching cycles and Taba's (1965) teaching strategies.

The main emphasis of the course of lectures is on the Flanders system and the first part of the course deals with the method of analysis, and the construction and interpretation of matrices. When the students understand the Flanders approach they study the Gallagher and Aschner categories for classifying teacher questions and pupils' thinking. Briefly, the four categories are Cognitive Memory, Convergent Thinking, Evaluative Thinking and Divergent Thinking. Each category comprises three or four subcategories, some of which are further subdivided. Cognitive Memory, for example, includes a subcategory of *recapitulation* which is further divided into *quoting, repetition, recounting* and *review*. Explanation of different types forms a major subdivision of Convergent Thinking, *structured judgement* is an example of a subcategory from Evaluative Thinking, and *elaboration, divergent association, implications* and *synthesis* are the subcategories of Divergent Thinking.

Students are encouraged to integrate the Flanders and the Gallagher and Aschner systems and are then introduced to the analysis of teaching functions developed by Hughes. These functions are those performed by the language of the teacher and include the seven broad categories of controlling, teacher imposition, facilitating, development of content, personal response, negative affectivity and positive affectivity. Finally the students are introduced to Taba's teaching strategies designed to raise the level of children's thinking. Briefly, Taba focused upon specific learning tasks and designed strategies tailored to the tasks by careful structuring and logical sequencing and in line with the psychological requirements of mastering tasks.

By concentrating upon the Flanders system the students obtain detailed insights into the rationale of a useful tool for analysing interactions. By considering, in addition, the other approaches, they become aware that the Flanders system is just one example of a general approach which can be adopted for a variety of specific purposes. They are, in fact, encouraged to draw on the various systems for inspiration in proposing appropriate approaches for the accomplishment of particular goals.

Finally the lecture course deals with research into teacher–pupil interaction and the important question of the function of category systems as feedback devices.

The workshop sessions are designed to put into practice the concepts discussed in the lecture and to develop skills in students, based on those concepts. Classroom tapes are played and classified according to the various category systems. Discussion of the tapes and role playing of different approaches from those on the tapes also take place. Students also use role playing for the development of skills in similar ways to those described in microteaching, the main difference being that this approach uses audio tape and role playing with fellow students instead of video tape and pupils. An additional difference would be that the students in the workshops would base their practice skills on the various category systems and combinations of the systems.

The seminar focuses on an analysis of the students' own teaching. This is done by playing tapes of the students' teaching, discussing and classifying the tapes, and role playing different methods of teaching together with preparing lessons and role playing in seminar and later in the classroom.

The lecture, seminar and workshop are designed to achieve the aim of providing students with a laboratory in which they have the opportunity to experiment with, practise and learn new teaching behaviours. It is hoped thereby to overcome the limitations of traditional practice teaching. It is also hoped, in our view not unreasonably, that once the students understand how to study their own teaching and are able to get an insight into their own classroom performance they will want to improve. The feedback from the various approaches to interaction analysis that they study should help them to do so.

THE EFFECTS OF INTERACTION ANALYSIS

There is, in fact, evidence that students trained in the use of interaction analysis differ from those not trained in that they are more accepting, less critical and less directive (Amidon 1966). The same research also found that student teachers trained in interaction analysis tended to have more pupil initiated talk, more extended pupil initiated talk and less silence or confusion. A further interesting and unforeseen difference was that students trained in interaction analysis showed a greater range of teaching behaviours than did other students. Bondi and Ober (1969) found that students trained in interaction analysis differed from others in the following ways. They used more praise, accepted and clarified pupils' ideas more, used more indirect teacher talk as opposed to direct teacher talk, used more extended praise, made more extended use of pupils' ideas, used more positive affective talk, accepted pupils' ideas more after teacher initiated pupil talk, used less corrective feedback, asked more questions, used less lecturing and gave fewer directions. Amidon *et al.* (1967) found similar results in a comparison of trained and untrained student teachers and also found more positive attitudes towards teaching among the trained students. Moskowitz (1968a and 1968b) found that foreign language teachers trained in interaction analysis had more positive attitudes towards teaching than other teachers; they used more indirect teaching patterns in grammar and conversation lessons, had more negative attitudes towards the class teachers cooperating with them, and were perceived more favourably by the pupils in their classrooms. She also investigated the effects of training in the system on in-service teachers using taped lessons of their own teaching with the teachers analysing their own lessons in the light of their knowledge of interaction analysis. The reception of the in-service teachers of the techniques of interaction analysis was extremely enthusiastic. One wrote in reply to a follow-up enquiry after the course: 'No experience I have had in teacher training comes anywhere near giving me the kind of guidance and inspiration that this course in interaction systems gave me.' There were many such testimonials of comparable fervour. One comment may shed light on the third finding of the student teacher investigation: that interaction trained students had more negative feelings to the cooperating class teacher. This teacher having returned to her school from the course found that the school programme was so highly controlled that she was unable to apply analysis and was extremely dissatisfied as a result. Something of the same conflict may have taken place between inter-action trained students and non-trained class teachers.

Amidon and Flanders (1967) review much research along lines similar to those discussed above and in summary declare that the evidence from these studies is conclusive and demonstrates that students trained in interaction analysis:

1 take more time to accept and use pupil's ideas
2 encourage a greater amount of pupil-initiated talk
3 use less criticism
4 use less direction
5 are more accepting and encouraging in response to pupil's ideas
6 have a more generally indirect teaching style

One problem that is not dealt with in these studies is one we referred to earlier. What evidence is there that approaches such as the one given have any effects on pupil learning different from those produced by other approaches? There is, in fact, evidence of such differential effects. Flanders (1960) found that pupils of indirect teachers learned more according to tests of written achievement. Amidon and Flanders (1967) report a number of researches by various investigators which found indirect teacher influence to be correlated with pupil achievement. These studies embraced subjects such as written language skills, reading comprehension, biological science, and general science, with one study using the Torrance creativity tests as the criterion. In this last, indirect teaching was found to produce higher pupil creativity scores than direct teaching. La Shier and Westmeyer (1967) found that pupils studying a B.C.S.C. laboratory block on animal behaviour learned more from indirect student teachers than from direct student teachers: Wragg (1971) used interaction analysis in conjunction with microteaching and found the combination more powerful than either used singly.

SOME QUALIFICATIONS

We have no doubt that the techniques described above can be of considerable use in preparing students for practical teaching. One point we should like to stress, however, is one we have made before, namely that student teachers should learn the general approach to interaction analysis rather than take any one as being *the* approach. It is not inconsistent with this proposal to help students to acquire competence in one particular method of analysis so long as they do not as a result think that there is only one way of doing it.

Some authors have pointed out various shortcomings in the different approaches to interaction analysis, and while these criticisms do not, we think, invalidate the method, the points made should be borne in mind by tutors and students when studying interaction analysis and applying the techniques to practical situations.

Greenberg (1967) compared the work of five researchers in the field and pointed out that they shared a very important assumption which may be open to question: namely that the teacher is the free controlling agent in the classroom. The teacher, it is assumed, controls the interaction, and the general theme, that if teachers are

E

made aware of different patterns of interaction they will be in a position to change the pattern, is based on that assumption. Greenberg suggests that Bellack's position is not quite like the others. She suggests that his position is close to one that sees the classroom as a system and his analysis, she suggests, is system-oriented rather than teacher-oriented as are those of Flanders, Hughes, Smith and Taba. The evidence from the researches referred to earlier certainly indicate that the teacher is sufficiently in control to be able to effect some modification of his behaviour, but Greenberg's point is a very important one which students and researchers might well give some thought to.

Greenberg makes another point which is also made by a number of other writers and which often occurs to teachers when they first come across the Flanders system. They feel that taping a lesson and more so, recording a lesson stenographically or analysing it according to a category system while it is taking place, results in a very incomplete picture of the classroom transactions. Tape recording, Greenberg points out, abstracts from the real situation and is therefore lacking in certain dimensions. This does not mean that recordings are inappropriate, but that they should be used with their limitations clearly in mind. She also suggests that there is loss of information because of the great reduction in cues as compared with the real situation.

Barnes (1969) raises an allied question, one that touches on the work of Bellack. He carried out investigations using a modified Flanders instrument but he paid particular attention to the nature of the language used in the course of interactions. He found that analyses of interactions might be misleading because of the conceptual gap between teacher and the pupil. Verbal interaction may take place and be codable but a close scrutiny of the nature of the language used in the interaction could well reveal that conceptual interaction was of a different order entirely. Barnes suggests a real lack of contact between the pupil and the teacher, created in part by the different language registers used by pupil and teacher. He considers that 'teachers need a far more sophisticated insight into the implications of the language which they themselves use, especially the register which we have called the language of secondary education'. Barnes also found like many other earlier investigators that teachers talk most of the time and that questions asked of pupils usually demand answers of very low conceptual content.

Focusing on the language of the classroom in this way may cope with some of the problems of interaction analysis, but it does not cope with another problem: the effects of non-verbal interaction. Galloway (1968) draws attention to the importance of the careful use of space and how rearranging the class furniture may influence the potential meaning of a learning context (Kohl (1969) spells this out graphically when he discusses the question of why there should be a 'front' of a classroom, or what happens when the teacher surrenders the 'teacher's desk' to the general use of the class). Galloway also discusses the significance of the way a teacher moves about the classroom, the non-verbal tactics he uses to control the class, for example raising his finger to his lips, raising his eyebrows. He proposes six dimensions of non-verbal behaviour all ranging from encouraging to restricting in their functions:

Congruity	Incongruity
Responsive	Unresponsive
Positive affectivity	Negative affectivity
Facilitating	Unreceptive
Supportive	Disapproving
Attentive	Inattentive

Galloway argues that the effects of non-verbal behaviour on class-room transactions should be studied by students in training.

Lail (1968) has used an adaptation of Flanders's system to incorporate Galloway's dimensions of non-verbal behaviour. She added the prefix 1 to the Flanders categories to indicate if the categories were non-verbally restrictive and left the category un-annotated if it were non-verbally encouraging. She gives examples of verbal responses that could give a misleading impression when divorced from their non-verbal context. For example, is 'good' always praise? It could be just a punctuation mark in the teacher's spoken repertoire. The prefix 1 would make it clear. Again, as with other examples, this approach adds an additional dimension to the student's concept of the processes of the classroom. Meux (1967) suggests that what is needed is an attempt to construct a super system which contains the best facets of the other systems and so overcomes their limitations. Until this is done it will be important that students get an idea of the variety of approaches possible.

We conclude this section by considering one other approach to the question of classroom interaction analysis which seems to us to raise some very important issues. Good and Brophy (1969) have pointed out that the assumption that interaction takes place between the teacher and the class as a whole can be questioned. They point out that, while this is probably true for all occasions when the teacher is lecturing, it is not necessarily so when other types of interaction are taking place. It is true that when lecturing is taking place there is no interaction in the normal sense of the word but in the various category systems it is usually one of the categories. In other classroom moves the category systems would record the teacher as having interacted with the class, whereas in fact he may have only interacted with one or two pupils but on repeated occasions. It is possible, for example, for a teacher to be recorded as medium to high in 'teacher warmth' whereas in fact she could be low in 'warmth' towards most of the class. This follows since the record of the interaction does not register the fact that her 'warmth' was extended over a very limited range of children. In order to get over this problem Good and Brophy argue that a more profitable line to take would be to consider the individual pupil as the unit of analysis in classroom studies. They believe that such an approach would not only give a truer picture of interactions but would also provide more powerful research designs.

There are two reasons why misleading pictures of teacher inter-actions may flow from using the class as the unit of interaction. On the one hand some of the categories in most of the methods of analysis refer to dyadic interaction. Such behaviours as praising, criticizing or accepting pupils' ideas are typically interactions between one pupil and the teacher. On the other hand the different category systems seem to assume that teachers are consistent across pupils in their classroom behaviour so that individual differences within a classroom are of little or no importance to inter-class differences. In fact there is a considerable amount of evidence that teachers do not treat all children in the same manner so it is more than likely that the phenomenon suggested in our example relating to teacher warmth could be found in other categories of interaction systems.

What are the implications of this argument for interaction analysis systems? It seems to us that the argument should not be disregarded. It does not mean, however, that the arguments render the various systems nugatory. Teachers do acquire and improve skills by learning about interaction analysis of the orthodox variety.

The development of techniques to guard against the problems raised by Good and Brophy within the framework of existing methods does not seem to be impracticable, while research and development in the techniques of dyadic interaction analysis may in the future add significant aspects to a super system such as Meux refers to. However, we would look at the question somewhat differently and suggest that it is more useful to look upon the various contributions as helping to make the mesh of the net of our theory finer without any implication that we have at any stage reached finality.

8 · Perspectives

The perceptive reader will have noticed a discrepancy between the way in which student teachers perceive their likely development after training, and the type of skills and attitudes that workers in such fields as microteaching and interaction analysis would like them to develop. The work of Shipman and Cohen (Chapter 2) indicates that students see themselves as becoming more authoritarian and less indirect when they leave college. They would use praise more sparingly, counsel children less and give them less opportunity to learn from mistakes. Compare this with the indications from interaction analysis that indirect teachers are more effective, and the work of tutors in microteaching who try to teach students the use of reinforcing techniques, which is virtually the antithesis of using praise more sparingly. It seems to us that this discrepancy highlights the danger of modelling the master teacher and illustrates its essentially conservative nature.

AIMS AND OBJECTIVES

All the more reason, therefore, to strive to master the teaching model, and to do this we need first to give some attention to the aims of the exercise. We cannot aspire to produce a set of objectives for practical teaching like producing a rabbit out of a hat. We should like, however, to suggest some guidelines for such a set of objectives. But first we would propose as a statement of a general approach to the problem some broad aims against which innovations may be appraised. In summary form we would say that practical teaching should:

1 Aim to make skilful teachers; skilful being defined as skilled in producing learning in pupils, and the skills being based on a consistent body of theoretical principles.

2 Aim to develop in students positive attitudes of acceptance of and respect for children, openness to change, commitment to self-awareness and self-evaluation.

3 Aim to prepare students for entry to the teaching profession with particular reference to appropriate professional behaviour.

We do not suggest that these are any more than very broadly stated aims and we recognize that they need considerable sharpening up before they can be accepted as working objectives. Nor do we naively consider that they would attract universal agreement although their lack of precision may make consensus more likely than if they were stated in precise and specific terms. The point is, of course, that it is the process rather than the product with which we are currently concerned. It is much more important that teacher trainers adopt the objectives-oriented approach to practical teaching than that they agree with our views and formulations.

Thus the process as we see it would involve the production of aims such as we propose *in the first instance*. These broad and general aims would then be analysed and the more specific objectives which they subsume derived from them. These more specific objectives would need to be couched in unequivocal terms so that when tutors agreed to them it would not be a spurious consensus such as is often obtained with broad imprecisely formulated aims. The objectives should, in our view, be stated in terms of what the student should be able to do at the end of the course; that is, they should be couched in behavioural terms.

The objectives reported by Cope (pp. 16–21), for all their specificity, are not presented in the way we suggest and need further interpretation if they are to be stated in terms of students' behaviour. Thus the first objective states that school practice should: 'provide the student with an opportunity of establishing an appropriate teacher-pupil relationship with children'. In elaboration of this objective we have the following:

An appropriate teacher-pupil relationship is characterized by:
a) reciprocity, i.e. mutual respect and the sharing of initiatives;
b) positive constructive and lively attitudes to work manifested by teacher and pupils;
c) a warm yet objective concern felt by the teacher for the general well being as well as for the intellectual progress of all the pupils.

We would endorse these sentiments without reservation, as indeed would almost all teachers. The crunch comes and disagreements are likely when we try to express these notions in terms of student behaviour. Perhaps we can make our point clearer by suggesting that what is needed is an indication as to how we should be able to distinguish between a student who had established the relationship and one who had not. Indeed, this is a useful way of sharpening up one's perceptions of objectives generally.

Although stating objectives in the way we propose is an abrasive operation, it seems much better to us than sweeping the problem under the carpet. Cope, herself, makes a very similar point when she discusses the relationship between college tutors and school staff. She reports this relationship as a delicate liaison characterized by social amiability and complete lack of educational interchanges which might cause embarrassment. Cope comments: 'a working partnership that has been vigorously hammered out can take more strain.' Objectives that are spelled out in behavioural terms offer more hope for meaningful working relationships than those presented in terms of processes such as 'providing opportunity for'.

Cope recognizes that the objectives she reports on are not presented in operational terms 'since [to ask] this would have imposed impossible demands on the groups involved in discussions'. These groups were students, college staff and teachers who prepared brief lists of objectives for Cope who then classified them in the groups we referred to in Chapter 1. There is a real problem here. Preparing objectives is a difficult task and in the context of Cope's investigation it was undoubtedly out of the question. However, experience in the Birmingham Area Training Organization suggests that it can be done on a group basis (Stones 1970b). Here groups of college tutors meeting to discuss the teaching of various aspects of the education course have thrashed out sets of objectives and stated them in behavioural or quasi-behavioural terms and thereby laid the foundation for genuine collaboration of teaching approaches to the different subjects; which is what we would hope for in a college–school liaison.

As an example of a very different approach we may consider a highly specific objective from the microteaching programme at Brigham Young University (Webb et al. 1968). This is not a general objective of teaching practice as are those reported by Cope, but one related to the teaching of a particular skill and for that reason cannot be compared with them. It states:

> Within a period of seven minutes, the pre-service teacher will teach a single concept within his major or minor field, and evaluate whether or not it has been learned.
>
> An evaluation of the microteaching will be made in terms of: the desirability and effectiveness of the materials selected to show the referent; application of the learning sequence; the amount of pupil involvement; whether or not the concept was learned; whether students were caused to think above the lowest cognitive level, and on the voice, poise and mannerisms of the teacher.
>
> The pre-service teacher will write a summary of the suggestions made for improvement, those he would select for implementation, and the steps he would take to implement them.
>
> Minimal performance shall require that 75 per cent of the pupils taught shall have achieved the teacher's objective and learned the concept taught, and that pupils shall be caused to function *at least once above the lowest cognitive level*.

Mager (1962) has made what is probably the most influential contribution in the field of behavioural statement of objectives. He counsels the reader to avoid the use of terms that can mean all things to all men. Few people would disagree with objectives that state that at the end of the course the student should 'know' this, that or the other; or that the course should 'provide each student with the opportunity to extend his creative potential to the full'. The trouble starts, of course, when different people attempt to state precisely what they mean by these terms. Hence Mager suggests that we use terms such as *construct*, *state* and *solve*, and eschew expressions such as *understand* and *appreciate*.

It is an interesting fact, however, that while all colleges make some sort of statement in their prospectuses about the broad aims of the theoretical element in their courses, few venture to do the same in relation to practical teaching. Most say such things as 'The practice of teaching will take place in infant, junior, or secondary schools', the main addition to this formula being 'for not less than X days'. Not that we would expect colleges to state their objectives in the detail of the example given above when compiling their prospectuses, but it does not seem unreasonable that some aims should be suggested.

We should be surprised if all readers were enthusiastic about the objective stated by Webb and his associates. Objectives, as we have suggested, seem to be amenable to consensus in indirect relationship to their level of specificity. The point about the Brigham Young objective, as with specific behaviourally stated objectives generally, is that it exposes possible points of difference which would otherwise be concealed under a cloak of ambiguity.

One further point which we consider to be of great importance in the specification of objectives is that they should constitute a logically and psychologically valid system. It would be quite possible to formulate aims such as the one in the example which had minimum relationships with each other. We could, that is, produce a collection of atomistic objectives, each one probably of some importance but the whole collection lacking the unifying principles which we referred to in our discussion of theory of teaching. Ideally, of course, we should like to see a taxonomic approach, but probably at the present stage of development in the scientific study of teaching, it is premature to entertain such hopes, although the argument by Snow about putting the teacher together again is clearly moving in the right direction.

Stones (1972), in a proposal for a taxonomy of objectives for educational psychology, has put forward a system that relates closely to problems of teaching practice. He takes the view shared by other workers in the field that the concepts and skills of educational psychology should be closely related to the actual practice of teaching. He makes the point that, while it is perhaps possible to assess students' grasp of those skills and concepts in orthodox tests, the only satisfactory test is the ability to apply them in teaching. Stones proposes three levels of skills as being the necessary objectives of a course in educational psychology. The highest level of skill is that which asks that the student should be able to apply the concepts of educational psychology to specific classroom situations. Thus the second section of his taxonomy, which is concerned with the psychology of teaching cognitive skills, has as its most general objective the following:

Given a teaching objective involving cognitive learning, decide on the type(s) of pupil learning most appropriate to the objective and specify the teaching and learning activities most likely to optimize the pupils' learning.

When subjected to analysis this objective yields eleven second-order objectives, one of which we may consider as an example: objective 7 states:

Decide whether the learning necessary to achieve a given teaching objective involves any element of concept learning and, if it does, specify the optimum conditions for such learning.

This objective in turn yields ten third-order objectives among which are the two following examples.

Objective 5: Specify the optimum conditions for the presentation of exemplars in specific teaching/learning situations involving concept learning.
Objective 6: Specify the optimum uses of feedback or reinforcement in specific teaching/learning situations involving concept learning.

The third-order objectives may themselves be analysed further but at this level we are moving into the field of task analysis where quite detailed specifications are made for student activity and the structuring of the teaching situation. We could, for example, take the sixth objective and derive from it an objective of the type and specificity of: 'the student praises a correct answer from a pupil'. Number five might be analysed to yield an objective such as: 'the student presents an ordered series of exemplars of a concept, designed to teach differentiation and classification'.

The reader will probably note the close similarity between the two third-order objectives and some of the teaching skills referred to by the practitioners of microteaching, and in fact many of those skills would fit satisfactorily into the categories of the proposed taxonomy. It may well be that this taxonomy or something similar could provide a first approach to the systematizing of objectives in the field of practical teaching.

TASK ANALYSIS

As has just been suggested, the pursuit of ever more specific objectives eventually takes us into the field of task analysis. At this stage we scrutinize the teaching task, in our case based on the objectives we have set for practical teaching, and attempt to identify the subtasks and the concepts and skills prerequisite to the adequate fulfilment of the task. Stones (1966) has produced a heuristic device as a guide to teachers planning teaching sequences which may illustrate a method of approaching task analysis. He suggests that when analysing the general content (i.e. the key concepts) of a teaching task it is useful to think about other aspects of the task at the same time. Although this approach was designed more for theoretical than for practical work it seems not inapposite to our present discussion. In outline the approach can be seen in Table 5. The tutor or teacher using this guide analyses the substantive content of the teaching task by working out what principles and concepts are subsumed by the general content area. This is done, as was suggested in our discussion of objectives, by working in a descending hierarchy from the most general concepts to the most specific ones. At much the same time he could be making tentative decisions about the nature of the specific exemplars of the concepts and the possible methods of presenting the exemplars to the students. A knowledge of the parameters of different types of learning would enable him to classify the learning involved and this would shed light on the other aspects of the analysis such as the nature of the student's response and the feedback most appropriate to the learning. All the foregoing analyses would be relatable to the problem of evaluation. In Table 5 the emphasis is mainly on the assessment of grasp of concepts but the suggestion for a skill criterion would chime well with our suggestions for the evaluation of practical teaching. The value of a device such as is presented in Table 5 is that it helps one to take a systematic approach to the problem but at the same time to have in mind the various aspects of the analysis and their likely interconnections.

EVALUATION

The implications of an approach to the specification of objectives and task analysis like the one we have suggested are antithetical to the present practices of assessment of practical teaching. So much so that we feel obliged to argue that the system cannot be mended and should be ended forthwith. Current practice is not only infinitely various in its manifestations, it is also based on a view of evaluation that is being increasingly questioned. Assessment as currently understood in relation to practical work is norm referenced – that is, it is based on criteria of competence in the subject under

Table 5 Task analysis (Stones 1966)

General content	Specific examples	Type of learning	Method of stimulus presentation	Student's response	Feedback	Evaluation
Main concepts rules, principles involved.	Actual examples to be used in instruction.	S-R. Concept learning. Problem solving.	Pictures. Film. TV. Teacher's speech. Actual phenomena. Visits. Etc.	Written communication. Recall of information. Discrimination. Motor activity.	Tutor's verbalizing. Matching with correct examples. Other students' verbalizing. Record of student's own activity.	Germs of items for final test, e.g. objective test, performance of psychomotor skill to specified criteria.

N.B. The entries in the columns are examples only and are not intended to be exhaustive.

scrutiny related to a set of norms drawn from a typical population (Stones 1970a). Like all norm referenced measures it is used mainly to grade students and, in fact, all grades quoted in relation to student achievement say nothing of an objective nature about his level of competence; they merely state that A is better than B and B is better than C and so on. Taking the view we have suggested for the specification of objectives and the analysis of the teaching task, and marrying this to some of the approaches for evaluating the teaching skills acquired by students under some of the proposed objectives-oriented training procedures, it becomes possible to think in terms of criterion referenced tests. The user of criterion referenced tests decides beforehand on the skills and concepts that he expects the students to acquire, devises a test to test these attributes and then scores students' performance according to the extent to which they demonstrate their grasp of those skills and concepts after instruction.

Stones (1970a) outlines the key differences between norm referenced and criterion referenced tests.

In norm referenced evaluation the discriminative power of the test instrument is all important and will often take precedence over its other functions. In instruments related to an objective criterion, discrimination will be unimportant and individual items in the instrument will be selected for reasons other than their power to discriminate.

The most obvious practical difference between the two approaches is that norm referenced measures will emphasize grading and the production of a rank order of examinees, while criterion referenced measures will not be concerned with ranking but will emphasize the achievement of predetermined standards. In norm referenced evaluation, examiners will probably have some notion of what constitutes a pass, or average, or distinction performance which they carry in their heads and which may lead to their working on a scale roughly following a normal distribution. Performance here is related to the performance of the group, and one student's distinction depends on the non-distinction of the rest of the group. Criterion referenced assessment is different. Theoretically all students could reach distinction level or all could fail. Since performance is related to an objective predetermined criterion, however, it is not enough for an examiner to conceive of an intuitive pass mark – say 50 per cent –

whenever he attempts to assess student performance. Nor is it enough for him to observe and perhaps record student perform- ance and then to rank on this performance and finally decide on cutting scores to determine pass, fail or other categories.

It may well be that in practical teaching it is difficult to get a truly objective criterion but the use of rating scales with high rater agreement or the consensus of a body of tutors upon clearly specified criteria would act as reasonably satisfactory measures of student performance. *Vis-à-vis* the question of certification, we conceive the most appropriate approach as being one that expects of students a certain basic minimum performance on a variety of key skills with individual excellencies in some of the skills according to the interests, personalities and specific competencies of the students. Students would be certificated on the basis of having attained the basic level on the key skills and the individual strengths would be based on this level to form a profile specific to each student. This profile would be of much greater value as a guide to student performance than the current highly suspect literal grading.

To help standardize certification the development of rating instruments would be of great use. A standardized profile form based on a nationally agreed statement of objectives of practical work would ensure that tutors are evaluating the full range of student teachers' behaviours, while an instrument similar to the Stanford Teacher Competence Appraisal Guide would reduce the subjective element in evaluation and prove helpful to the students' self-evaluation. Used, as has been described, by tutors, the student teacher himself, pupils, and student peers, the objectives and criteria would be made fully explicit and the process of evaluation would be less personal so that the student being evaluated would be more likely to take a dispassionate view of the process and even make his own contribution to the evaluation.

THE CONCEPT OF TEACHING PRACTICE

We have consistently argued for a *rapprochement* between the theoretical elements of a course in teacher preparation and practical teaching: we would now like to suggest a view of the course which might contribute to this *rapprochement*. It seems to us that it would be useful to consider the whole college course as having theoretical and practical elements. Thus, for example, the study of geography would be conceived of as involving the mastery of bodies of theoretical concepts and principles and the application of these principles in the practical situation of field work; science studies would be similarly conceived. In essence this is the way these subjects are viewed at the moment, but the same reasoning can be applied to other subjects. Thus English could be concerned with mastering given sets of concepts concerned with literary style, methods of communication, aspects of linguistics and spoken English, which would have their practical correlates in such things as the production of unique communications by students which utilized this body of knowledge. Applying this reasoning to the study of education we would be concerned to build up bodies of concepts in the fields of the philosophy, history, sociology and psychology of education together with curriculum studies. These concepts would be applied to practical situations at the appropriate opportune time and not held over to a period of teaching practice which could well be remote in time from the first learning of the concepts. Nor would the practical work necessarily take place in schools as is the case at present. It would be organized in a variety of places according to the learning requirements of the students, such as the college itself, school, community centre, nursery, play group, clinic or any other appropriate institution. Often it will not be necessary to distinguish this type of activity from other professional course work, but when it is, the term *practical professional work* could be used; this would also distinguish it from practical work in other fields and denote a wide unified concept of practical/theoretical teaching activity.

OBJECTIVES-ORIENTED PRACTICAL PROFESSIONAL WORK

Taking an objectives-oriented approach to practical professional work, such as we suggest, makes it possible to end the haphazard visiting of schools, 'because there is good work going on', and sending students to schools on an apprenticeship basis, in favour of a systematic approach to providing student practical professional experience in schools and other institutions. The student's learning objectives will then govern the type of institution he attends, the points in the course when he attends and the duration of his stay.

The approach to practical teaching that we suggest will make use of the various techniques we have discussed in earlier sections. We find it useful to classify the techniques available according to the two major divisions of model the master teacher – master the teaching model, and the simulated – actual division. Figure 1 relates these two divisions to form four cells into which we can fit the

	Model the master teacher	Master the teaching model
Simulated	Role playing in imitation of teacher or audiovisual recording of teacher Cell 1	Dossier work Microteaching with peers Interaction analysis with specially prepared material Cell 2
Actual	Orthodox teaching practice Cell 4	Microteaching with children Interaction analysis of actual classroom transactions Minicourse Group practice? Cell 3

Figure 1 Suggested method of classifying teaching behaviour according to the two major divisions: the *model the master teacher* approach versus the *master the teaching model* approach and the *simulated* versus the *actual* teaching situation.

various types of teaching activities. The argument we have presented throughout this book leads us to prefer activities that can be allocated to cells 2 and 3 and to prefer cell 3 to cell 2. Some of the examples given could possibly be allocated to more than one cell depending upon the precise nature of the specific activity. For example, the extent to which dossier work, say, is purely based on mastering the teaching model, will be a function of the specific dossiers. The same could possibly be said of some of the other examples. The point is, however, that these approaches *could* be entirely based on the mastering of the model: the potential is there and we would hope that in time sufficient experience and theoretical understanding will be gained to enable us to allocate these methods unequivocally to cells 2 or 3. Similarly with the simulated – actual dimension. Microteaching is real teaching and therefore belongs in cell 3 or 4. As it is normally practised it would be placed in cell 3 but when used in role playing situations with the use of peer students it becomes simulation and is then more rightly placed in cell 2. The case of group practice, which we place between cells 3 and 4, is interesting. It is in fact a current practice which could be placed in cell 3 but probably in fact it is usually likely to be conducted in a way consistent with placement in cell 4.

The assigning of the teaching activities to the various cells will give some indication as to the most suitable location for the activity to take place: thus simulation work is probably most appropriately and conveniently carried on in college, whereas current practice, mainly tied to cell 4, cannot but be carried out in school. We suggest that the basic teaching skills and skills of observation, analysis and evaluation should be taught largely in college by means of various simulation techniques, microteaching and allied activities using visiting groups of children as the microclasses and involving peer groups of students in the critique sessions. These activities should be concurrent with and related to the theoretical studies in education. Certain activities, however, need much more prolonged contact with children in a school community; for example, learning how an area in a junior school could be most effectively organized for a variety of pupil activities (this could have been prepared for by simulation techniques). Or, in a secondary school, how best to organize groups of different sizes in team teaching (this, also, could be preceded by simulation work). These types of activity can probably only be school based. Similarly, work that involves such things as establishing a relationship over time with a group of children, or learning how to work with other teachers, will require periods of several weeks in school. However, there seems no reason why some of these activities should not be preceded by simulation work in college once the techniques have been developed.

Scheduling the practical work in relation to objectives, taking an experimental approach from college work into schools, and the development of a working partnership between college tutors and teachers in which explicit objectives and criteria are shared fully, would facilitate the careful structuring of the students' learning experiences in schools. It should not be difficult in these conditions to devise for students a programme of observation and analysis of children and teachers; to grade the students' teaching from individual and small group work to teaching half and finally whole classes; to vary the students' mode of teaching from individual to collaborative teaching in pairs and teams; and to involve them in discussion and decision-making in the field of teaching methods and curricula. Regular observation by a fellow student working in partnership for part of the school period and using an evaluation instrument of the type suggested earlier, coupled with regular observation by supervising teachers, would provide the student with essential feedback. It may seem pie in the sky at the moment, but we suggest here that the use of simple video systems would enable the student to record his teaching and view it with cooperating teachers or even send it to college to be viewed by his supervisor. What is certainly more practicable at the moment is the use of audio tape both in microteaching sessions in the practice school and in interaction analysis exercises of the type discussed in Chapter 7. This gradual phasing in of the student to the 'real' teaching situation is of course very much in line with some of the work going on in America and in the Universities of Ulster and Stirling.

It seems likely to us that the development of more objective approaches to practical teaching and the development of agreed sets of unequivocally stated objectives would facilitate the sharing of ideas on values, aims, curricula and teaching methods by teachers, tutors and students and thereby lead to mutual understanding and a lessening of tension among the three. The growth of a partnership between school and college would enable the student to feel that he belongs equally in both institutions. If the learning of the basic skills takes place in college the student would enter the school for a period of practical work as a beginning teacher rather than as a student, and this, we think, would be likely to diminish the role conflict that he would otherwise probably experience. The elimination of assessment along the lines we suggested above, in addition to diminishing the student's anxiety, would also de-emphasize his role as student and strengthen his role as beginning teacher.

THE ORGANIZATION OF PRACTICAL PROFESSIONAL WORK

In colleges the organization of practical professional work and its integration with theoretical studies will require a great deal of close cooperation between subject specialists and education staff. Identification of the teaching skills to be developed in students, the development, production and analyses of *protocol materials* (see p. 91), the linking of teaching theory with methods of teaching specific subjects and bodies of knowledge, will all necessitate, as normal practice, the collaboration that is beginning to grow in a few colleges (Cambridge Institute of Education 1970). In many colleges staff will need training in microteaching techniques, simulation, observational methods and use of video tape, and technical resources for the production of teaching materials will be needed.

In schools and other institutions used for practical work the selection of key staff and their appointment as teacher-tutors would constitute a first step in developing a partnership with colleges (Cope 1971, Bell and Mundy 1966, Cambridge Institute of Education 1970). Officially constituted and regularly held conferences between school staff and college representatives would take the idea of cooperation and partnership a stage further and could lead to a formal, semi-permanent relationship between a group of schools and a college which might result in a school/college committee (Collier 1970). The concept of a working group of several schools and a small team of college staff might be productive (Owens 1970). The collaboration of college staff, teachers and students in flexible teams for short periods of practical work in both college and school would clearly be valuable in developing the partnership.

A partnership, however, depends on reciprocity. Services that colleges could perform for schools, related to students' practical work, include advice on curriculum development, help with the evaluation of new curricula and teaching methods, freeing teachers for in-service training by allocating a team of students and staff to take over classes completely for a time, giving help with specialist services (diagnostic, remedial, etc.) and with technical resources (A.V.A. equipment, etc.).

The prerequisite for the success of such a partnership would be the in-service training of cooperating teachers by the colleges in new curricula and teaching methods and above all in methods of supervision and techniques of evaluation. Moves in this direction are being made in parts of the U.S.A. under a variety of titles. The University of Maryland has developed a teacher education centre which provides a specific example of the type of institutions that are developing and incorporates many of the features we have been discussing. Full details are provided in Part 3 (pp. 245–51) but we give here the salient features of the centre. It involves the close partnership of schools of all types with the University in providing a unified approach to the study of teaching and supervision for in-service and pre-service training. Emphasis is placed on individualized learning, and methods are being developed making use of microteaching and methods of analysing teaching and supervisory behaviour. The centre provides the site and facilities for the study of teaching, and research is going on to test the efficiency of such things as modelling and the use of video tape recordings.

The Maryland centre seems to us to be moving in the right direction but B. O. Smith (1969) sounds a warning on some possible problems.

At the present time, training centres and laboratories are springing up all over the nation. But they tend to be poorly planned and inadequately staffed, and they lack a clear conception of the training function they are to perform. Such a centre too easily becomes merely a new base for the traditional program of student teaching with a few catch phrases and gimmicks and a lot of fanfare about school participation. If ever there was a time when insightful planning for teacher training was needed, it is now. The federal government is poised to spend more millions of dollars on the training of teachers. Universities and colleges are rising to meet the growing demands for educational personnel. Public schools are making every effort to enter the field of teacher education. Yet all these resources are in danger of being used to bolster up old programs disguised as revolutionary developments by catchwords and empty phrases.

Apart from the unlikely spectacle of a government poised to spend millions on teacher education, and the possibility of teacher training centres 'springing up' ubiquitously, much of what Smith says applies only too accurately to present conditions in England and Wales.

INNOVATION OR ENERVATION?

The keen young teacher with his mind full of 'new' ways of teaching this, that and the other, with notions of the teacher 'as manager', of team teaching, of individualized learning, could possibly suspect that many of the techniques we have discussed are essentially linked to traditional ways of teaching. We think that this could be the case but that it need not be. The point is that the techniques of microteaching and what-not have been applied to existing teaching situations and we have reported on those situations. However, the techniques are by no means bound up with those situations and in fact they have been used in conditions quite different from those of the 'orthodox' classroom. Microteaching has been used in work with college staff and in developing techniques of counselling where individuals replace the microclass. Similarly, the concepts of interaction analysis were used by Bales (1955) to analyse interactions in conferences, situations that differ considerably from those of the classroom. The work of Taba and others, in classroom situations aimed at developing higher levels of thinking and the formation of concepts, has a clear application to work with individual pupils. This point is close to that made by Good and Brophy in their argument about the essentially dyadic nature of classroom interactions. Simulation, of course, has been used in a very wide variety of settings, from complex 'war games' involving many participants to individual training situations such as are embodied in the link trainer for pilots or simulated car driving. The point we wish to make is that *whatever the teaching set-up*, if the teacher is playing any part at all then the techniques we have discussed are applicable.

A crucial feature of our argument for the systematic deployment of varied approaches to the mastering of the teaching model is the planned programming of the teaching/learning activities of the student. As we said in the beginning, the experiences of the student at the moment are unorganized and unsystematic, and watching another person perform cannot give the range of experience necessary to build comprehensive concepts as to what teaching is and how the multitude of teaching skills is best orchestrated. The planned approach we advocate is one that makes use of the psychological principles of concept formation and the application of these principles to the acquisition of teaching skills. This approach involves the planned presentation, through the various approaches we have suggested, of a variety of exemplars of teaching activities. By presenting this variety of exemplars we enable students to acquire the *class* of teaching behaviour without the idiosyncratic features of any single model's performance. This is in line with the findings of Bandura, Ross and Ross (1963) on the effects of using a variety of models of a class of behaviour. It is also connected with the point made earlier that the carefully planned approach in microteaching produces not teachers who copy the models they are provided with, but teachers who develop their personal styles on the basis of a general approach. Resnick and Kiss (1970) conducted an experiment which illustrates a further effect of this type of approach. They provided student teachers with a variety of models of a limited class of teaching skills related to the effective testing or diagnosis of children in a tutorial setting; other students did not get this variety of models. All students received practice and verbal feedback from the supervisor. The experimenters found that the students who had the variety of models were better able subsequently to monitor their own performance when teaching.

This finding is encouraging additional evidence to suggest that the techniques outlined in previous chapters offer a possibility for a greater emphasis on self-instruction than is possible at the moment. Unwin and McAleese's point about the students acting as their own critics, and the extremely well developed ideas of the minicourse, clearly indicate that much can be done to develop the student's independence in this field and give him much more responsibility for his own learning. The use of a tape recorded analysis of one's own classroom interaction, whether with a traditional class or in other sorts of groupings, has already been referred to and has had a fair amount of practical testing. Simulation methods lend themselves to the production of packages with feedback geared to them. All these approaches seem to us to be moving in the right direction, from considerable dependence upon teacher and tutor, to a position of shared responsibility which holds the possibility of ever increasing emphasis on individual self-instruction.

We see no reason, then, why the methods of conducting practical professional work, such as we have described, and as are already being conducted in some centres, should be inimical to any new developments in approaches to teaching. We believe that the techniques stand a better chance of being seen to be valuable than many innovations in the field of teacher preparation, since, unlike many of those innovations, they depend upon explicitly stated objectives and criteria, and we hope that colleges and other institutions will take them up and use them in ways that explore their possibilities in the varied conditions of British schools.

GOODBYE TO NELLIE?

Neither of us is so naive as to think that what we have described in these pages will render Nellie redundant at a stroke. With the Association of Headteachers calling for students to spend more time at her feet, and evidence to the James Committee from A.T.O.s saying much the same thing, we expect her to be around for a little longer yet. We deplore this since we think that much of current practice is little better than a charade, and a pretentious charade at that when one considers the learned discussions as to whether a student should be awarded a C or a C+ for teaching practice and when a student is denied the chance of reading for a B.Ed. degree because his grade was a point below the cut-off grade. There is no suggestion, either, that any of our proposals are to be considered as universal panaceas. What we do hope for is an open-minded reappraisal which takes note of existing evidence about the inefficacy of current methods of conducting practical teaching and the promise (to some extent already being fulfilled) of alternative approaches.

We cannot conclude without some expression of appreciation of the pioneering work of those institutions who have developed new approaches – in particular, of course, the workers at Stanford. We are also extremely conscious that many of the suggestions we have made have already been adopted by some institutions, and in the United Kingdom the work of the New University of Ulster and the University of Stirling is outstanding. We hope that their examples will be followed by an increasing number of colleges and departments of education, not necessarily merely to imitate, but to develop the ideas in creative ways according to their own circumstances.

Part 3 · Papers

1 · The assessment of practical teaching

E. STONES and S. MORRIS

Introduction

The investigation reported here was undertaken as a contribution to the discussion of the problems of the assessment of practical teaching. This is a subject which has been attracting increasing attention in recent years as is evidenced by journal articles and increasing research activity in universities and colleges. The problem of assessment is, of course, just one aspect of the larger problem of reappraising the aims and procedures of teaching practice.

We are aware that any scrutiny of methods of assessment raises the question of criteria: how can you tell a good teacher when you see one? We are also aware that this question has in itself generated an enormous amount of research and a vast literature without producing a consensus view on the subject. This report does not contribute directly to the debate about criteria, but it may do tangentially since one of the key elements in our survey was the collection of data about criteria currently being used in colleges and universities in England and Wales. However, we were of the opinion that discussion about criteria, about methods of supervision, about methods of agreeing final teaching practice mark and other related matters would be helped by some general information about current practices, which we lack at the moment, and this is what our survey sought to provide.

We believe that the question of practical teaching is one that is in urgent need of appraisal. But this is not because we think we have the answers. On the contrary, we believe that in the past the complexity of the problem has scarcely been grasped. Human learning is one of the most complex things in the universe and

Reprinted from *Educational Research*, 14 (1972), 2.

getting other human beings to learn (which is what *we* take teaching to be about) must, by the same token, present enormous problems. It is not surprising, then, that faced with such complexity those engaged in teacher preparation perforce make use of methods that are open to question. The investigation we report below reveals what we take to be weaknesses in current practice. We present them to our readers not because we wish to be associated with current criticisms of colleges and departments of education, which we think in the main completely fail to understand the problems of teacher preparation, but because we hope to contribute to the debate with a little more information and objectivity than often seems to be the case.

Method

In order to collect the information required a questionnaire was prepared and revised twice on the basis of comments from staff in colleges and a university department of education. The final version of the questionnaire comprised six sections dealing with the form of assessment, the evidence used in assessment, the staff involved in assessment, the criteria used, feedback to students, and the weighting of the practical teaching mark in total assessment. The questionnaires were sent to heads of education departments in colleges of education and to tutors in charge of courses for the post-graduate certificate in education in university departments of education. 188 questionnaires were sent out and 122 returned, a response of 65 per cent.

i) THE FORM OF ASSESSMENT

The pros and cons of different forms of assessment have been debated for many years. Commonly used approaches such as rating scales have been subjected to criticism (Cattell 1931, Evans 1951). The fifteen point scale was found wanting by Downes and Shaw (1968) and Morris (1970) advances a number of arguments against the use of rating scales in the assessment of practical teaching and suggests the use of a teaching profile. Despite the general doubts about the efficacy of measures such as five and fifteen point scales we thought it not unlikely that such measures were still in widespread use. This section of the questionnaire put seven questions which sought to collect information about current practices in this field.

ii) EVIDENCE USED IN ASSESSMENT

An important question in the discussion of any type of assessment is whether the approach adopted is impressionistic or analytic. In some instances impressionistic assessment can be effective especially when several judges are involved in assessing *the same piece of behaviour*. However Robertson (1957) found a low correlation among eighteen supervisors' ranking of the attributes that contribute to success in practical teaching. We therefore asked whether assessments were impressionistic or analytic and what elements in the students' performance contributed to the final grading. We also asked whether assessors had in mind the likely development of the student as distinct from his present performance.

iii) THE ASSESSORS

This section sought information about the people who actually do the assessing. We were interested in such things as the extent to which opportunities for multiple assessor gradings were provided, the extent of involvement of the external examiners, and the formal provision for exchange of views among assessors.

iv) CRITERIA

The problem of criteria is, of course, the question that has attracted most attention over the years. Apart from the questions of validity and reliability of criteria there is a not inconsiderable problem in merely classifying the criteria used into some sort of taxonomic framework (Mitzel 1960). Our question here therefore invited respondents to indicate the criteria they used in assessment.

The standardizing of criteria is another major problem which would seem to be of great importance in the assessment procedures. The Stanford Teacher Competence Appraisal Guide is an example of an American approach to the problem which has been developed over a number of years, but there seems to be little attempt in Britain to develop work along these lines. We therefore asked questions aimed at discovering whether any college or university was using approaches of this nature. Finally, in this section, we enquired about the bases upon which distinctions and failures were determined.

We hoped that the answers provided to the questions in this section would throw light on the key problem of whether tutors could say exactly what they are looking for in their student's teaching. There is some evidence that they cannot (Lantz 1967) and clearly if this is the case it does not seem possible to judge the performance or to communicate the judgement in meaningful terms to others.

v) FEEDBACK TO STUDENTS

Learning theorists of a variety of theoretical persuasions are agreed on the value of feedback in learning. Student teachers are in very complex learning situations. What arrangements are made to provide feedback when they are in the practical teaching situation? Some recent techniques such as microteaching using video tape recorders and the self-analysis of taped lesson using some form of interaction analysis are attempting to cope with this problem, but we were anxious to establish the extent to which this fundamental element in efficient learning was being allowed for in current practice.

Results

i) THE FORM OF ASSESSMENT

122 institutions replied to the questionnaire and in all cases a final teaching mark of some kind was awarded. Of the institutions that provided information about the use of rating scales (111), the five point scale was the most popular (65 institutions) followed by the three point scale (17 institutions) and the fifteen point scale (10 institutions). Fifty-two institutions averred that they used a profile but there is strong indication that the word 'profile' was interpreted in two main (different) ways. Some respondents clearly equated the term with 'pen portrait' and we received one or two examples of this type of 'profile'. An example of the kind of content of this type of return might read: 'Miss X has largely followed the existing regime in the classroom and consequently her work has been less ambitious and imaginative than one would like . . . she has raised

the standard of the children's writing. . . .' We received only seven examples of profiles in the sense in which it is used in rating procedures. A typical profile of this type lists attributes being rated along one side of a matrix and the rating along the other side. A student is given a rating on each of the attributes and these ratings may be plotted on the same scale and joined up to produce a 'profile' which presents a picture of a student's teaching performance along the different dimensions provided.* The profile that provided for the largest number of dimensions had thirty-two items in eight sections and the profile with the lowest number had four. The most common form of scoring along the dimensions was a five point scale but one profile had a three point scale and one made provision for the assessor to draw lines the length of which was a measure of the student's performance along the different dimensions. The criteria used in the dimensions of the profiles are discussed below but typical examples are 'relationship with children', 'appropriate use of audiovisual aids', 'questioning ability'.

Twenty-eight institutions reported that they used other methods of expressing practical teaching assessment. Sixty said they did not, and thirty-four did not reply to the question. In many cases the method referred to was a written report provided by the practice school, the tutor or the practice school headteacher. The only other method mentioned was record cards but few respondents provided examples. Presumably, however, 'record cards' is just another way of referring to written reports.

A final question in this section asked respondents to provide information about the distribution of marks for practical teaching. Forty institutions said they worked to a notional distribution, fifty-seven said they did not and twenty-five did not reply to the question. In the main, notional distributions are suggested by area training organizations and it was possible to identify six distinct patterns. These are set out in Table 1 on p. 150.

Many respondents reported that D and E were bracketed and pointed out that failures were few because unsatisfactory students usually dropped out of the course before they reached the final practice. Some respondents stressed that the distribution suggested was not operated rigidly and others said that past experience had

* See Poppleton, P. K. (1968) 'The assessment of teaching practice: what criteria do we use?', *Education for Teaching*, Spring 1968, for a discussion of profiles in the assessment of practical teaching.

led them to believe that a given distribution was appropriate. One institution said they would hope for a 'reasonable' distribution. One institution said that they would expect 15 per cent distinctions but that they would be quite prepared to award more if they thought it

Table 1 Patterns of notional distribution of marks.

ATO	Grades				
	A	B	C	D	E
A	5%	25%	40%		30% (bracketed)
B	5%	30–40%		50% (bracketed)	less than 3%
C	7%	27%	49%	17%	
D	10%	25%	40%	23%	2%
E	10%	20%	60%		10% (bracketed)
F	10%	20%	40%	20%	less than 10%

justified. One A.T.O. is moving towards a simple pass/fail grading but one institution in this A.T.O. said it still made use of a scale internally. The most common percentage of distinctions was 10 per cent.

ii) EVIDENCE USED IN ASSESSMENT

The bulk of respondents (69) used impressionistic methods of assessing. Some (17) used a combination of impressionistic and analytic and only 17 reported using analytical methods alone (19 did not reply to this question). Almost all institutions (107) base their assessments on the students' performance in a series of lessons. The number of lessons reported as forming the basis for assessment ranged from 1 to 23.

However, only single institutions reported numbers at the extremes of the distribution, the most popular frequencies being: 3 (by 7 institutions); 4 (4 institutions); 5 (6 institutions); 6 (12 institutions); 7 (9 institutions); 8 (14 institutions); 9 (6 institutions); and 10 (9 institutions). The crude mode is thus 8 lessons (mean = approximately 7). Very few institutions (10) reported using the final lesson as the basis for their assessment but 40 institutions reported that it was used in conjunction with a series of lessons. The impression given by the replies to these questions, then, is that students are being assessed continuously throughout their school practice.

Few institutions reported using methods other than observation by staff for student assessment. Methods mentioned were head-teacher and school reports (3) and teaching practice notes (2). 106 institutions reported that they made some allowance for the 'difficulty' of the school in their assessment, almost all indicated in some way that this allowance was impressionistic or subjective. Comments on this subject included remarks such as 'very impressionistic and highly suspect, not valid or reliable'; 'in theory'; and 'the difficulty of making accurate allowance for this is *one* reason why we think assessment at this stage is a pretty blunt instrument'. One institution reported that although they tried to make allowance for the 'difficulty' of the school they found that there was a correlation between school and student grades. Factors institutions attempted to take into consideration when determining the 'difficulty' of a school included the absence of head or class teacher, the cooperation and sympathy of the staff, the level of the facilities in the school, school environment, the number of 'problem' children, and the degree to which the regular teacher has difficulty in coping. One return declared that experienced staff are able to make allowance for the ability, age, social background and aptitude of the children.

We asked a question in this section which proposed a number of factors such as 'pupil's work', 'pupil's learning', 'student's note-book', which might be taken into account in assessment. The returns from this section yield no information in themselves but corroborate the findings of the first question in the section. Since assessment is so overwhelmingly impressionistic it is not surprising that the bulk of replies to this question merely said that all the factors are taken into consideration but weightings cannot be accorded to them.

The final question in this section asked institutions whether they made allowance for a student's likely development as distinct from his present performance. Forty-five respondents said they did. Of these seventeen made allowance of between 20 per cent and 40 per cent for future performance (one said $37\frac{1}{2}$ per cent!); twelve institutions allowed between 40 per cent and 60 per cent and eight allowed between 60 per cent and 80 per cent. Other replies were 'too subjective', 'supposedly' and 'I wish I knew'.

F

iii) THE ASSESSORS

The analysis of returns under this head produced the findings summarized in Table 2.

Table 2 Staff involvement in assessment.

Person(s) assessing	Percentage of students							No reply
	0	0–19	20–39	40–59	60–79	80–99	100	
Supervisor alone	50	6	3	6	15	6	0	36
Supervisor and other tutors	0	4	10	7	8	12	68	12
Supervisor and external examiner	9	22	63	7	0	0	0	19
External alone	72	3	4	0	0	0	0	43

Numbers in cells = number of institutions making those choices.

The picture presented by this analysis indicates that assessment is usually a cooperative exercise among members of staffs with external examiners moderating about 20 per cent of assessments. Additional information given in this section indicated that in a number of institutions tutors act in teams in an attempt to get standardization of assessment and in some cases individual members of staffs act as moderators. Staff involved sometimes included the principal and the vice-principal and often the head of education department. Several respondents made the point that problem students would be seen by several tutors.

The majority of institutions reported that they made provision for some type of formal assessment meeting. Thirty-one said they held one formal staff meeting on assessment, forty-seven held two and five held three. The external examiners were usually involved in the final meeting. Others instanced different methods. Five reached their decisions on the basis of discussion among members of supervisory teams. Two reported that senior staff discussed individual students with supervisors before deciding on assessments. The general procedure, then, seems to be one where assessment is based on the field work of two or three tutors followed by the collective deliberations of one or two meetings of the full staff.

iv) CRITERIA

Institutions were first asked to state whether they made use of a printed or duplicated schedule of criteria, and were invited to send a copy of any such schedule. Out of the total of 122 institutions replying to the questionnaire fifty-one sent copies of printed schedules. Fifteen institutions which did not use printed or duplicated schedules sent detailed lists of criteria. Thus sixty-six sets of criteria were available for analysis. The total number of criteria used was 148. The main groupings of criteria and the numbers of institutions mentioning the criteria are shown in Table 3.

Table 3 Main groupings of criteria mentioned.

Criteria	Number of mentions
Planning and preparation of lessons	221
Teaching performance	495
Desirable traits in the student	153
The pupils' learning	14
Students' ability to evaluate self and pupils	31
Professional characteristics and behaviour	70

The number of criteria mentioned by individual institutions ranges from three to thirty-three and a similar variation may be seen in the variety of levels of generality as well as the terms in which the criteria are expressed, by inspection of the following five representative sets of criteria offered:

A.
    1 Teaching ability.
    2 Personal relationships.
    3 Application to the work, etc.
B.
    1 Preparation.
    2 Classroom procedure.
    3 Content.
    4 Rapport with pupils (questioning, etc.).
    5 Use of aids (blackboard).

C.
  1 Contact with children.
  2 Understanding of work.
  3 Preparation of work.
  4 Varied use of teaching techniques.
  5 Ability to communicate simply and effectively.
  6 Positive attitude.
  7 Willingness to teach children from where they are, yet to try for standards that show growth of individuals.

D.
  (I) Management of children
      1 Discipline.
      2 Relations with class.
      3 Enthusiasm and liveliness of manner.
      4 Giving praise.
 (II) Teaching skill
      1 Questioning.
      2 Initiative and imagination.
      3 Material of lesson: preparation: notebook.
      4 Exposition.
      5 Use of teaching aids.
      6 Organization of practical work.
(III) Personal qualities
      1 Reliability, conscientiousness.
      2 Sincerity.
      3 Keeness and cooperation in school activities.
      4 Acceptability with school staff.
      5 Voice and appearance.

E.
  (a) Relationship with children
      1 Atmosphere of classroom.
      2 Responsiveness and cooperation of children.
      3 Consideration of children's individual problems.
  (b) Preparation and organization
      1 Teaching practice file:
          a Adequacy of schemes of work.
          b Adequacy of lesson notes.
          c Suitability to age and ability of children.
          d Consideration given to children's activity.
          e Student's knowledge of the subjects.

2 Classroom organization:
   a Arrangement and distribution of materials.
   b Use of space and equipment.
   c Use of teaching aids.
   d Organization and planning for group and individual activities.
   e Marking and display of children's work.
(c) Class control
   1 Ability to establish suitable conditions for learning to take place.
   2 Ability to secure and retain children's attention.
   3 Anticipation and avoidance of disorderly behaviour.
   4 Firmness and consistency when required.
(d) Communication with children (spoken and written)
   1 Clarity and audibility of voice.
   2 Appropriateness of vocabulary.
   3 Awareness of children's linguistic needs.
   4 Success in communicating with children.
(e) Effectiveness of teaching
   1 Ability to elicit interest and enthusiasm of children.
   2 Degree of children's activity.
   3 Purposefulness of children's activity.
   4 Progression of learning sequences.
   5 Initiative and resourcefulness.
   6 Adaptability to needs of the children.
(f) Under this heading, comments are invited on:
   1 a Appearance.
      b Punctuality.
      c Relations with colleagues.
   2 Any aspect of the curriculum in which the student shows particular competence or weakness.

Eight institutions gave two schedules each, one issued to the schools in which the students were practising, one for tutors. Seven institutions use the same schedule for schools and tutors; five give only the schools' form. The statement of criteria is normally linked with the actual assessment of practice teaching and is embodied in a report or assessment form, though seven institutions issue notes dealing with criteria alone, to tutors. In four institutions preparations are actively in hand to produce written schedules; in two institutions existing schedules are under review. One institution mentions efforts that were made to produce a schedule but says that these have not been successful. There are two cases of two institutions using the same schedule, suggested by the local school/institute of education. Of the criteria given, the following, each offered by one institution, are not classified in the appendix:

1 Grasp of essential principles.
2 Ability to foster the development of integrated personalities.
3 A sense of values.
4 Sense of direction.
5 Grasp of fundamental principles.
6 Constructive attitude to difficulties.

An attempt was made to ascertain how the criteria had been arrived at and fifty institutions gave details of this. Forty-three

Table 4 Methods of communicating criteria.

Method of communication	No. of institutions mentioning the method
Meetings and discussions	9
Letters and memoranda	4
Notice board	1
Apprenticeship	1
'Folklore'	1

mentioned discussion among staff. Of these, nineteen gave no details of the discussion process, twenty-two gave details of formal discussions involving official committees of the institutions. Eight mentioned consultation with parties other than the staff of the institution, and of these eight, four instanced consultation with schools, two with university schools and departments of education, and two mentioned discussion with staff/student committees. It is interesting to note that a small number of respondents interpreted this question as asking for details of the bases on which the criteria were founded. Of these, two institutions mentioned an analysis of teaching situations and of the mechanics of teaching; five said their criteria arose out of articles in journals and schedules worked out by other institutions; two instanced modification of earlier schedules of their institutions; and four mentioned the practical experience of tutors.

How, in institutions where written schedules do not exist, are the criteria communicated to tutors? Details are set out in Table 4.

Questions were asked about the bases on which distinctions and failures were awarded in practical teaching; 110 institutions gave details for the award of distinctions and 109 for failures. The answers may be divided into three types:

Type 1: Answers stressing the ways in which distinction and fail marks were awarded, referring to the actual grades, the participants in the assessment and the type of judgement made.
Type 2: Answers stressing the criteria on which distinction and fail marks were based.
Type 3: Answers giving a brief, global summary only, e.g. 'outstanding', 'extra dazzle', 'inability to cope'.

Details of the numbers of institutions giving answers of the different types are set out in Table 5.

Table 5 Numbers of institutions giving answers of different types as bases for failure or distinction.

	Type of answer	Number of institutions
Distinction	1	67
	2	39
	3	22
Failure	1	44
	2	40
	3	27

The main criteria subsumed by the type 2 answers and referring to failure and distinction together are set out in Table 6. Of type 1 answers (for both distinctions and failures), sixteen characterized their methods of assessment as 'impressionistic' or 'subjective'. In one institution the practice of awarding distinction in practical teaching has been discontinued. Two institutions mention that a distinction is not awarded in practical teaching unless a satisfactory standard has been reached in educational theory. One institution reports that a distinction is not awarded in practical teaching, but a 'general' distinction on performance over the whole certificate may be given.

Table 6 Criteria used for identifying distinction and failure and the number of institutions mentioning the criteria.

Criteria	Number of institutions
Teaching ability	44
Personality traits	24
Professional behaviour/attitude	7

Although details of the percentage of distinctions and fails and the literal marks used were not asked for here, twenty-four institutions vouchsafed information. The percentage of students awarded a distinction in practical teaching varied from 2 to 15 per cent; of fails, 1 to 2 per cent (cf. Table 1 above). Literal marks for distinction varied from B+ to A, and for a fail, from E to D+.

In order to check whether any meaningful clusters of criteria could be isolated from the relatively heterogeneous collection mentioned by respondents, a principal components factor analysis was carried out using the data from sixty-six institutions giving thirty-seven identifiably discrete criteria. The idea of this procedure was to see whether institutions perceived criteria as hanging together in fairly broad categories such as, for example, 'deportment' or 'organization'. Twelve factors with roots greater than unity were rotated to the varimax criterion. The results of this analysis did not, in fact, reveal any distinct groupings. The factor that loaded highly on the largest number of variables was still fairly heterogeneous conceptually. Thus this factor included items such as 'planning, aims and objectives' (loading 0·81), 'promotes children's participation' (loading 0·91), 'maintains discipline and order' (0·67), 'creating and sustaining interest' (loading 0·64) and 'appearance and social climate of the classroom' (loading 0·61). Another factor grouped lesson notes, use of aids, exposition and demonstration techniques, and appearance and dress. Few other loadings were high enough to merit consideration as identifiable factors.

v) FEEDBACK TO STUDENTS

The first two questions in this section asked about the communication to students of lesson assessments and final assessments. Of the 120 replies, ninety-nine replied that the assessments of individual lessons were normally communicated, and forty-five replied that the final assessment was communicated. Eighteen communicate the final teaching mark to students. Of the 102 that do not communicate the final teaching mark, three point out that the final teaching mark is communicated to, and discussed with, students who fail. Four respondents comment that the regulations of the school/institute of education do not allow the final teaching mark to be divulged to students.

A further question sought to ascertain whether students were informed of the criteria that were being used by tutors in their assessment of the students' teaching. Of the 113 answers received, eighty-eight were in the affirmative. Eighty-two replied that this was done verbally and twenty-two mentioned the use of 'handouts', including students' handbooks, duplicated notes and written assessments of lessons, giving the criteria.

vi) CONTRIBUTION OF FINAL TEACHING MARK TO TOTAL ASSESSMENT

Institutions were asked to give the percentage of the total assessment for the final certificate contributed by the final practical teaching assessment. Fifty-four institutions replied and their responses are given in Table 7. Forty-one respondents made the additional comment that a pass in practical teaching is essential for

Table 7 Percentage of total assessment for the final certificate contributed by practical teaching assessment.

Percentage	No. of institutions giving this proportion
0–19	2
20–39	42
40–50	10
over 50	0

the award of the certificate. We hoped in this section to obtain some idea of the importance attached to practical teaching within the context of the Certificate of Education as a whole. One quarter of the respondents were prepared to quantify their weighting. An appreciable number (thirty) of those who refused to quantify said that, as in their institutions practical teaching was a distinct part of the certificate and as its assessment was quite separate from the assessment of the other elements, it was difficult, if not impossible, to show the contribution of the practical teaching assessment to the total assessment.

Although the questionnaire was not concerned with the assessment of the certificate as a whole, in the course of answering this question respondents revealed a wide divergence, presumably between area training organizations rather than between individual institutions, in the elements that make up the assessment of the whole certificate. Some respondents mention two elements (practical teaching and educational theory), some three ('practice of education, principles of education and academic studies'), some four ('practice of education, theory of education, main subject, professional studies' and in one case 'practical teaching, theory of education, main subject, qualifying English'), some five, and some seven. A difference between a university department of education and colleges is, of course, to be expected as academic studies are not assessed in U.D.E.s.

Discussion

If we were to attempt to draw a profile of the typical procedure for the assessment of practical teaching we could sketch with confidence only some of the broader organizational aspects of the operation. We can say that in the majority of cases institutions award a final teaching mark of an impressionistic nature on a five point scale after the student has been visited on about seven occasions by his supervisor and other college staff. The student's final teaching mark will come up before a meeting of the staff but it is unlikely to be the subject of close scrutiny unless it is borderline distinction or fail in which case the external examiner is likely to be asked to adjudicate. The number of failures likely to result from the assessment procedures is very low since unsatisfactory students will have left earlier in the course. The number of distinctions awarded, on the other hand, will depend upon the institution but the most likely percentage will be about ten.

The note of uncertainty introduced by our reference to the award of distinctions pervades most of the rest of our findings. There is no uniformity in the distribution of marks, the use of profiles, or the use of external evidence. The sceptical note struck by some respondents when asked whether they take into account the 'difficulty' of the practice school and whether they make allowance for the student's future development provides an interesting counterpoint to the many respondents who claim to make such allowances, but again there is no distinct pattern.

Nor can we find a clear pattern when we consider the nature of the criteria used as the basis for assessment. Here the factor analysis confirmed the findings of our scrutiny of the questionnaires. The conceptual strain involved in identifying the common elements in factors that sorted together such things as standard of lesson notes, use of aids, and appearance and dress was too much, and we concluded that there was little evidence of conceptual unity in the factor analysis. This conclusion was, of course, strengthened by the general lack of clearly identifiable groupings in the analysis.

One other very important feature of some of the criteria was the vagueness of expression. Probably few would disagree with the desirability of 'fostering the development of integrated personalities' or of being able 'to grasp essential principles', or even 'the possession of a sense of direction'; precisely how to decide when these criteria are met is another thing to being able to decide, when awarding a distinction, whether or not a student has 'extra dazzle'.

Scrutiny of the returns relating to the criteria used in assessment reveals that approximately half of the institutions replying to the questionnaire do not use a written schedule or list of criteria and cannot, or will not, say what their unwritten criteria are. One can only conclude that in these institutions informal discussion between tutors and formal staff meetings for assessment of teaching practice perform a normative function in developing broad sets of values against which students' practical teaching is subjectively assessed. And yet the emergence of no clear pattern from the factor analysis raises doubts as to how far this development of sets of values takes place.

Three important features arise from the analysis of criteria. First, their extremely wide variety; a variety that seems to arise from idiosyncratic selection with few attempts at standardization within area training organizations. Second, the criteria as presented by many institutions lack logical arrangement or structure although much work has clearly gone into the drawing up of many of the schedules (see the comments on the factor analysis). In a handful of institutions only is there evidence of a taxonomical approach. Third, very little attention is paid to what the children actually learn from students, and even less to the ability of students to evaluate what the children have learned. While teaching performance receives overall the overwhelming number of mentions as a general criterion, this crucial aspect of teaching performance is strangely neglected.

In sum, a reasonable conclusion, based on this survey of criteria, seems to be that individual institutions and area training organizations are looking for, and assessing, different behaviours and qualities in their students.

Whatever criteria may be adopted, the question of informing students about their performance as assessed by those criteria is clearly of importance. Nearly one sixth of all respondents said they did not communicate the assessment of individual lessons to students. Despite the fact that the distinction was clearly made in the questionnaire between *assessment* and *teaching mark*, it may well be that some of the respondents confused the two.

The fact that 23 per cent of respondents did not inform students of the criteria on which the assessment was based somewhat weakens the effect of the impressive number of respondents saying that they fed back the assessments of individual lessons. And it will not have escaped the notice of the observant reader that although eighty-eight respondents said that they informed students of the criteria used, only sixty-six respondents could, or would, specify their criteria.

We do not feel that we can conclude this section without referring to the question that poses itself insistently as one considers the evidence in the returns: the question of comparability. The wide diversity of assessment patterns among institutions, the variety and vagueness of many criteria and the idiosyncratic nature of their selection by institutions suggest to us that the certificates of the different area training organizations may be rewarding quite different student behaviours.

We remarked in the beginning that we are not interested in joining in the sniping at the colleges and departments of education which is currently fashionable and which we think is in general quite uninformed, and we are convinced that many of the snipers are equally if not more vulnerable. The problems our survey exposes are not unexpected but we hope that by providing some detail institutions will be helped in their grappling with a very difficult problem and that discussion about the problem will be more informed and more lively than it has been hitherto.

Coda

The returns from two respondents illustrate both the problems of current approaches to the assessment of teaching practice and the possibilities for fruitful reappraisal. One respondent declared: 'I found this extremely difficult to complete. Somehow the spirit of the questionnaire is alien to the way we approach things.' The other said: '. . . we are largely committed to the view that teaching practice is probably of little value in modifying student teacher attitudes and behaviour. Instead we focus on children's learning during Year 1, microteaching in Year 2 and a $2\frac{1}{2}$ day "teaching studies" per week in term 2 of Year 3.'

References

Cattell, R. B. (1931) 'The assessment of teaching ability'. *British journal of educational psychology*, 1, 1.

Downes, L. W. and Shaw, K. E. (1968) 'Innovation in teaching practice'. *Trends in education*, 12, 42–5.

Evans, K. M. (1951) 'A critical survey of methods of assessing teacher ability'. *British journal of educational psychology*, 21, 2, 89–95.

Lantz, D. L. (1967) 'The relationship of university supervising teachers' ratings to observed student teachers' behavior'. *American educational research journal*, 4, 3, 279–88.

Mitzel, H. E. (1960) 'Teacher effectiveness'. In Harris, C. W. (ed.) *Encyclopedia of educational research*. 3rd ed. New York: Macmillan.

Morris, S. (1970) 'Assessment and evaluation of teaching practice'. In Stones, E. (ed.) *Towards evaluation: some thoughts on tests and*

teacher education. Educational review occasional publication
No. 4, 64–70.

Poppleton, P. K. (1968) 'The assessment of teaching practice: what
criteria do we use?' *Education for teaching*, 75, 59–64.

Robertson, J. D. C. (1957) 'an Analysis of the views of supervisors
on the attributes of successful graduate student teachers'.
British journal of educational psychology, 27, 2, 115–26.

2 · Model the master teacher or master the teaching model

L. M. STOLUROW

The educational psychologist probably does not think that he works at a weaver's trade, but in many ways he does. He is concerned with the fabric of behaviour. In fact, some of the real problems he faces are those of planning its warp and woof and of determining its pattern. He works with conceptual tools and experimental devices to determine the threads and the weave. He is concerned with the loom, and with the way it is used to develop a behavioural fabric that suits a teacher's taste and a student's needs.

The educational psychologist who not only is concerned with achieving an understanding of teaching as a psychological process but also wants to help in the weaving is faced with a dilemma. Either he must begin by looking at the craftsmen who have been weaving by tradition and intuition, or he must think of the design and engineering problems necessary for automation. He either looks at teachers and extracts a list of characteristics, or he manipulates variables which he thinks are important factors for improving the process. The former is essentially a passive approach; the latter, an active approach.

The passive approach is insufficient (e.g. Ryans 1960, Ryans 1963). If the objective is to understand teaching rather than teachers, and to find ways of redesigning education, then the educational psychologist needs to study the process of teaching by analysing and then synthesizing. Traditionally, the research on teaching has been passive and analytical and has consisted of describing teacher characteristics rather than specifying the necessary and sufficient teaching behaviours and the way in which the behaviours are inter-related with one another. Often, research has attempted to study an

Reprinted and abridged from J. D. Krumboltz (ed.), *Learning and the Educational Process* (© 1965 by Rand McNally & Company, Chicago), pp. 223–47.

unarticulated, incompletely defined and poorly controlled set of activities which were called a 'method'. Furthermore, the so-called method was used as if it were a replicable variable that was derived from a unidimensional theory.

It is now possible for the research on teaching to be an active scientific process which does not involve the nominalism just mentioned. Experiments can be conducted in which the variables are derived from a model and are replicable. Models of the teaching process can be formulated (see Gage 1963), and their variables can be studied both individually and jointly. In addition, it is possible to study the variables in conceptual isolation while operating *in situ*. There are many problems that must be dealt with in using this approach, but with it there is the possibility of advancing the knowledge about teaching by several orders of magnitude. One of the first problems is the laboratory capability that permits work with complex variables under conditions that can be replicated. This is now technologically possible by means of a computer-based teaching machine system, at least for the study of tutorial instruction. This technological capability alone is a necessary step and an important advance towards the solution of old and persistent problems, but it is not sufficient (see Stolurow and Davis 1965).

Modelling the master teacher

Once the laboratory hardware is obtained, there is the problem of mastering the software. The question is how to get a grasp of this problem. One suggested answer is to model the master teacher.

This idea of modelling the master teacher has not worked. When this solution to the problems of instruction is examined, many reasons for its failure become apparent. One potentially important factor working against this approach is the complexity of the behaviour being observed and the associated difficulties of controlling behaviour so that it can be studied. Observations of teaching produce an effect which can be associated with the Rorschach and other projective tests in that different factors are identified by different observers and each observer interprets what he sees in a different way. The experimental demonstration by Skinner (1948), that superstitious behaviour is readily learned, presents a related point. Skinner showed how irrelevant but correlated events can become the cues for behaviour. This is especially possible in view of the fact that the conditions for learning about teaching are typically so highly variable, and the critical result (student learning) is not readily relatable to particular teacher behaviours.

Since there probably are fewer ways to teach effectively than there are to teach ineffectively, it is more likely that ineffective teaching behaviours would be identified in observational studies of teaching behaviour. Even master teachers are likely to engage in ineffective behaviour, and these ineffective correlates of master teacher performance would be misleading to investigators and students who are unguided by validated concepts of what to look for. Thus, they would be more likely to learn the wrong way to teach than the right ways.

THE MYTH OF THE SINGLE METHOD

While there has been a vain search for a single effective method of instruction, there also has been a widespread practice of recommending the virtues of variety. An excellent example of the fruitless search for the one grand method is that which sought to show that learner-centred instruction was superior to teacher-centred instruction (see Anderson 1959). Like many other efforts to locate the instructional pot of gold, the learner-centred method turned out to be an ill-defined, unspecified and unreplicable collection of methods. The results of its use show a normal distribution of outcomes. Intimately involved in the search for the single but undefined method are the deception of nominalism and the treacheries of reification.

An alternative is to dissect the psychological threads of a teaching fabric so that particular operations can be individually related to their effects on learning. In this way, useful relationships can be identified and effective combinations of them formed to produce an efficient teaching method.

The most significant conclusion that can be drawn from efforts to use teachers as a basis for information about teaching is that effective instruction can be produced by a variety of combinations of characteristics and conditions rather than by one unique combination. If this were not the case, efforts to enumerate the characteristics of good teachers would have resulted in the identification of at least one or two critical characteristics. However, neither the observation of master teachers nor that of a large number of effective teachers (e.g. Ryans 1960) has led to findings that are either substantial or sufficient for the understanding of teaching as a process. Thus, an alternative approach is needed.

GOING BEYOND DIRECT OBSERVATION

It seems reasonable to consider the possibility that it is undesirable to limit one's attention to only those factors that have been revealed by observations of teachers. Doing so might impose unnecessary restrictions upon an effort to understand teaching as a process, although it might add to an understanding of individual teachers.

There are several points to be made here. It may be possible to do a better job of teaching than that which has been observed. This may not be a popular position, but it is one that an objective analysis of the situation suggests. If this is tenable, then it is unwise to *restrict* one's concern to what teachers are doing now. There would be little point to the study of teaching if we did not want to improve it. Another possibility is that many of the things that teachers are now doing may be accomplished more effectively by other means. An efficient combination of resources must be found if effectiveness is to be improved.

Mastering the teaching model

THE PROCESS OF MODELLING

It is important to consider the appropriate use of models in the solution of teaching problems. The term 'model' is used a great deal, and although it is assumed to have only one meaning, there are different kinds of models and different reasons for developing models. Some models are built to predict, while others are designed to describe. These are very different purposes, although they may not appear to be at first.

While a descriptive model also should predict at least one dimension of a system's output, it is not the case that the predictive model also describes the real phenomena. Adequacy of prediction often is confused with accuracy of description. Although a watch can predict time very adequately, it cannot accurately describe the solar system. A mathematical model of a mechanical system may provide an adequate basis for predicting an outcome, but it does not necessarily tell us the position of each of the parts at any point in time. Similarly, mathematical models of learning provide an adequate basis for the prediction of a set of outcomes but may not give an accurate description of the processes going on within the learner.

Another example relates to the molar and molecular relevance of models. A model such as a chemical formula does not describe what any particular set of ions is doing at a particular point in time; rather it describes the mode or median effect. Thus while it is perfectly useful on a statistical basis, it is not useful for predicting what an individual molecule is doing. It seems useful therefore to distinguish models designed to predict individual cases from those designed to predict group outcomes.

An algorithm is a procedure for accomplishing a transformation. Many people have learned algorithms to accomplish such arithmetic operations as long division and the extraction of square roots. However, the algorithms learned in the past are not the only means by which these transformations can be accomplished. In fact, a large number of new algorithms are being developed so that modern computers can perform these very operations. Certain algorithms are efficient for one computer, but not for another. Similarly, while an algorithm may be efficient for a computer, the same algorithm does not permit children or adults to accomplish the same operations. Thus, algorithms differ in their suitability to the system using them. Models that are equivalent in one respect are not equivalent in all other respects. For example, one model used to predict a particular outcome or class of events may be as accurate in its prediction as another model, but it may not do other things that the first one will do. Obviously, the more outcomes a model accounts for, the more useful it is.

IMPLICATIONS OF MODELLING

What are the implications of modelling for the process of mastering the teaching model as contrasted with the modelling of a master teacher? Assume that we set out to develop a teaching model which has the prediction of a set of learning outcomes as its objective. It does not also follow that the model will describe the behaviour of a master teacher. If the model is built to predict learning outcomes, it may not describe the procedures that a teacher might use to accomplish the same objective. If, however, one is attempting to develop a descriptive model of instruction, then the procedures used could be the prototype of those employed by a teacher.

The constructed model may focus on the development of a set of elements sufficient to achieve a particular objective; however, the set of elements used may not be a necessary set. Other models using other elements may be just as effective. Just as different models of internal combustion engines can be used to convert chemical to mechanical energy, so a variety of different teaching models can be used to convert teacher activities into student learning. Consequently, the relationship between a model of teaching and a model of learning is not a one-to-one correspondence. On the other hand, knowledge about the critical variables in learning would affect the design of a model of teaching. Nevertheless, different teaching models might be developed to account for the same set of dependent variables used to measure learning.

If there is no unique solution, then why use models? An important reason is to make explicit the elements and relationships needed to account for the phenomenon in which we are interested (e.g. a student's performance on a learning task). A model is a commitment to a position and can be tested if properly formulated. It is not a loosely assembled, inarticulated set of statements that some theorists can point at with pride in their eclecticism.

Why build a model for teaching? There seem to be a number of reasons in addition to those already mentioned. Each time research is done to study conditions that affect students' performance on a learning task, five or six factors are suggested that were not taken into account as possible reasons for the results. In short, there is a widely held belief that teaching is a complex process, and that a large variety of variables affect what students do, even in a tutorial situation. If this is the case, a model of teaching must be developed that will do at least two basic things. First, it must make the large set of relationships explicit. Second, it must permit the correction of mistakes made in trying to find out about teaching and indicate the nature of the required corrections. To achieve these things, either lists can be developed and the loose state of the eclectic maintained, or a set of factors can be articulated to see how much explanatory power can be obtained from a model. In this latter way, clarification and continuity can be increased, while control is gained over nominalism and reification.

References

Anderson, R. C. (1959) 'Learning in discussions: a resume of the authoritarian-democratic studies'. *Harvard educational review*, 29, 201–15.

Gage, N. L. (1963) 'Paradigms for research on teaching'. In Gage, N. L. (ed.) *Handbook of research on teaching*. Chicago: Rand McNally. 94–141.

Ryans, D. G. (1960) *Characteristics of teachers, their description, comparison and appraisal: a research study*. Washington, D.C.: American Council on Education.

Ryans, D. G. (1963) 'Assessment of teacher behavior and instruction'. *Review of educational research*, 33, 415–41.

Skinner, B. F. (1948) ' "Superstition" in the pigeon'. *Journal of experimental psychology*, 38, 168–72.

Stolurow, L. M. and Davis, D. J. (1965) 'Teaching machines and computer-based systems'. In Glaser, R. (ed.) *Teaching machines and programmed learning: data and directions*. Washington, D.C.: National Education Association. 162–212.

3 · A conceptual model of instruction

B. STRASSER

The motivation that led to the evolution of the Conceptual Model of Instruction is common to all who are in education: a desire to understand more of what teaching is all about.

A point of departure for this work was the notion of teaching strategies and tactics as evolved by Taba (Taba and Elzey 1964, Taba 1963). To what aspect of instruction does the term teaching strategy refer? What activities of the teacher can be described as tactics? What do the learners do while a teacher is engaged in such activities? And finally, how does this notion of strategies, tactics and learners' responses interrelate in a picture of instruction?

To begin with, a series of lessons ranging in grade level from first grade through college was studied in an attempt to identify various tactics and strategies of teachers in order to evolve an operational definition of each of the terms. As a frame of reference for his observations and reflections, the author accepted a definition of teaching by B. Othanel Smith (1963), which he outlined as follows: 'Teaching is a system of action involving an agent, an end in view, and a situation including two sets of factors – those over which the agent has no control (class size, size of classroom, physical characteristics of pupils, etc.) and those that he can modify (ways of asking questions about instruction and ways of structuring information or ideas gleaned).'

Smith points out that it is by means of the set of factors the agent can control that the particular end in view is reached. It might be concluded, then, that the dimension of the instructional situation that includes those factors the agent can modify is, in sum, the *strategies* and *tactics* of the teacher. This definition of teaching is also of aid in identifying those elements of teaching over which

Reprinted from *The Journal of Teacher Education*, 18, 1 (1967), pp. 63–74.

teachers have little or no control, thus helping one to be consciously aware of the limitation of the model, that it focuses only on factors over which the teacher has control.

Some assumptions about instruction used as a basis for observations

1 *What the teacher does is a critical factor in determining what the pupil learns.*
   Implied in this assumption is the notion that teachers have to display some behaviour so that the learners will know what is expected of them: what goals they are to work towards, what they are expected to do, and how they are to do it.
   James Gallagher (1963), in reporting his study of productive thinking, stated, 'The teacher is the key in the *initiation* and *stimulation* of productive thinking in the classroom.'
2 *Children can set goals in the instructional situation; teacher behaviour determines if they will.*
3 *Children can do productive thinking in the instructional situation; teacher behaviour determines if they will.*
4 *Some aspects of learner behaviour in an instructional situation may be directly related to specific units of teacher behaviour; that is, learner behaviour is influenced by the behaviour of the teacher.*
   In a meeting at the Manhattan Beach Unified School District in 1965, Marie Hughes stated, 'There is a syndrome of teaching acts that will (1) lead to good order and management in the classroom, and (2) lead to the development by the learners of higher mental processes; and there is also a syndrome of acts that will lead to involvement and self-commitment on the part of the learners.'
5 *Some aspects of teacher behaviour in an instructional situation may be directly related to learner behaviour; that is, teacher behaviour is influenced by the behaviour of the learners.*
6 *Other factors being equal, certain units of teacher behaviour (tactics) generally elicit learner behaviour within a given range.*
   This is not to imply that all teachers need do is to behave in a certain way and the learners will respond accordingly. Certainly teaching is not so simple. But with students of our culture, our range of socioeconomic backgrounds and kinds of past experiences, the responses of the learners in a given

learning situation are generally predictable. The work of J. Richard Suchman in the Illinois Studies in Inquiry Training is interpreted as evidence in support of this assumption. When a teacher creates a certain kind of structure (conditions for enquiry among the structural factors), learners usually do enquire – and in a more or less predictable fashion.*

Strategies and tactics

From the observation and analysis of forty-nine tape recorded lessons, the following operational definitions of strategy and tactic, as these terms apply to instruction, were developed:

Strategy: A generalized plan for a lesson(s) which includes structure, desired learner behaviour in terms of the goals of instruction, and an outline of planned tactics necessary to implement the strategy. The lesson strategy is part of a larger development scheme – the curriculum.

Strategies are, in a sense, the 'why' of specific teacher behaviour. Some are a function of more explicit 'now' goals, or 'one-lesson-accessible' strategies; others, which take more than one lesson to develop and usually continue over a period of several lessons, are referred to as 'overtime' strategies.

Either one-lesson-accessible or overtime strategies may be changed, modified or discontinued (with another substituted perhaps) as a lesson proceeds and the teacher interprets feedback from the students. One factor which may give rise to such change in a lesson strategy is the nature of that strategy in relation to the hypothesized and real readiness and rate of progress of the unique group of students (pupils).

Strategy planning is done at a time other than that at which the teacher is teaching; however, this is not to deny that the teacher may get some ideas for future strategies while in the process of teaching.

Tactic: Goal-linked influenced/influencing behaviour of the teacher – the way a teacher behaves in the instructional situation in working towards the development of the strategy; units of teacher behaviour through which the teacher fulfils his various instructional roles with the students of his class from moment to moment; the

* This assumption is drawn from the author's experience in Inquiry Training during the last five years and from many discussions with Dr Suchman.

components of teacher behaviour through which the teacher, the students and the subject matter interact.

A tactic may range from no overt teacher behaviour (e.g. using silence for a specific purpose) to one question or statement to a complex of verbal or purposeful non-verbal teacher behaviour interlaced with student behaviours.

In the lessons observed, it was found that one lesson may vary from one tactic for the whole lesson to a highly complex interweaving of several different tactics. In some cases, while using one tactic with an entire class, a teacher may employ several different tactics at different times or at the same time with different individuals within the total group. Some tactics may be directed towards one child and some towards a group of children; some may be in the form of one teacher behaviour directed towards one learner response, while others are more complex and dependent upon a sequence of teacher–student interactions; still others may be directed to learner responses at some time in the future.

It also became evident that a given lesson may illustrate two different kinds of teacher tactics, *planned tactics* and *responsive tactics*. The difference between the two is that planned tactics are those a teacher decides to use to implement his strategy; they are planned before the lesson takes place. Then, as the teacher uses these tactics with the class, certain responses by the children may clue him to apply a different tactic with a particular child in terms of the goals established or in order to enhance the child's self-concept. In this case, the teacher draws from his tactic repertory, or he may consciously or subconsciously invent a new (new to the teacher) tactic to meet the specific situation.

Instruction

After an operational definition of tactics and strategies had been built, attention was turned to searching for the ways in which tactics and strategies fit into the total picture of instruction; that is, an attempt was made to seek relationships among tactics, strategies, teacher behaviour, goals of education and the learners.

Smith provided the idea that led to the development of the Conceptual Model of Instruction:

Everyone knows that the teacher not only influences student

behaviour, but that he is also influenced by student behaviour. The teacher is constantly observing the student and modifying his own behaviour in terms of his observations. . . . We may therefore say that instructional behaviour consists of a chain of three links – observing, diagnosing, acting. (Smith 1963, p. 296)

The idea of influencing/influenced teacher behaviour seemed most intriguing, as was the picture of the teacher as behaver, observer and diagnoser. By applying these two ideas, the following four aspects of instruction were identified:

1 *Teacher planning* – in terms of what the teacher knows of the learner, the curriculum, the situation.
2 *Teacher behaviour, initiatory* – to create a focus for thinking and working, what the teacher does to get things started.
3 *Teacher observation, interpretation and diagnosis of learner behaviour* – in terms of the situation, knowledge of prior experiences of the learner, prior observations of learners' behaviours, enhancement of child's self-concept, the curriculum (affective, cognitive and action dimensions).
4 *Teacher behaviour, influenced/influencing* – influenced by the observations, interpretations and diagnosis of learner behaviour and influencing to the degree that teacher behaviour stimulates further learner behaviour.

Consideration of the flow of those aspects during the process of instruction led to the development of the Conceptual Model of Instruction (Fig. 1), from which it can be seen that the potential lesson takes shape as the teacher, making decisions about goals, structure and planned tactics, begins the development of the strategy. *Teacher planning* (1) is completed.

Teacher behaviour, initiatory (2) is a tactic(s) that creates the focus for the lesson and sets the appropriate structure. As a result of the teacher behaviour, initiatory, the children become aware of some of the goals that will direct their activity as well as their evolving responsibilities in the specific instructional situation. The lesson begins to unfold.

At the same moment the initiatory tactic takes place, *teacher observation, interpretation and diagnosis of learner behaviour* (3) take place. The teacher observes the consequences of his influencing

behaviour. Some observations may be singular in nature, leading
directly to influenced teacher behaviour; some may take place for a
longer period of time over a more complex series of learner–teacher
behaviours as related to the purpose of the tactic; some may yield
information about the learners that is not directly related to follow-

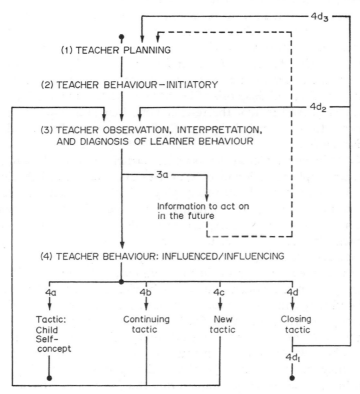

Figure 1 A conceptual model of instruction.

ing the teacher behaviour. For example, while a group of third
grade children were working to make a compass, one said, 'The
north part of one magnet will attract the north part of another
magnet.' Rather than stop the lesson to attempt to correct this
misconception, the teacher made a mental note of the response,
which became *information to act on in the future* (3a) and possibly the
basis of planning for a future lesson. In this case, the observation,

interpretation and diagnosis of the learner behaviour did not lead to influenced teacher behaviour˙– at that particular moment.

As the lesson continues, the teacher's observation and interpretation may lead to the diagnosis that the initiatory tactic is developing according to plan, and the tactic is therefore continued (4b – *continuing tactic*). It may be, however, that the initiatory tactic is not achieving the intended purpose, and the planned teacher behaviour is consequently modified or discontinued and another initiatory tactic started (4c – *new tactic*); or the lesson may be aborted (4d – *closing tactic*). Thus, *teacher behaviour, influenced/influencing* (4) is initiated. The teacher behaves according to a previous observation, interpretation and diagnosis of learner behaviour (*influenced teacher behaviour*). And in that the teacher behaviour is intended to feed forward to new learner behaviour (back to 3), the teacher behaviour is *influencing*.

Once having achieved the focus and structure for the lesson, the strategy implementation tactic(s) evolves. A 4, 3, 4, 3 . . . behaving–observing cycle develops; this 4, 3 cycle is the interactive heart of instruction. During this sequence, one kind of tactic a teacher might use which is an exception to the development of the lesson strategy is teacher behaviour designed to enhance immediately a child's self-concept (4a – *tactic: child self-concept*).

If the strategy is won or time has run out, a closing tactic (4d) is employed. In one case, the topic may be closed off, not to be reconsidered ($4d_1$); in another case, the closing tactic may set the stage directly for work next time ($4d_2$). The teacher may say, 'We will not be able to complete this work today. Tomorrow, let's begin just where we left off. When you come into the room after recess you may get the materials with which you were working and continue.' The use of $4d_3$ implies that the day's closing tactic provides information which the teacher will consider in planning the next lesson.

The ways in which the strategies and tactics relate to the four aspects of instruction visualized in the model are:

1 The first step, *teacher planning*, is devoted to developing a strategy for a lesson or for a series of lessons in terms of selected goals. Planned tactics are decided upon.
2 *Teacher behaviour* in the class situation initiates the tactics in action.

3 *Teacher observation, interpretation and diagnosis* are made in terms of the purpose for which the tactic was initiated.

4 Teacher behaviour proceeds with tactic as planned or the tactic is modified as a result of prior observation, interpretation and diagnosis. In reaction to students' interactions, teacher may draw on responsive tactics to pull certain students into class interaction, to take advantage of problems, questions, etc., which arise.

It may be concluded, therefore, that the central directive element of instruction is the lesson strategy, and the essence of classroom interactions, the lesson tactic(s).

Tactical elements

As attention is turned to classroom interaction, all tactics, whether they are directed towards a convergent behaviour such as interpreting a contour map or a more divergent behaviour such as setting

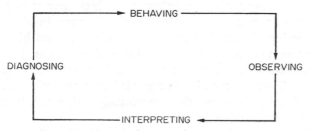

Figure 2   Tactical element loop.

the stage so that the students can generate theories about a given event, consist of the four elements introduced in the model as *teacher behaviour, influenced/influencing* (4) and *teacher observation, interpretation and diagnosis* (3). A behaving–observing cycle develops.

In the light of some previous diagnoses and in terms of explicit goals, a teacher behaves. Simultaneously, he observes the students. Such observations are interpreted in terms of the purposes of the tactic. With this information, diagnoses about continuing or new teacher behaviours are made which lead to continuing behaving. Thus, a tactical element loop takes shape which involves *diagnosing, behaving, observing* and *interpreting* by the teacher.

Teaching as experimenting

In making a diagnosis, the teacher generates a hypothesis about a relationship between his potential behaviour and its effect upon the students. In effect, he is saying, 'If I . . ., then the learners will. . . .'

Following the formulation of such a hypothesis, the teacher experiments: he behaves and observes the responses of the students, viewing such responses largely as a consequence of his behaviour. These observations are then interpreted in terms of the purposes that motivated his behaviour in the first place. Thus, if a tactic does not seem to be successful in helping the learners move towards the purposes for which it was hypothetically designed, the teacher, either by drawing on his repertory of tactics, by creating a new tactic (spontaneous teacher behaviour), or by modifying the purpose for which the tactic was designed, may change his behaviour sequence.

Viewed in this way, instruction is experimental in nature. Knowing the goals appropriate for a child or group of children, a teacher hypothesizes about his own behaviours which may stimulate certain kinds of productive behaviour of the learners. In his behaving and observing, the teacher experiments. He interprets his observations in terms of their relevancy to the goals of instruction. Hypotheses may then be discontinued, modified or discarded in favour of new ones. Thus, instruction is regarded as a dynamic and, over a period of time, self-correcting, continually redirected, influenced/influencing, interactive process.

Smith points out that teaching includes two sets of factors. One of these sets is those (factors) over which the agent (teacher) has no control. Other extrasituational factors which add the dimension of the past and future to the tactical element loop affect that loop to an unknown degree. The following diagram identifies some of these factors as well as the points at which they affect the elements of the loop (Fig. 3).

As attention is directed to some of the 'knowns' in instruction, the question of relative uncertainty about instruction arises. One group of such knowns is those factors which Smith defines as being modifiable by the teacher; another is the body of educational goals which motivate teacher behaviour. As the teacher interacts with the students, a third group of knowns – the teacher's past experience (strategy and tactic repertory) and present awareness – is marshalled in directed effort. To what degree, however, are all of these knowns in instruction *operationally* known?

When these groups of factors are combined (the one set over which the agent has no control, extrasituational factors and the limit of the degree to which the 'knowns' are known) with the idea

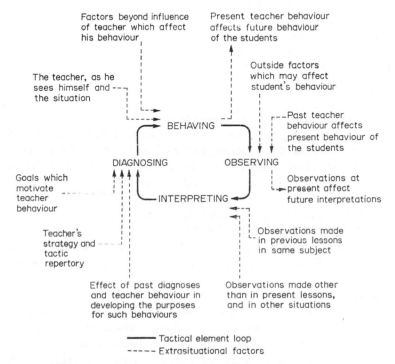

Figure 3 Some extrasituational factors that affect the nature of instruction.

that in instruction attention is directed towards new or future experiences in which the instructional knowns are largely of value only in a predictive sense and in which every instructional excursion is in reality an unknown, it is readily apparent that the number of 'unknowns', 'barely knowns' and 'I-think-I-know's' in any instructional situation necessitates an experimental approach: continually redirected, influenced/influencing teacher behaviour founded on a continuing stream of data from and about the learners.

Limitations of the model

Most of this paper has been centred on communicating the various dimensions and development of the model. But models are simplifications or generalizations of that which they are designed to represent; hence it is useful to direct some attention to looking at and thinking about what they don't do, to look at their limitations.

In this case, the limitations discussed serve to identify some holes in the tactical element loop. Although they have been alluded to in prior discussion, the following list has been included in order to make them more explicit.

1 *Instruction is not a closed loop as implied.*
   In considering the tactical element loop of instruction at any one moment of instruction, two kinds of extrasituational factors that affect the nature of instruction may be identified. These include one group which is more or less bound to the specific situation, such as class size, district policies, size of the classroom, availability of instructional materials, etc. A second group of factors adds the dimension of outside experiences of the learner, which may affect his behaviour, and his outside observations, which may affect the teacher's interpretation and diagnoses.

2 *Instruction is not purely linear in nature.*
   The model suggests that, first, there is a teacher behaviour, then learner behaviour, then teacher behaviour, then learner . . . This, however, is not necessarily the case. A kind of feed forward and feedback exists. That is, teacher behaviour in previous situations and on previous days may affect the present behaviour of the learners, and present teacher behaviour may affect the future behaviour of the learners in like manner. In addition, a present observation of a learner may provide the key through which prior observations may be more clearly understood.

3 *Observing, interpreting, diagnosing and behaving are cumulative.*
   The longer a teacher works with a given group of children the more data he brings to each observation, interpretation and diagnosis; thus, hopefully, the more rational is his behaviour.

4 *The behaviour of a learner at any one moment is the result of a*

complex of affective factors, rather than of teacher behaviour alone as implied.

5 *The behaviour of one student in a class may affect the behaviour of another student(s).*

The effect of the behaviour of one child on another is not discussed as a factor of the instructional situation. It is recognized, however, that such influence may be significant in some classes in some instructional situations.

6 *Tactical elements may occur simultaneously.*

Human behaviour is such that a teacher may be behaving and at the same time observing the effects of that behaviour, interpreting it, and forming diagnoses. Thus, teacher behaviour may appear to be continuous even though the discrete tactical elements are aspects of that continuous teacher behaviour.

Implications for instruction

After a look at the Conceptual Model of Instruction and consideration of some of its more apparent limitations, attention is turned to what this model implies about instruction, how it ties together past experiences and opens up some new hypotheses for further consideration.

1 *Instruction is viewed as a two-way situation.*

In one case, students are growing towards the stated curricular goals; in the other, teachers are learning about the children or their classes, the effect of their behaviour upon a specific group of students, ways to behave in terms of certain goals, and the limitations of present instructional goals: students grow towards curricular goals and teachers' tactic and strategy repertoire is empirically extended.

2 *One relationship between learner behaviour and ongoing instruction is indicated.*

The tactical element loop illustrates the role of the learner behaviours in instruction and identifies some specific points at which learner behaviours affect the nature of instruction.

3 *The necessity for continuous feedback (completing the tactical element cycle) in shaping instruction is highlighted.*

According to the model, it may be predicted that if part of the tactical element loop were eliminated the effectiveness of

G

instruction would become limited. When the loop of tactical elements is destroyed, effectiveness is diminished and the cumulative learning effect of instruction for *both* teacher and student is impeded.

4 *Use of the model provides one basis from which some aspects of instruction may be observed, discussed and experimented with.*

The notion of tactics and strategies provides one useful organizer for observing, classifying and experimenting with teacher–learner behaviour.

5 *Implicit in the model is the goal-directed behaviour of the teacher; the control points at which goals affect the behaviour of those involved in instruction are suggested.*

The model indicates the specific points at which goals affect the instructional process – as the bases for strategy decisions, as planned tactics are decided upon, as responsive tactics come into the situation, and as the tactical element loop proceeds from moment to moment during instruction.

6 *Evaluation in instruction is not something unique to the instructional situation; rather, it is a part of the tactical element loop.*

Viewed from the perspective of the tactical element loop, instructional evaluation proceeds *while* the students learn, during instruction rather than apart from it (although it is recognized that for some purposes some evaluation takes place apart from instruction).

7 *One route to increasing teacher effectiveness is through a purposeful experimental approach to instruction.*

Implied is a relationship between a teacher's tactic repertory (both planned and responsive) and the variety of instructional goals accessible through his behaviour. Thus, one route to extending one's tactic repertory may be through reflecting on his spontaneous behaviour as well as purposeful experimenting to discover the real effect of a certain hypothesized tactic upon the students.

8 *The model provides a unifying element through which some of the studies about various aspects of instruction may be related.*

The model may serve to place goals, curriculum, pedagogy, teacher, students, materials, etc., in perspective so that increased understanding of what such factors are and how or where they relate to the total picture of instruction may be further hypothesized.

In summary, perhaps the essential implication of the model about teaching is that teaching is enquiring and invites a teacher's thinking and behaving in terms of certain goals or enduring purposes. In another sense, teaching is viewed as learning – learning about the learners; learning about the effect of one's behaviour on the learners, based on a continuing stream of feedback from and about the learners; and learning as the teacher extends the goals which direct his activity.

A model for what purpose?

The model is an attempt to make sense out of experience. It may serve to facilitate educational dialogue about the topic, that is, a way to talk and think about instruction. Models also suggest what is to be observed and imply the meanings ascribed to such observations. They also outline ways certain facts may be organized, classified and interrelated. Furthermore, models usually stimulate the derivation of hypotheses and/or new questions which may serve to substantiate the relationship postulated or suggested a new model.

In *Theories of Instruction*, Ryans (Macdonald and Leeper 1965) indicates that the chief function of theory (a model) is to serve as a framework for observation and analysis rather than a once-and-for-all description of how certain kinds of phenomena operate.

The criterion by which a model is judged is its usefulness in tying together past experience and ideas and in opening new doors for continuing research. At this time, the Conceptual Model of Instruction provides some basis for looking at and thinking about instruction: the limitations pointed out illuminate several paths for reflection and the ideas generated suggest inviting explorations. As it now stands, the model is incomplete; it represents only a point on the time line of our growing understanding of the nature and essence of instruction. Hopefully, many new questions about instruction may arise which will demand our attention and lead to the extension of our awareness. If so, this model will have served us well.

References

Amidon, E. and Simon, A. (1965) 'Teacher–pupil reaction'. *Review of educational research*, 35, 130–9.

Amidon, E. and Giammatteo, M. (1965) 'The verbal behaviour of superior teachers'. *Elementary school journal*, 65, 283–5.

Bellack, A. A. (ed.) (1963) *Theory and research in teaching*. New York: Bureau of Publications, Teachers College, Columbia University. See articles by Aschner, Flanders, Hughes, Medley and Mitzel, and Smith.

Cyphert, F. R. and Openshaw, K. (1964) 'Research in teacher education: practices and promises'. *Theory into practice*, 3, 1.

Eisner, E. W. (1964) 'Instruction, teaching and learning: an attempt at differentiation'. *Elementary school journal*, 65, 115–19.

Flanders, N. A. (1963) 'Intent, action and feedback: a preparation for teaching'. *The journal of teacher education*, 14, 251–60.

Gage, N. L. (1964) 'Toward a cognitive theory of teaching'. *Teachers college record*, 65, 408–12.

Gallagher, J. (1963) *Problems in stimulating productive thinking of the gifted*. A presentation made at the California Teachers Association in Los Angeles.

Hughes, M. M. (1962) 'What is teaching? One viewpoint'. *Educational leadership*, 19, 251–9.

Macdonald, J. B. and Leeper, R. R. (eds.) (1965) *Theories of instruction*. Washington, D.C.: Association for Supervision and Curriculum Development. See articles by Beatty, Bellack, Macdonald and Ryans.

Scheffler, I. (1965) 'Philosophical models of teaching'. *Harvard educational review*, 35, 131–43.

Smith, B. O. (1963) 'A conceptual analysis of instructional behaviour'. *The journal of teacher education*, 14, 294–8.

Taba, H. (1963) 'Teaching strategy and learning'. *California journal for instructional improvement*, December, 3–12.

Taba, H. (1965) 'Strategy for learning'. *Science and children*, 3, 21–4.

Taba, H. and Elzey, F. F. (1964) 'Teaching strategies and thought processes'. *Teachers college record*, 65, 524–34.

Taba, H., Levine, S. and Elzey, F. F. (1964) *Thinking in elementary school children*. San Francisco State College.

Withall, J. (1963) 'Mental health teacher education research project'. *The journal of teacher education*, 14, 318–25.

4 · Teaching strategies for cognitive growth (the work of Hilda Taba)

J. R. VERDUIN

Professor Hilda Taba and associates (1964) have focused their intensive research largely on the development of a strategy for the generation and enhancement of independent thought processes on the part of elementary school children in the area of social studies. The central goal for the study was to examine the development of thought under three training conditions: (*a*) a curriculum designed for the development of thought, (*b*) teaching strategies focused explicitly and consciously on the mastery of the necessary cognitive skills, and (*c*) a sufficient time span to permit a developmental sequence in training. A subsidiary objective was to develop a method of categorizing thought processes for analysing thinking as it occurs in a classroom setting. A further subsidiary goal was to develop the teaching strategies for the development of cognitive skills. However, the transaction between teaching acts and student behaviour was a significant aspect of the analysis of this work.

The essence of this paper on Taba's work will focus on the thought processes or cognitive tasks as defined by her and the teaching strategies needed for the mastery of these cognitive skills. To ignore the curriculum aspect of this research is ill advised, but it is felt that once understood and mastered, the thought processes and strategies can be utilized in any type of the curriculum and even in areas other than the social studies area (the focus of this research). Therefore, the processes involved will be discussed with an understanding that the curriculum content is an essential ingredient for the successful execution of the processes. The social studies curriculum will be brought out only to afford meaning to the important cognitive processes (Taba *et al.* 1964).

Reprinted from J. R. Verduin, *Conceptual Models in Teacher Education* (Washington, D.C., American Association of Colleges for Teacher Education, 1967), pp. 16–26.

Taba identified three categories of thought processes or cognitive tasks: (a) concept formation, (b) interpretation of data and the making of inferences, and (c) the application of known principles and facts to explain new phenomena, to predict consequences from known conditions and events, or to develop hypotheses by using known generalizations and facts (Taba 1965b). These three cognitive tasks were analysed from two different angles: the operations or elements involved, and the sequential steps necessary for mastering them.

Concept formation

Since concept formation is considered the basic form of cognition on which all cognitive processes depend, Taba, for her study, utilized basic concept formation and defined it as consisting of three different processes or operations: (a) the differentiation of the specific properties of objects or events, such as differentiating the materials of which houses are built from other characteristics of houses (this differentiation involves the process of analysis, in the sense of breaking down the global complexes representing objects and events into specified properties); (b) grouping, or a process of assembling specified properties across many objects and events, i.e. grouping together hospitals, doctors and medicine according to some semi-intuitively identifiable basis such as representing something to do with health, or the fact that their availability serves as an index for the standard of living; and (c) labelling or categorizing, i.e. explicitly identifying the basis for grouping, and subsuming the items under some label or category.

In the classroom differentiation may be called for in the act of enumeration, either by recall from previous experience, or by specifying items noted in a complex presentation, such as a film or a story. For example, pupils could list the materials used for building houses, or name things and events noted in a film. Grouping is putting together diverse items which have some common characteristics, such as grouping schools, hospitals and parks as community facilities. Usually, this process of searching for a basis of grouping leads to a discovery that the items can be grouped in multiple ways, depending on the purpose and the basis used.

Categorization occurs in the form of making decisions about what labels to use for groups, what to subsume under which category, such as whether weather is to be subsumed under climate, or vice versa. This involves an awareness of orders of subordination and superordination.

In teaching these operations, as well as in analysing them, the hierarchical nature of concepts must be kept in mind. As the process of abstracting continues, the categories or labels become increasingly more abstract and encompassing, and thereby more remote from the initial concrete reference. This increasing abstraction also enhances their power as cognitive tools for organizing information. In the classroom, concepts on different levels of abstraction may be suggested simultaneously, which creates the problem of differentiation. For example, students may enumerate materials for building housing in specific terms, such as tar paper and fibre glass, or in classes, such as insulation.

A graphic representation of the cognitive task of concept formation and the skills for using it appears below:

Concept Formation (Taba and Hill 1965)

Overt activity	Covert mental operation	Eliciting questions
1 Enumeration and listing.	1 Differentiation.	1 What did you see? hear? note?
2 Grouping.	2 Identifying common properties, abstracting.	2 What belongs together? On what criterion?
3 Labelling, categorizing.	3 Determining the hierarchical order of items. Super- and sub-ordination.	3 How would you call these groups? What belongs under what?

Interpretation of data

Interpreting data and making inferences from them is essentially an inductive process of developing generalizations, although never accomplished without some application of what is previously known. This task involves four basic operations. One is that of assembling concrete information, either by instigating a process of recall and retrieval of previously learned information, or by being presented new information and identifying the specific points in this set of data. This is a basic operation and somewhat similar to the first step in grouping and classifying. Second is that of explaining or giving reasons for certain events, such as explaining why the way of life in California changed when harbours opened for free trade, or why the early colonists desired to change their form of government.

The third operation consists of relating different points of processed information, such as is involved in comparing the proportion of white population in Brazil and Argentina, and relating the information thus obtained to its possible connection with standards of living in the two countries. The fourth operation is that of formulating generalizations or inferences, such as that the countries in Latin America with predominantly white population tend to have a higher standard of living.

While these processes are generic, there are differences according to whether the content being interpreted is scientific or literary, whether the data is couched in quantitative or verbal symbols, or whether it is concrete or abstract. Greater precision is required, and fairly rigorous limits are set, for extrapolation and interpolation when interpreting quantitative data, while 'reading between the lines' is almost a necessity in interpreting literary passages (Taba 1962).

A graphic representation of the cognitive task of interpretation of data and the skills for using it appears below:

Interpretation of Data (Taba and Hill 1965)

Overt activity	Covert mental operation	Eliciting questions
1 Identifying points.	1 Differentiation.	1 What did you note? see? find?
2 Explaining items of identified information.	2 Relating points to each other. Determining cause and effect relationships.	2 Why did so-and-so happen?
3 Making inferences.	3 Going beyond what is given. Finding implications, extrapolating.	3 What does this mean? What picture does it create in your mind? What would you conclude?

Application of principles

A third cognitive task has to do with applying previous knowledge – principles, generalizations or facts – to explain new phenomena and to predict consequences from known conditions. For example, if one knows what a desert is like, what way of life prevails there, and how water acts on the soil, one can predict what would happen in a desert if water were available.

Essentially, two different operations are involved: that of predicting, and that of establishing the parameters either of logical relationships or of information with which to test the validity of predictions. The level of a prediction or a hypothesis can be judged according to the extent of the leap from a given condition. But equally important is the completeness of the parameter – the chain of links which connects the prediction and the conditions. For example, the prediction that grass will grow in the desert if water is available is a prediction of a lower order than is the prediction that nomads will become farmers, and the former entails a shorter and a simpler chain of causal links.

Application of principles invites a greater degree of divergence than either of the preceding cognitive tasks. Each condition presented as data invites a divergent line of predictions. For this reason, this process contains opportunities for creative and divergent use of knowledge. In fact, some tests of creativity use situations involving prediction, but they use conditions that set few constraints and therefore permit an unlimited exercise of ingenuity.

In social situations, these processes also provoke value judgements and stereotypes. For example, in explaining why delinquency exists or in predicting how it will change if certain measures are employed, it is necessary to consider not only the factors affecting human behaviour, but also what beliefs prevail about equality, justice, democratic values, deviate behaviour and adolescence (Taba 1962).

The operations involved in applying principles are quite crucial to developing productive patterns of thought. This process is the chief vehicle for transfer of knowledge. This process is, therefore, crucial for getting mileage out of the little that students can acquire directly during their schooling. It is a chief means for creating new knowledge by logical processes, and a way of acquiring control over wide areas of new phenomena. It is also the process by which models for hypothesizing can be created, freeing the individual from the necessity of being bound to the immediate stimulus.

A graphic representation of the cognitive task of application of principles and the skills for using it appears below:

Application of Principles (Taba and Hill 1965)

Overt activity	Covert mental operation	Eliciting questions
1 Predicting conse-quences. Explaining unfamiliar pheno-mena. Hypothesizing.	1 Analysing the nature of the problem or situ-ation. Retrieving rele-vant knowledge.	1 What would happen if . . .?
2 Explaining, support-ing the predictions and hypotheses.	2 Determining the cau-sal links leading to prediction or hypo-thesis.	2 Why do you think this would happen?
3 Verifying the pre-diction.	3 Using logical prin-ciples or factual know-ledge to determine necessary and suffi-cient conditions.	3 What would it take for so-and-so to be true or probably true?

As conceptualized in the study, these three cognitive tasks have several things in common. First, the mastery of operation in each task – concept formation, interpretation and inference and applica-tion of principles – entails a sequence of steps. For example, in order to form general concepts from diverse specific information, the operations need to be mastered in a certain sequential order: enu-meration combined with differentiation $\rightarrow$ grouping, which in-volves determining the basis for grouping $\rightarrow$ categorizing and labelling, which involves creating superordinate classes (Taba et al. 1964).

Despite the difference in the operations and in the specific steps, the sequences involved in mastering these steps are similar in that all involve hierarchies of levels of abstraction and complexity. Each successive step in all the cognitive tasks involves more complex operations than does the preceding one. In a sense, each step also represents an increment in the leap from that which was originally given.

Finally, the sequence of operations required in the successive steps involves different proportions of intuitive performance and of conscious awareness of the principles involved in the performance.

Indirectly, this conception of the hierarchical difficulty in levels of mental operations also involves the principle of rotation of assimilation and accommodation. This principle implies that in-formation is at first fitted into and interpreted according to the existing conceptual system. This is followed by a type of mental activity which calls for the extension and reorganization of that conceptual system. In interpretation of data, for example, accumulation of descriptive information is followed by explanation. In the sequence involved in applying principles, the offering of intuitive and fairly unconstrained predictions or hypotheses is followed by challenging their validity by constructing the informational and logical parameters to justify them.

Teaching strategies for cognitive development

For the training of teachers and the design of this study, Taba evolved a paradigm of teaching in which, instead of treating teaching as a global process, specific learning tasks were defined and teaching strategies were focused on these cognitive tasks. To bring about particular behavioural changes in pupils, the strategies were arranged into sequential order to meet both the logical requirements of the nature of the tasks and the psychological requirements of mastering them. This means that the nature of the strategy depends on the kind of task. For example, each cognitive task (i.e. concept formation, interpretation of data and application of principles) requires a special set of questions and a special sequencing of them. Each question is designed to elicit a special kind of overt activity, such as enumerating or explaining. This overt activity in turn fosters or requires the covert mental operation, such as differentiating in case of enumeration and seeing causal relations in case of explaining. Taba states that these covert mental operations are the ones that actually determine the sequence of learning activities and of the eliciting questions for the teacher. For example, in the task of grouping and classifying, the first question will take the form of 'What did you see, hear, note?' This calls for enumeration or listing of the items for consideration. From there the pupils must decide what belongs together. This overt activity calls for identifying a property or a characteristic that is common to all items. This characteristic becomes the basis for grouping. Finally, it is necessary to label the groups and to decide what belongs under which label.

In these operations each step is a prerequisite for the next one. One cannot label or categorize until some prior grouping has taken place, and one cannot group until the items have been listed and enumerated.

For the cognitive task of interpretation of data (see chart p. 190), the overt activities are identifying points, explaining these identified items and then making inferences or generalizations. These in turn require the covert mental operations of differentiating, explaining by comparing and contrasting, and finding implications beyond what is given. Taba suggests that a variety of learning experiences can foster this kind of cognitive task. Pupils may read, review audio-visual materials, observe, and do other things which furnish the data for interpreting and inferring. The learning experience must provide opportunity to differentiate the relevant from the irrelevant, to contrast and compare, to seek cause and effect relationships, and to generalize beyond what is given. This latter is difficult for many youngsters to do, because they have never been required to go beyond what is given in a book. The requirement of looking for specific answers has conditioned them against inferring from the data.

The strategy for the application of principles, the third cognitive task (see p. 192), starts with the requirement to predict conse-quences from described conditions. The eliciting question would be, 'What would happen if . . . ?' The corresponding covert mental operation would then require the pupils to analyse the nature of the problem, retrieve relevant information and use available information in order to make a valid prediction. From this point the teacher can move the pupils to the second step, explaining and supporting the prediction or hypothesis, by stating the question 'Why do you think this will happen?' This requires the pupils to search for causal links leading from condition to prediction. Then the final overt activity is to verify the prediction, in which case the pupils are required to use logical principles or factual knowledge to determine the neces-sary and sufficient conditions.

There is also a more or less natural placement for these tasks in the sequence of the units. Taba suggests that the beginning of the unit usually affords good opportunities for grouping and classifica-tion of information. The task of interpreting data is best performed at points at which new information, such as research, reading or viewing of films, is gathered. The task of applying principles is usually most appropriate at the end of a unit of study, of course, after some previous knowledge has been gained and after concept formation and the interpretation of data have occurred.

Taba suggests further that the questions should be viewed as serving specific pedagogical functions. One is that of focusing. The questions should set the stage for both the kind of mental operation to be performed and the topic or the content on which this operation is to be performed. In other words, the question should tell the pupils what they are to talk about (such as materials used to build houses), and what they are to do with this content (whether they are to list the materials or group together materials that serve similar functions, etc.).

Another pedagogical function is that of extending thought on the same level. For example, when pupils are explaining events they noted in films, it is not enough for one pupil to give his notion. It is important to encourage others to add their ideas also. The teacher should seek additional information on already established levels of thought or elaboration and clarification of information already provided.

Finally, there is a pedagogical function of making a transition from one level of thought to another (or from one step to another), such as from assembling descriptive information to explaining certain items in that information, or from offering predictions to establishing their validity. This is a form of changing the focus, or 'lifting of thought to another level'.

An important consideration in all these intellectual operations is to so form the questions that the pupil can and will perform the operations themselves. Teachers must refrain from a temptation to offer a category, a generalization, when pupils have difficulty in developing one themselves. Otherwise, the pupils are deprived of the opportunity to learn the process. For example, in case of grouping, the pupils must see themselves what relationship exists between different items they have listed and devise their own categories. They must also discover that things can be grouped in different ways. An orange can be grouped with other round objects and also with the group called fruit. However, clarity of specific items is important to achieve adequate groupings, and the teacher should assist in eliciting clarification when necessary.

Naturally, the end outcomes are not perfect, especially in the first attempts. For example, the explanations of information or the generalizations and predictions may be quite defective at first, because the pupils have not yet mastered all the necessary processes. In time, as the work on these tasks is repeated, the responses will become more sophisticated.

An important aspect of the teaching strategy to promote autonomous performance on these cognitive tasks is that of pacing the main three questions on each task. Taba suggests that ample time should be spent on each step so that the majority of the class can participate in the practice of all three steps of each cognitive task. The class should remain on a particular step long enough to permit pupils who learn at different speeds to become involved and to master the needed skills.

For interpretation of data this strategy of pacing involves the following:

1 Drawing out the 'what's', including questions eliciting the 'who', 'how', 'when', and 'where'. The teacher must pursue these questions long enough to: (a) have the wherewithal for later comparisons, and (b) to make sure that even the slowest pupils are involved. If they are not included at this level of intellectual activity, they will not be able to function at subsequent levels. Where several content samples are involved, the same line of questioning must be pursued regarding each.

2 Eliciting explanations and comparisons by using questions which get at similarities, differences, changes, and the 'whys'. This group of questions requires the students to move to higher levels of thinking and the number of pupils involved at this point will be closely related to the number of pupils who participated at the earlier level. Dealing with these questions prepares the ground for interpretation, the making of inferences that go beyond the actual data at hand and for formulating hypotheses.

3 Probing for generalizations or consequences, which seem the likely result of selected events or series of events, by questions such as: 'What does/will this mean?' Such questions set the ground for the discovery of the principles and the development of generalizations.

To summarize, pacing of the question in the sequences is all-important when the strategy involves a sequential mastery of cognitive skills where one is a prerequisite for each succeeding one. It is important also to remain at one level until a variety of responses accumulate. This case accumulation assures the availability of a wide range of information from which the pupils can generalize. This procedure also increases the involvement of the pupils, helps the majority to practise the skills and enhances the quality of thinking at the same time.

The pacing of the transitions from one step to another radically affects the ultimate productivity of the class. Premature lifting of the thought to the next level usually brings two results: (a) fewer and fewer pupils participate as discussion moves on; (b) the class discussion, instead of ending on a higher level of thought, is likely to return to the most primitive level, namely, the giving of specific information (Taba and Hill 1965).

Implications for improved teacher education

Professor Taba's investigation into teaching strategies for cognitive growth has many significant implications for improving the preparation of classroom teachers. Probably the most significant is the fact that her model has been developed to a point where it can be used immediately. She was able to train teachers in these skills in ten days in a public school situation. The recent development of the *Teacher Handbook for Contra Costa Social Studies, Grades 1-6* by Taba and Hill (Taba and Hill 1965) brings to the reader a thorough discussion of the cognitive tasks, of the curriculum, and of the appropriate teaching strategies in the setting in which these strategies were used. A complete review of this *Handbook* should provide the teacher educator and his students some insights into the important aspects of teaching pupils to think. The exposition is sufficiently explicit to show the kind of curriculum organization in social studies that is needed and to give concrete guidance for designing teaching strategies for cognitive growth.

Even though this investigation was set in the social studies curriculum, Taba sees these processes as generic processes capable of being used in areas other than the social sciences, such as the 'new' science and mathematics. These new curricula are presumably predicated on the same general notions. If the central concepts in these new areas are identified, the strategies for developing these concepts should be similar to those employed in the social studies. A reanalysis of the content so that the teacher can identify the basic ideas, combined with an understanding of the three basic cognitive processes, should provide for effective cognitive growth in these new curricula. These processes can be utilized at a secondary level also, if a knowledge of the content and an identification of the important concepts and principles are sought.

Taba assumes that three prerequisites are necessary for the use of her research in any curriculum area. A teacher must: (a) know the processes of thinking, (*b*) possess a good knowledge of the pupils, and (*c*) know the content to be taught. This demands a great deal from the teacher educator in his work with future teachers and has definite implications for the content of education courses.

Taba's investigation further emphasizes the interaction in the cognitive domain between teacher, pupils and content. A careful examination of the curriculum is imperative within the framework of this research, thus pointing to the fact that teacher education students must familiarize themselves with the elements of the curriculum and the selection and use of the significant major ideas to be taught. Teacher educators should be aware of this important aspect of content selection when working with teacher education students.

Another implication important for the teacher educator to consider is that of the art of questioning. Taba has offered some excellent suggestions within the context of her research for use in effective cognitive development. Focusing, extending and lifting within the three major cognitive processes are important functions for the teacher. Care should be taken when working with the prospective teachers in this area. They need sufficient time and practice and must experiment with formulating open-ended questions and developing appropriate sequences during their teacher preparation work.

Professor Taba has regular sessions in which she trains teachers to utilize the various processes and strategies. Part of the training consists of experiencing the same kinds of things that school children would do. This same practice could also be employed in training new teachers: the teacher education students could learn to classify and categorize things, make inferences and apply ideas to new problems. The introduction of such practices would require development of appropriate materials by the teacher educators. Both magnetic and video tapes that focus on definite strategies for cognitive development are beginning to be available for purposes of analysis and demonstration. Since this entire idea is a new experience for young teacher education students, a whole new frame of reference must be developed.

Finally, this entire research has significant implications for enhancing the ability of pupils to think. This writer will not make any judgements regarding thinking as an important goal in education. However, if one were to review current statements about goals for education, he would not find it difficult to note the central emphasis on cognitive development in the last ten years. If teacher educators want to keep abreast with this emphasis, they can find significant support from Taba's efforts for fostering the higher level of cognitive processes.

References

Taba, H. (1962) *Curriculum development: theory and practice.* New York: Harcourt, Brace & World.

Taba, H. (1963) 'Teaching strategy and learning'. *California journal for instructional improvement,* December, 3–12.

Taba, H. (1965a) 'The teaching of thinking'. *Elementary English,* May, 534–42.

Taba, H. (1956b) *Teaching strategies and cognitive functioning in elementary school children.* San Francisco State College.

Taba, H., Levine, S. and Elzey, F. (1964) *Thinking in elementary school children.* San Francisco State College.

Taba, H. and Hill, J. J. (1965) *Teacher handbook for Contra Costa social studies, grades 1–6.* Hayward, California.

5 · Interaction analysis: recent developments

E. AMIDON and E. HUNTER

There are a number of category systems for analysing verbal inter-action in the classroom, and in the past fifteen years, the interest shown in category systems as research tools has increased tre-mendously. In a recent survey, for example, Amidon and Simon (1965) found that educational researchers reported over twenty systems for classifying verbal classroom interaction. We have found that our own colleagues and students are developing category systems at an increasing rate.

Hough (1966), Honigman (1966), Amidon and Hunter (1966) and Simon and Agazarian (1966) have developed systems which include many features of the ten-category system of Flanders, but which also branch out from and differ somewhat from Flanders's interaction analysis. The first issue of *The Classroom Interaction Newsletter* (1965) presents summaries of a number of studies in which other new category systems have been developed. So many observational systems are now being produced that it is difficult to keep informed about them. While there is a wide field here for innovation and invention, it seems that in order to increase our understanding of classroom verbal interaction and generalize from present findings it would be important to conduct future careful research with presently existing systems or modification of systems that will allow for reference back to current data. The modifications of Flanders's interaction analysis which will be suggested here would allow a researcher to compare any data he collected with that collected using the original system. In addition, the modified system presented here has a unique training potential that allows for a selective analysis of specific aspects of teaching, such as, for example,

Reprinted from E. Amidon and J. B. Hough (eds.), *Interaction Analysis: Theory, Research and Applications* (Reading, Mass., Addison-Wesley, 1967), pp. 388–91.

a teacher's questioning behaviour, the type of student talk occurring in the classroom, or the way the teacher uses praise and encouragement in his teaching. This modified system is presented as an example of how the original system of interaction analysis can be expanded to provide a highly flexible research and instructional tool.

Table 1 Modified categories

Teacher talk	1 Accepts feeling
	2a Praises
	2b Praises using public criteria
	2c Praises using private criteria
	3 Accepts idea through: *a*) description
	b) inference
	c) generalization
	4 Asks: *a*) cognitive memory question
	b) convergent question
	c) divergent question
	d) evaluative question
	5 Lectures
	6 Gives direction
	7a Criticizes
	7b Criticizes using public criteria
	7c Criticizes using private criteria
Student talk	8 Pupil response: *a*) description
	b) inference
	c) generalization
	9 Pupil initiation: *a*) description
	b) inference
	c) generalization
	10a Silence
	10b Confusion

The Flanders system describes only verbal interaction between teachers and pupils. Only verbal behaviour is analysed because of the difficulty at the present time in reliably categorizing non-verbal behaviour. All teacher–pupil interaction is divided into ten categories, seven of teacher talk, two of student talk and one of silence or confusion.

The modified system presented in this paper retains the basic ten categories, but includes some ideas of other researchers in the field. Additional categories are added (Table 1) so that more data might be collected in classrooms, and also so that student teachers being trained in the use of a category system may look at their classroom verbal interaction more discriminatingly and may thus gain more insight into their own teaching behaviour. A wide variety of expansions and contractions of categories are possible to meet specific training or research needs. For example, a teacher who wishes to analyse his own teaching with specific emphasis on patterns of questioning could use a thirteen category system composed of the basic ten categories with a category 4 expansion (categories 4a, 4b, 4c and 4d). A teacher who wished to focus on the effect of clarification on level of student thinking could use the basic ten categories with an expansion of categories 3, 8 and 9. Such an analysis would involve the use of a sixteen category system.

Proposed modification of the Flanders system of interaction analysis

The modification retains the use of the matrix, so that a person using the twenty-four categories described in this paper would enter data into a 24 by 24 matrix, a 13 by 13 matrix, a 16 by 16 matrix or a matrix of varying size determined by the particular categories being used. In each case, however, the categories may be collapsed back into a 10 by 10 matrix.

In creating the flexible system presented here, the authors have drawn from the work of Marie Hughes, Hilda Taba, and James Gallagher and Mary Jane Aschner. The contribution of each of these people to the flexible category system is presented below.

Category 1 (accepts feeling), category 5 (lectures) and category 6 (gives directions) are left as they are in the Flanders system. Category 2 (praises or encourages) is modified by using Marie Hughes's ideas about public and private criteria (Hughes *et al.* 1959). If a teacher praises by saying, 'good', or 'fine work', and uses no criteria, then category 2a would be tallied. If a teacher gives the kind of reasons that are logical and explicit, then 2b would be tallied. Examples of 2b would be 'Your report was particularly helpful because you used those graphs to show us exactly how production changed income levels', or 'Your quiet voices are helping the rest of us concentrate on our written work'. If a teacher gives reasons for praise that involve his own likes and dislikes, 2c (or private criteria) would be tallied. Examples of this would be 'I was proud of your behaviour in the halls today', or 'A report like John's makes me very happy'. These additions should help student teachers think about and use praise in ways which encourage pupils to grow and become more self-directing.

Taba's levels of thinking (Taba 1964) have suggested the modifications in category 3 (accepts ideas). Three subcategories have been added to category three: describing, inferring and generalizing. Examples of these subcategories would be:

Student: 'They built their houses out of snow.'
Teacher: 'So they used snow to provide shelter.' (Acceptable through description.)
Student: 'They had to use snow.'
Teacher: 'You mean that if they had had wood or stone available they probably would have used that instead.' (Acceptance through inference.) 'People in primitive cultures have to use the materials in their immediate environments for their homes.' (Acceptance through generalization.)

By dividing acceptance of ideas in this way, student teachers are helped to think about their pupils' levels of thinking, and also to be aware of whether or not their own responses to pupils will be most helpful if kept on the same level, or if moved to another level.

The categories of Gallagher and Aschner (1963) are used in the modifications of Flanders's category 4 (asks questions). Examples of cognitive memory, convergent, divergent and evaluative questions follow in the order in which they are listed: (4a) 'What is the largest city in New York state?' (4b) 'What is there about the position of New York City which accounts for its importance?' (4c) 'How might the lives of the people of New York City be different if the city were located in the torrid zone?' (4d) 'Would you like to live in New York City?' According to Gallagher and Aschner, cognitive memory questions ask for recall and require no additional thinking, convergent questions require some analysis of data, divergent questions call for imagination and a move in new directions, and evaluative questions ask for judgement. By dividing questions into these broad and narrow categories, student teachers are helped to formulate questions in a more varied way than they might otherwise do.

Category 7 (criticizes or justifies authority) has been modified in the same way that praise has been, by adding public and private criteria; and for the same reasons, so that pupils will be provided with reasons for criticism when this is appropriate. An example of criticism (7a) would be 'wrong'. 7b (criticism using public criteria) might be 'Your answer is wrong because you divided with a nine instead of a seven'. An example of 7c (criticism using private criteria) would be 'I don't like your attitude'.

The Flanders categories 8 and 9 have been modified in the same way as category 3, by the addition of the subheadings, description, inference and generalization. The reasons for this change are to help student teachers to think about the levels of pupils' contributions, to help them move from one level to another, to back up if necessary, to be aware of what Taba calls 'jumpers' (those pupils who may skip levels when others are not ready), and so forth.

The Flanders category 10 (silence or confusion) has been divided into two categories. Silence following a question, for example, is quite different from confusion following a question. It would seem helpful for student teachers to learn to allow silence after truly thought-provoking questions.

Obviously, the potential creation of subcategories is not restricted to those derived from the work of Hughes, Taba, and Gallagher and Aschner. Many other subclassifications could be created so long as the behaviours categorized can be identified in spontaneous classroom behaviour and so long as the categories are mutually exclusive.

The modifications in interaction analysis suggested in this paper result in twenty-four categories rather than ten. However, there are only ten main categories, with the others being subheadings. Thus, the category system would not be difficult to learn, or to use. The system is particularly designed for use as a feedback tool; to analyse one's own teaching, to think about and formulate questions, to role-play behaviours in the college classroom, to observe teaching patterns, and to diagnose teaching problems.

References

Amidon, E. J. and Hunter, E. (1966) *Improving teaching: the analysis of classroom verbal interaction.* New York: Holt, Rinehart & Winston.

Amidon, E. J. and Simon, A. (1965) *Implications for teacher educa-*

tion of interaction analysis in student teaching. Paper presented to the annual conference of the American Educational Research Association.

Classroom interaction newsletter, 1965, vol. 1 (ed. A. Simon). Temple University, Philadelphia.

Gallagher, J. T. and Aschner, M. J. (1963) 'A preliminary report: analysis of classroom interaction'. *Merrill-Palmer Quarterly*, 9, 183–94.

Honigman, F. (1966) *Testing a three-dimensional system for analyzing teachers' influence.* Unpublished doctoral dissertation, Temple University, Philadelphia.

Hough, J. B. (1966) *An observational system for the analysis of classroom instruction.* Ohio State University, Columbus (mimeo).

Hughes, M. *et al.* (1959) *The assessment of the quality of teaching: a research report.* U.S. Office of Education, Cooperative Research Project No. 353, University of Utah, Salt Lake City.

Simon, A. and Agazarian, Y. (1966) *Sequential analysis of verbal interaction.* Temple University, Philadelphia (mimeo).

Taba, H., Levine, S. and Elzey, F. (1964) *Thinking in elementary school children.* San Francisco State College.

6 · Microteaching

D. W. ALLEN and A. W. EVE

From its inception as a simple device for the training of secondary school teachers in a few selected teaching skills, microteaching has grown to the point where multiple specific applications are being made at all levels of education, from the elementary school to the university. Pre-service as well as in-service microteaching clinics and workshops have been established in many universities and public school systems throughout the country. Microteaching techniques and research have also been implemented with increasing frequency in new and different ways outside of teacher training, as in medical education.

There are numerous examples of usage within the field of education. At the University of Massachusetts, the regular pre-service microteaching clinic is supplemented by an intensive summer workshop to train school personnel who can then return to their systems and establish microteaching clinics and practices on a local basis. At the University of Illinois, Arye Perlberg utilized microteaching in the preparation of vocational education personnel and in the refinement of teaching skills among university professors.* At the University of Maryland, David B. Young has used microteaching in teacher education centres to (1) train centre faculty members to work with student teachers within the centres, and (2) to develop the teaching skills of student teachers. Young and his associates have also used microteaching and selected self-analysis techniques at Johns Hopkins University to individualize pre-service training and internships for prospective teachers.

* Arye Perlberg, Professor of Education at Technion Institute in Haifa, Israel, was a Visiting Research Professor at the University of Illinois during the 1967–8 academic year.

Reprinted from *Theory Into Practice*, 7 (1968), 5, pp. 181–5.

The use of microteaching to train Peace Corps volunteers is an excellent example of its flexibility with unique teacher training objectives. The microteaching clinic was adapted specifically to the preparation of the Peace Corps volunteers for the Philippines and has since become a model for other Peace Corps training programs. Objectives for the Philippine Peace Corps clinic were (1) to equip the volunteers with teaching skills directly related to English as a second language, (2) to acquaint them with special materials for teaching English as a second language, and (3) to provide a reality test during which the volunteers could decide if they really wanted to become elementary school teachers in the Philippines for the next two years. Since the microclasses were made up of Philippine students who had been in the United States less than six months, the microteaching sessions were much more directly related to the reality to be faced by the Peace Corps volunteers than would have been possible in a regular classroom situation.

An example of how microteaching concepts and techniques have been utilized in counselling and guidance has been provided by Allen Ivey. He and his associates developed the concept of micro-counselling, which is a video method of training counsellors in the basic skills of counselling.* Microcounselling training procedures focus on these skills: attending behaviour, reflection of feeling and summarization of feeling.

Microteaching techniques and principles have been used with some effectiveness in the area of medical education. Hilliard Jason, director of the Office of Medical Education Research and Development in the College of Human Medicine at Michigan State University, has utilized microteaching techniques in assisting medical students to acquire the skills of relating to patients. He is developing a series of process skills utilizing patient simulation, video taped patient–doctor relationships, immediate video playback and super-visor–doctor critique and analysis.

Additional areas exist, both within and outside of education, where microteaching techniques and principles appear to be useful. For example, microteaching could be useful within education for pre-employment prediction as a framework for selection or rating of experienced teachers seeking employment within a school

* The original research was conducted while Ivey was the Director of the Counseling Center at Colorado State University. He is currently at the University of Massachusetts.

district. This concept could also be extended to include the evaluation of current employees for possible promotion; however, it would be necessary to indicate clearly to teachers those occasions when their microteaching sessions would be utilized as the basis for evaluating their competence.

Microteaching principles and techniques might be effectively applied in the training of administrators to improve presentation skills, particularly in the area of administrator–parent communications. Such prior practice, combined with an effective supervisory critique of the administrator's micro-presentation, might result in a significant improvement in the administrator's ability to communicate with his community and might also result in an increase in the number of bond issues which are subsequently approved.

Another example of the possible application of microteaching is the training of personnel such as secretaries or receptionists. They might be trained in specific interpersonal relations skills to become more effective in dealing with the public. Teacher aides who would be working primarily with students (e.g. in open laboratories, resource centres or cafeteria duty) could also receive such training.

Potential areas outside of education would include those service areas where information is obtained by a specialist from individual clients or from groups of clients such as social workers, psychiatrists and police officers. In-service teachers in diverse preparation institutions (hospitals, police academies, the military and schools preparing social workers) could increase their competence through the use of microteaching procedures. Microteaching can also help to train people in the techniques of oratory and debate. Law school students could practise the skills of set induction, closure and probing questions before a small audience. High school students, politicians and ministers could improve speaking skills in a microteaching setting in which they could practise specific speaking skills on a small audience.

The normal classroom setting contains so many variables that precise research is virtually precluded. A major attraction of the microteaching format is that it simplifies the teaching act and provides an opportunity for real experimental control and manipulation of variables.

As a teacher training technique, microteaching is in its infancy, and many issues related to its most effective use have not as yet been resolved. There is no convincing research evidence regarding the optimal number of students for microteaching sessions. It would be useful to examine the impact of student characteristics upon the success or failure of the teacher training session and the impact of a variety of different timing and sequencing arrangements within the microteaching setting. Finally, how to increase the effectiveness of the self-confrontation critique and the feedback that it supplies in training teachers to acquire specific teaching skills must be determined. The important point here is that microteaching as a teacher training technique should proceed in light of a careful investigation of the contributions of each of its components.

The microteaching situation suggests that a second major category for research experimentation might focus upon the process of learning itself. Some of the learning situations which might be investigated relate to the use of models in the training of specific teaching skills. As noted in Allen and Ryan (1969), the key issues which might be examined are as follows. (1) Is a model of a skill a more efficient aid to learning if it contains the positive and negative instances of the skill or if it contains only the positive instances? (2) To what extent does extreme exaggeration of teaching techniques in a model add to or detract from its usefulness in a training situation? (3) Is transfer of the skill to the real classroom by the teacher trainee improved by the use of models in several different contextual situations (e.g. one in a microteaching situation, one in a regular classroom and one in a large group lecture hall)? (4) Are modelling procedures more effective in producing learning if they contain segments that show the model being reinforced for performing the desired skill?

The supervisory sessions within microteaching also provide an opportunity for investigating some basic learning phenomena related to self-confrontation situations. Examples of the kinds of issues involved are: (1) the effectiveness of various schedules of reinforcement in training particular skills; (2) the effectiveness of different verbal and non-verbal reinforcers in training particular skills; (3) the relative training effectiveness of pointing out positive and/or negative instances of a training use of a particular skill in a self-confrontation situation; (4) the effects of training on different attitudinal sets and expectancy on the part of a supervisor; and (5) the investigation of supervisory techniques and cueing devices which can eventually eliminate the role of the supervisor and can make the trainee himself an adequate critic of his own teaching behaviour.

A third major category of microteaching research would focus on the interactions between students and teachers. Teacher trainers must begin to face the problems of determining the relationships between teacher performance and student performance so that they can build empirically based justification for the objectives of their training programs. Video tapes on which the students and the teacher are recorded simultaneously will make it possible to do this. In addition to observing the immediate effect upon student behaviour of a particular teaching skill, appropriate achievement measures could be given to the microclass students to determine the long range impact of the teaching skill upon student learning. As researchers begin to gather evidence in this area, we can begin to utilize teacher training programs where the skills, attitudes and understandings required by prospective teachers are supported by the empirical evidence of their efficacy in producing learning.

Microteaching can and should be used as a research tool to investigate which training strategies are most effective for teacher trainees with different backgrounds and aptitudes. At the same time, it can be used as a training strategy to give individual teachers the kind of teaching most suited to their particular abilities. Such research into alternate training routes should provide educators with a means of approaching the problem of individualizing instruction within teacher education. There is a strong probability that teachers who are prepared in such an individualized program will subsequently be much more able to develop and implement individualized instructional approaches with their students.

While the four specific microteaching research categories which have been discussed are only those areas which today appear to be most fruitful, the most promising thing about microteaching as a research device is the extent to which it is open to new implementation and as yet unconceived experimental issues.

Microteaching stands today as one of the few experimental techniques which by its very structure encourages a combination of theory and practice, research and training, innovation and implementation. The phenomenal growth and diversity of microteaching should not obscure the fact that the technique is still in its infancy. The ultimate potential of this most promising tool for both research and training depends entirely upon our imagination and our ingenuity in developing and testing new ways of applying micro-teaching principles and techniques to the problems of education.

References

Allen, D. W. and Ryan, K. (1969) *Microteaching*. Reading, Mass.: Addison-Wesley.

7 · The model in use (microteaching)

D. B. YOUNG and D. A. YOUNG

In teacher training programs on campuses and in schools alike, microteaching is coming into its own. It is being used successfully in a wide variety of settings as a major teacher training technique in both pre-service and in-service programs. Descriptions in this article of exemplary programs in which microteaching is an integral part illustrate the many purposes it can serve.

At the University of Maryland microteaching is a major technique in a program that focuses on continuous educational personnel development. It is conducted in a unique teacher education centre, a cooperative effort of the university and several public schools that are geographically contiguous. Although it is coordinated by a full-time joint appointee, university personnel assume major responsibility for training centre personnel for significant roles in the induction of student teachers into full-time professional teaching.

One of the major problems in attempting to establish microteaching as a major component is a shortage of trained personnel to conduct microteaching sequences. A second problem is the availability of pupils. To bring them to the campus often presents a major logistical obstacle. The University of Maryland has overcome many such problems in the teacher education centre.

The major focus of work at the centre is analysis and modification of teaching behaviour. The instructional sequence is organized to prepare teachers to use Flanders's interaction analysis, Galloway's non-verbal continuum, and other systems for analysing teaching including microteaching, video tape feedback and simulation to

Reprinted from *Theory Into Practice*, 7 (1968), 5, pp. 186–9. D. B. Young is Director of the Educational Personnel Development Center, University of Maryland; D. A. Young is Nursery/Kindergarten University of Maryland College Park Instructor, Montgomery College.

modify behaviour. A major portion of the instruction is 'learning by doing' as centre teachers use the systems with student teachers.

Microteaching is being incorporated into the program at three points: junior year experiences, pre-student teaching in methods courses and concurrent with student teaching. The junior year experience consists of an observation to complement course work in psychology and human development and seminars with coordinators in teacher education centres. During these seminars, student teachers learn to use one or two basic teaching behaviours in a microteaching sequence. Prior to full-scale teaching, student teachers in several pilot projects are engaged in microteaching as a part of the 'methods' courses. Following discussion of the relationship of a given dimension of teacher behaviour to learning, student teachers identify specific teaching behaviours within that dimension and practise them in a microteaching sequence. For example, if the dimension of teaching behaviour is developing alternative teacher responses to a pupil's questions and responses to questions, comments and challenges, the following teaching behaviours would constitute the performance criteria:

1 Given a student question, comment or challenge, the teacher can respond with: (a) praise accompanied with criteria for the praise; (b) a clarification question; (c) a counter-example; (d) reproof with criteria; (e) acceptance of feeling of student; or (f) statements using or building upon the student contribution.

2 When the teacher responds to a pupil, he discriminates in choosing responses 'a' to 'f' by weighing: (a) student non-verbal communication of anxiety; (b) student level of thinking; and (c) student statement of fact or opinion.

3 Given a student comment, the teacher can summarize the student's comment accurately.

4 After a pupil's response, the teacher can withhold verbal comment.

5 While a pupil responds, the teacher can establish and maintain eye contact.

6 After a pupil's response, the teacher can discriminate between, select and administer reinforcement for correct answers.

7 Given a pupil's response, the teacher may: (a) probe the pupil for additional responses; (b) solicit a counter-proposal or

opinion; (c) non-verbally reinforce the answer or act of responding by writing the response on the chalkboard, smiling at the pupil, gesturing or nodding approval, approaching pupil, or physically contacting pupil; (d) solicit peer reinforcement of pupil's response; or (e) redirect the question to other pupils.

Microteaching sessions are conducted in the centre using students from study halls or related content classes. Sessions may also be conducted after school with volunteer pupils. Students assigned to the material centres operate the video tape units. Three types of conferences have been used – supervisor, supervisor and peer, and peer alone. In each, the conference focuses on developing and using the specified behaviour. In addition to viewing and discussing the teacher's performance, a video taped model may also be shown. The effectiveness of different conference strategies is currently being investigated.

During the student teaching experience in the centre, supervising teachers conduct microteaching sessions for student teachers who are experiencing difficulty with certain teaching behaviours or seeking to experiment or refine a particular teaching strategy.

At Johns Hopkins University, microteaching with video tape feedback is used to teach interns systems for self-analysis of teaching behaviour. Stressing such verbal and non-verbal classroom interaction provides continuous and individually prescribed training modules for the acquisition of teaching behaviours as well as graduated experiences prior to classroom teaching.

A microteaching clinic is conducted during the academic year preceding internship. Initially, each intern prepares and teaches a five-minute diagnostic lesson to four pupils. This performance is coded and analysed using Hough's Observation System and/or Medley and Mitzel's Observation Scale and Record. Based on this analysis and inventory, a series of four microteaching training modules are prescribed for acquisition of the selected behaviours. In each, the number of times the intern reteaches is not predetermined but depends on his success. Following this series of four, the intern again teaches a 'diagnostic' lesson, and another series of microteaching training modules are prescribed and conducted.

Microteaching sessions are held in private and public schools near the college campus. This not only alleviates the problem of obtaining pupils for the microclasses but interns become more familiar with the school environment. Prior to engaging in micro-teaching sequences, on-campus seminars are held to study the relationship of the designated teaching behaviours to pupil learning and to develop performance criteria. Constructed models of the behaviour provide a basis for developing the performance criteria and also become an integral part of the supervisor conference in the microteaching session.

Subsequent to these individualized sequences, each intern teaches a twenty-minute lesson to ten students to be analysed by his peers and retaught to a different group of pupils. The intern's next graduated experience is student teaching during the summer between the academic year and the internship. Microteaching sequences are arranged to provide the intern the opportunity to acquire additional teaching behaviours and/or to practise those behaviours with which he is experiencing difficulty.

Follow-up video tape feedback is also an integral part of the internship. This process applies some of the same basic principles. A portable video recording unit is used periodically to record the intern's classroom performance in order to analyse it, and a specific teaching behaviour is selected for practise in a subsequent class period. This performance is also recorded and a confirmation conference held. The follow-up recording and analysis are made of the same or a similar lesson but in a different class.

Besides use over a period of time in such extensive projects as the University of Maryland and Johns Hopkins University programs, microteaching has been incorporated effectively in a variety of short-term workshops and clinics. Several brief examples of use in such abbreviated settings follow.

In-service workshops. In Hinesville, Georgia, elementary teachers participated in a four-day workshop on teaching physical education, which focused on the intensive study of the 'content' of physical education. Instructors, representing the President's Council on Physical Fitness and the American Association for Health, Physical Education and Recreation, demonstrated and led the teachers in various 'learning by doing' instructional units in physical fitness activities, sports fundamentals, rhythmic movement, games and posture exercises. In addition, specific teaching behaviours were identified for teaching the various units. Concurrent with these instructional sessions, other teachers were microteaching.

Four teaching stations were arranged, each equipped with a

H

portable video tape recorder. All of the teachers paired and rotated a teacher/supervisor role.

Each teacher taught a lesson of his own choosing and then selected a teaching behaviour to practice and analyse during the ensuing conference and to reteach. Each taught in two micro-teaching sequences.

In-service days. In Howard County, Maryland, forty new teachers participated in a microteaching teach–reteach sequence during a one-day workshop. Four teaching stations with video tapes were arranged. Each teacher selected a topic and taught and retaught a group of four students. The teacher then selected a dimension of teaching behaviour and constructed specific criteria to use in analysis of his performance during the intervening critique. Selection of participants in the critique was at the teacher's option, and some chose a colleague and others a supervisor.

Training leadership teams. For a three-week conference sponsored by the National Science Foundation at the University of Maryland, microteaching was an integral part of a National Leadership Training Conference for teachers, supervisors, and university professors for the Earth Sciences Curriculum Project. The training program consisted of instruction on earth science, human factor analysis (a form of sensitivity training), and analysis and modification of teaching behaviour. Each was conducted concurrently throughout the three weeks.

Each team developed a set of performance criteria (specific teaching behaviours) for different aspects of the investigative approach, and each team member (teacher, supervisor, professor) prepared and taught a five-minute lesson on some segment of earth science to five junior high students. They rotated the roles of video recorder operator, supervisor and teacher. Each lesson was retaught to a different group of pupils following a conference which focused on the analysis of the performance using the specific criteria previously identified.

Although video tape recording is used in most of the programs described here, it is not requisite to conducting microteaching sessions. However, video tape feedback adds a potentially powerful dimension. Acheson and Olivero report that a conference with video tape feedback, compared with a conference without it, is significantly more effective in modifying a teacher's behaviour. When a supervisor and teacher discuss a lesson, many times they do not share the same mental or visual-auditory frame of reference. Not only do they typically have somewhat differing attitudes about the content but they also see and hear different things. This lack of a common frame of reference complicates an already difficult talk. However, video tape makes it possible to obtain a simple and objective record so that a supervisor and teacher can see, hear and analyse the same phenomena.

The teacher may also want a respected colleague to help him analyse his performance. This has not been practised extensively because it has not been feasible. Most teachers are teaching at the same time; however, with microteaching and a video recording, the two can sit down and view a lesson together. Besides giving them a common frame of reference, the important parts of the tape can be replayed as often as desired. There is great power for improvement in this type of vivid feedback and focused critique, and the very fact that colleagues are sitting down and discussing teaching together is of definite value to both.

Video tape recording provides the supervisor the means to provide discrimination training. As the video tape progresses, he can reinforce the teacher for each instance of the behaviour by stopping the tape and telling the teachers 'You did that well, let's watch it again'. He then replays that portion. Or, if the supervisor has noted in advance when he wants to reinforce the teacher, he can stop the tape and say 'Now, watch how well you respond to this student'. Also, without stopping the tape, the supervisor can reward the teacher as the lesson progresses.

Another technique is to have the teacher contrast a variety of his behaviour instances and reflect on their effectiveness, considering such things as the effect on pupils. The supervisor might also stop the tape following a given situation which is a cue for a teacher response and ask the teacher 'What could you do here?' The supervisor may want to prompt the teacher's response and/or suggest alternative behaviour.

One of the most promising training modes is to present a model to the teacher during the conference in the microteaching sequence. Two basic kinds of modelling have been developed – perceptual and symbolic.

A perceptual model refers to a video taped teaching episode which exaggerates a specific teaching behaviour. It is a constructed teaching–learning situation in a microteaching format. To prepare such a model, a teacher selects a topic and assembles a fifteen-minute lesson lending itself to the teaching skill to be modelled. The lesson is taught and retaught several times to different groups of pupils (normally four to five in number). On each occasion, as many distracting stimuli (behaviours other than the one desired) as possible are eliminated. The final modelled performance is usually five to seven minutes in length.

A symbolic model is a detailed written description of a specific teaching behaviour to be acquired by the teacher and includes examples of the behaviour and a rationale for its use.

Studies investigating the relative effectiveness of perceptual and symbolic modelling reveal that teachers and interns viewing a perceptual model incorporate more of the modelled teaching behaviour into subsequent teaching than when studying a symbolic model. But, a combination of the two modelling modes is more effective than either alone.

Both the perceptual and symbolic models have served as a basic format for modelling studies in teacher education. Research on imitation learning (modelling) in fields other than teacher education has indicated that it is an effective means of accelerating the learning process. In teacher education, modelling has been demonstrated as an effective training variable in modifying a teacher's behaviour in a microteaching sequence.

As an instrument which focuses on specific teaching skills, microteaching has many advantages. As these examples have shown, microteaching provides both the experienced and novice teacher the opportunity to analyse and modify teaching behaviour with or without the assistance of a colleague or supervisor. For the experienced teacher, it offers the opportunity to acquire and practise new teaching skills and to refine existing ones. For the novice participating in this approach, it can eliminate much of the trauma, discouragement and failure often accompanying a sudden immersion into the complexities of teaching.

References

Allen, D. W. and Ryan, K. A. (1965) *A new face for supervision*. Stanford University (mimeo).
Allen, D. W. and Young, D. B. (1967) 'Video tape techniques at

Stanford University'. *Television and related media in teacher education*, August. Baltimore: Multi-State Teacher Education Project.

Allen, D. W. *et al.* (1967) *A comparison of different modeling procedures in the acquisition of a teaching skill.* Paper presented at the annual meeting of the American Educational Research Association.

Bush, R. N. and Allen, D. W. (1964) *Microteaching, controlled practice in the training of teachers.* Stanford University (mimeo).

McDonald, F. J., Allen, D. W. and Orme, M. J. (1966) *The effects of self-feedback and reinforcement on the acquisition of a teaching skill.* Paper presented at the annual meeting of the American Education Research Association.

Orme, M. E. J. (1966) *The effects of modeling and feedback variables on the acquisition of a complex teaching strategy.* Doctoral dissertation, Stanford University.

White, F. J. (1968) *Observational learning of indirect verbal behavior through the medium of audio tapes.* Doctoral dissertation, University of Maryland.

Wodtke, K. H. and Brown, B. R. (1967) 'Social learning and imitation'. *Review of educational research*, 37, 514–38.

Young, D. B. (1968) 'Try microteaching with videotape feedback'. *Tennessee teacher*, 35, 7, 9 and 10.

Young, D. B. (1968) *The effectiveness of self-instruction in teacher education using modeling and videotape feedback.* Paper read at the annual meeting of the American Educational Research Association.

Young, D. B. (1968) *The analysis and modification of teaching behavior using microteaching and videotape feedback.* Paper presented at the National Association of Secondary School Principals' convention.

8 · The minicourse: a new tool for the education of teachers

W. R. BORG, P. LANGER and M. L. KELLEY

The three aspects of teacher education

Both in-service and pre-service training can be broadly classified into three major areas of instruction: (1) curriculum content, (2) professional knowledge and (3) classroom skills.

Curriculum content refers primarily to the 'subject matter' or course content that the teacher is expected to transmit to the pupil. During the training phase most content materials are presented through language and/or abstract symbols. Subsequently, in the classroom the teacher duplicates the instruction and evaluation processes received during training; that is, he teaches using language and/or symbols, and evaluates pupil performance with objective tests. Considering this marked similarity between the training process and the teacher activities in the classroom, it is small wonder that most teachers consider content courses the most useful part of their training.

Professional knowledge pertains to the pedagogical concepts and behavioural science principles teachers need in order to understand and deal with problems related to the pupil and the educational process. These concepts normally are taught in courses such as educational psychology, child development and educational evaluation. Unfortunately, far too often these courses are organized and presented as a body of theoretical-abstract principles, with trainee performance measured by paper and pencil tests stressing the acquisition of the content. The conceptual leap from the predominantly abstract-academic orientation of these courses to the grim performance realities of the classroom must be made by the teacher. Many teachers are unable to bridge this gap between theory and performance, and subsequently complain that these courses are of little practical value.

Reprinted from *Education* (February–March 1970), pp. 1–7.

Classroom skills, the third area in teacher education, deals with the specific teaching skills and behaviour patterns the teacher needs to function in the classroom. Such training is usually assigned to the so-called methods courses. In these courses the trainee is confronted with an unbridgeable gap between the content presented and the skills actually needed to teach effectively. Instructors in methods courses employ lecture and discussion techniques for the most part (Willis 1968) and it simply isn't possible to learn complex teaching skills by talking about them. What teachers get out of such courses is an academic knowledge about teaching.

But, the reader may argue, surely student teaching makes up for the deficiencies of 'methods courses'. This long cherished assumption is based more on fancy than fact. B. O. Smith (1969) in his perceptive blueprint for teacher education observes that '. . . student teaching is not training but a type of reality experience in which the individual learns by trial and error and by the inadequate direction that the supervising staff is able to give him. Student teaching came into being before the concept of training was developed and should be phased out as quickly as possible.' (page 102)

In a series of studies by Joyce (1969) he compared the performance of trainees at the beginning and end of student teaching. He found that student teachers actually became more direct and more punitive as a result of their student teaching experience. The reasons are not difficult to establish; student teaching traditionally consists of (1) observations of a supervising teacher who usually uses as many bad techniques as good ones, (2) practice teaching in which the learner has virtually no idea of what he is supposed to be practising, and (3) intermittent feedback from the supervising teacher and/or the college supervisor consisting mostly of undefined generalities which the learner cannot translate into specific classroom behaviour.

Having reviewed the current state of most teacher education programs, the staff of the Far West Laboratory for Educational Research and Development decided to concentrate on the classroom skills component. This decision was influenced by two major considerations: first, we believe that methods courses are relatively less effective in meeting their objective than are courses in the other two major components of teacher education.

Second, preliminary findings suggested that the microteaching technique being tried at Stanford University could be developed into a powerful tool for improving teacher performance.

The minicourse program

Thus, over the past three years, the Teacher Education Program of the Far West Laboratory for Educational Research and Development has focused a major research and development effort on developing and/or modifying specific classroom skills and behaviour patterns required for effective teaching. The instructional model around which the Laboratory has developed in-service training courses is an adaptation of the microteaching approach developed at Stanford University and employed in the Stanford Intern Program (Bush and Allen 1964, Allen and Fortune 1966). As developed at Stanford University, microteaching has the following basic characteristics: (1) the intern studies a specific teaching skill; (2) attempts to apply the skill in a short video taped lesson, usually five to ten minutes in length, with four or five pupils; (3) watches a replay of the lesson with a supervisor who provides feedback; (4) replans the lesson, reteaches it to another group of four or five pupils, and receives further feedback.

The in-service courses we are developing are called 'minicourses' to differentiate them from other instructional models that employ the microteaching approach. The minicourse model differs from the Stanford model in several ways. The minicourse model provides a self-instructional package that can be used in any school where a video tape recording system is available. The minicourse provides feedback through self-evaluation and/or peer interaction while the Stanford Intern Program employs supervisors to provide feedback. The minicourse relies heavily upon illustrations by model teachers rather than supervisory feedback to provide the trainee with an operational definition of the behaviour patterns or skills to be learned. Research evidence suggests that models are more effective than supervisory feedback, and, of course, their use makes it possible for the minicourse to be self-contained (Orme 1966). Our first minicourse, Minicourse 1, deals with twelve specific skills that a teacher in the intermediate grades can use to improve his use of questions in a discussion lesson (see Table 1). A review of the teacher's experiences during the first five days of the fifteen-day course will help clarify the minicourse instructional model.

On the first day an *Introduction* film is shown. This film describes microteaching and the minicourse. The teacher then receives a handbook which provides more information on the skills to be learned and contains forms to be used by the teacher in evaluating his performance during the course. A practice lesson is also provided to familiarize teachers with the microteaching technique. This lesson includes the *Practice Instructional* film and *Practice Model* film which give him specific classroom examples of the skills he is to learn. He then plans a microteaching lesson which incorporates these skills.

Table 1 Minicourse 1 skills

Instructional Sequence I

Skills Covered:
1 Ask question, pause 3 to 5 seconds, then call on pupil.
2 Deal with incorrect answers in an accepting, non-punitive manner.
3 Call on both volunteers and non-volunteers in order to keep all pupils alert and distribute participation.

Instructional Sequence II

Skills Covered:
4 Redirection – directing the same question to several pupils.
5 Framing questions that call for longer pupil responses.
   a) Ask for sets or groups of information when framing information level questions.
   b) Avoid yes–no replies.
6 Framing questions that require the pupil to use higher cognitive processes.

Instructional Sequence III

Skills Covered:
7 Prompting to improve a weak pupil response.
8 Seeking further clarification of the pupil's response.
9 Refocusing the pupil's response.

Instructional Sequence IV

Skills Covered:
10 Teacher should not repeat his questions.
11 Teacher should not answer his own questions.
12 Teacher should not repeat pupil answers.

On the second day the teacher conducts the practice microteaching lesson, records it on video tape and evaluates his performance using the objective self-evaluation forms provided in the Teacher Handbook.

On the third day the teacher views the first regular instructional film which describes three specific skills illustrated with scenes from classroom discussion sessions. The model film, which shows the teacher applying the three skills in the context of an ongoing lesson is then viewed. The teacher's attention is focused on the specific teaching skills as they occur in the model lesson. The teacher then prepares his first microteach lesson designed to apply the skills he has seen in the instructional and model films.

On the fourth day, the *microteaching session* is held. The teacher conducts the microteach lesson with five to eight of his own pupils and records it on video tape. After dismissing the pupils, the teacher replays the video tape and, using a check list, evaluates his performance on the specific skills. He then replans his lesson based on what he has learned.

On the fifth day the teacher reteaches his lesson with different pupils, recording it on video tape. Again he studies the replay and evaluates his own performance. Days three, four and five make up a complete sequence of instruction, microteaching and reteaching. Minicourse 1 is made up of four such sequences.

Advantages of the minicourse model

When compared with conventional teacher education programs, the minicourse model appears to have the following important advantages:

1 Minicourses are designed to provide a complete package that can be used in any school, regardless of local resources.
2 Since the teacher works with a short lesson and few students, he can try out new methods and ideas in a less difficult situation than that found in the regular classroom.
3 Microteaching gives the teacher a chance to learn teaching skills through actual practice. In Minicourse 1, for example, about 10 per cent of the course involves telling the teacher, 20 per cent involves showing the teacher and in the remaining 70 per cent the teacher is practising the skills and watching his own performance.
4 The teacher gets *immediate feedback* (much of it reinforcing) from the video tape replays of his teaching. Thus, he can promptly evaluate his progress, eliminate bad habits and more firmly establish the new methods he is learning.
5 Minicourses focus on *specific skills* rather than generalities.

The development of a minicourse

Building Minicourse 1 included four major development stages. In the first stage we searched the literature, defined our goals, developed an initial form of the course and conducted a preliminary field test to determine where improvements were needed. After the results of this preliminary field test had been evaluated, we revised the course and conducted our main field test. The purpose of the main field test was to determine whether the course achieved its objective of changing teacher performance in class discussion lessons. The results of the main field test, in turn, were used to make a third version of the course. This revision was used in the operational field test which is carried out in the schools without help from the Laboratory and is designed to determine whether the course package contains everything needed for operational use by public schools. The last stage of development involves making a final revision of the course based upon the operational field test results and preparing the course for production by a commercial publisher.

Do minicourses work?

The main field test provides us with the quantitative performance data we need to determine if the minicourse achieves its objectives. Forty-eight teachers in twelve schools participated in the main field test of Minicourse 1. Twenty-minute video tape recordings were made of each teacher conducting a discussion lesson with his entire class before and after taking the course. These tapes were then scored for the specific behaviour patterns the course was designed to change. One of the twelve skills, calling on both volunteers and non-volunteers, could not be scored because of technical problems. The other eleven techniques covered in Minicourse 1 were analysed, however, and the results are reported in Table 2.

The first skill reported, *redirection*, changed markedly. Redirection is the technique of framing questions in such a way that the question can be directed to several pupils rather than to a single pupil. For the forty-eight teachers in the main field test, the mean number of redirections made by teachers in the twenty-minute pre-course tapes was 26·69. On the post-course tapes, these teachers

Table 2 Analysis of Minicourse 1 pre-course video tapes and post-course video tapes (N = 48)

Behaviour compared	Pre-tape mean	Post-tape mean	t
1 Number of times teacher used redirection.	26·69	40·92	4·98***
2 Number of times teacher used prompting.	4·10	7·17	3·28***
3 Number of times teacher used further clarification.	4·17	6·73	3·01***
4 Number of times teacher used refocusing.	0·10	0·02	0·00(ns)
5 Number of times teacher repeated his/her own questions.	13·68	4·68	7·26***
6 Number of times teacher repeated pupil answers.	30·68	4·36	11·47***
7 Number of times teacher answered his/her own questions.	4·62	0·72	6·88***
8 Length of pupil responses in words (based on 5 minute samples of pre- and post-tapes).	4·63	11·78	5·91***
9 Number of 1-word pupil responses (based on 5 minute samples of pre- and post-tapes).	5·82	2·57[1]	3·61***
10 Length of teacher's pause after question (based on 5 minute samples of pre- and post-tapes).	1·93	2·32	1·90*
11 Frequency of punitive teacher reactions to incorrect pupil answers.	0·12	0·10	0·00(ns)
12 Proportion of total questions that called for higher cognitive pupil responses.	37·30	52·00	2·94**
13 Proportion of discussion time taken by teacher talk.	51·64	27·75	8·95***

[1] Means would have been approximately four times larger if entire tapes had been analysed, t-test would have been higher.
* = $p < 0.05$ ** = $p < 0.005$ *** = $p < 0.001$

used redirection an average of 40·92 times, an increase of about 50 per cent in the use of this specific technique.

Probing describes a class of techniques designed to lead the pupil to a more adequate or complete response. Minicourse 1 attempts to increase the teacher's use of three probing techniques. These are:

prompting, in which the teacher gives the pupil clues or asks him leading questions; *further clarification*, in which the teacher attempts to get the pupil to clarify, elaborate or explain his initial response, and *refocusing*, in which the teacher attempts to get the pupil to relate his initial response to other topics that the class has studied.

On the first two of these behaviours, although statistically significant differences were obtained, the magnitude of these changes is not very large from a practical standpoint. The next revision of Minicourse 1 was substantially strengthened in these areas. As for refocusing, the behaviour was virtually non-existent in either the pre-course or post-course tapes. In most discussion lessons, opportunities to use refocusing seem to be limited. The failure of the course to develop this skill may indicate that the mini-course model is not useful in shaping teacher behaviour that can be practised only infrequently in a microteaching lesson.

Let us now consider changes in three negative teacher behaviours which the course attempts to reduce or eliminate. These behaviours are *repeating the question, repeating the pupil's answer* and *answering one's own questions*. Repeating the question is generally considered a poor practice since it wastes discussion time and encourages pupil inattention. Repeating pupil answers also increases teacher talk and in addition conditions pupils to listen to the teacher rather than to one another since they can expect the pupil's answer to be repeated by the teacher.

The disadvantages of the teacher answering his or her own questions are obvious. If carried to an extreme, this behaviour results in the teacher giving a monologue rather than conducting a discussion lesson. The reader will note in Table 2 that all three of these poor practices were drastically reduced after teachers had completed the course.

Another objective of the course is to train teachers to ask questions that call for longer pupil responses and avoid questions that can be answered by a single word. The average word count of pupil responses nearly doubled on the post-course tapes. This increase was accompanied by a significant decrease in the frequency of one-word pupil replies.

The course is also designed to train teachers to pause for three to five seconds after asking a question and before calling on a pupil in order to give pupils time to think about their answers. Although a statistically significant gain was obtained, teachers did not change the length of their pause enough to make a practical improvement in this behaviour. Additional emphasis was placed upon this behaviour in the next revision of the course.

The course also attempts to reduce the teacher's use of punitive reactions to incorrect pupil answers. Virtually no instances of this teacher behaviour occurred on either the pre-course tapes or post-course tapes, suggesting that we were trying to eliminate a behaviour that rarely occurs (at least under video taping conditions).

Finally, the course attempts to increase the teacher's use of higher cognitive questions. Research (e.g. Floyd 1960) has demonstrated that many teacher questions require little of the pupil except the recall of isolated facts. Our analysis indicated that only 37·30 per cent of the teachers' pre-course questions called for higher cognitive processes, while on the post-course tapes higher cognitive questions increased to 52 per cent. (Questions not related to the discussion, such as procedural questions were not included in the analysis.)

One major objective of the course that relates to several of the specific skills taught is to reduce the percentage of time during class discussion when the teacher is talking. Previous studies have shown that teachers talk as much as 70 per cent of the time during class discussions, thereby severely restricting the amount of time available for pupil contributions (Floyd 1960, Adams 1964). Analysis of Minicourse 1 data revealed that the average teacher talked nearly 52 per cent of the time before the course and only 28 per cent after the course. Reducing teacher talk by nearly half resulted in a profound change in the discussion atmosphere on the post-course video tapes. Pupils were generally more interested and more willing to participate; direct interaction between pupils was more in evidence; and teachers no longer dominated and restricted the discussion.

In order to estimate the permanence of behaviour changes brought about by Minicourse 1, video tapes were made in April 1968 of the teacher who completed the main field test course the previous November. Analysis of the delayed post-course tapes indicated that only prompting decreased. Three skills were significantly increased, while the remaining skills were virtually unchanged by the nearly five-month interval. Since most learning studies report marked drops in performance after training has ceased, the permanence of the skills learned in Minicourse 1 seems quite remarkable.

In April 1970 a commercial version of Minicourse 1 became available from Macmillan Educational Services. Since the commercial revision incorporated many improvements over the main field test version, it seems likely that this revision will produce even greater changes in teacher performance than those reported herein.

Progress since Minicourse 1

The success of Minicourse 1 led to additional minicourses designed to test the generalizability of the instructional model across a wide variety of teaching skills. Four minicourses have been taken through our complete development cycle and are ready for commercial production The main field test data indicate that each of these courses brought about substantial changes in teaching skills under a wide variety of teaching conditions (Langer 1969).

In addition, several other minicourses are now undergoing preliminary and main field tests.

What of the future?

Several objectives loom large in the future of the Teacher Education Program. Two new courses are being developed, which involve substantial changes in the instructional model. These changes were necessitated by the recognition that not all skills can be taught effectively using the original microteach model.

Second, enough minicourses have been identified and developed to think in terms of a system of teacher training in the area of classroom skills and behaviour patterns. It is anticipated that within five years the Far West Laboratory will have developed courses that improve teaching skills in virtually all of those areas essential for maintaining an effective learning situation.

References

Adams, T. H. (1964) *The development of a method for analysis of questions asked by teachers in classroom discourse.* Doctoral dissertation, Rutgers State University.
Allen, D. W. and Fortune, J. C. (1966) 'An analysis of microteach-

ing: new procedure in teacher education'. In *Microteaching: a description*. Stanford University.

Bush, R. N. and Allen, D. W. (1964) *Microteaching – controlled practice in the training of teachers*. Paper presented at the Santa Barbara Conference on Teacher Education of the Ford Foundation.

Floyd, W. D. (1960) *An analysis of the oral questioning activity in selected Colorado primary classrooms*. Unpublished doctoral dissertation, Colorado State College.

Joyce, B. R. (1969) Personal letter to Dr W. R. Borg, Director, Teacher Education Program, Far West Laboratory for Educational Research and Development, 2 July.

Langer, P. (1969) *The range of teaching skills that can be changed by the minicourse model*. Paper presented at the meeting of the American Psychological Association.

Orme, M. E. (1966) *The effects of modeling and feedback variables on the acquisition of a complex teaching strategy*. Unpublished doctoral dissertation, Stanford University.

Smith, B. O. (1960) *Teachers for the real world*. Washington, D.C.: American Association of Colleges for Teacher Education.

Willis, D. E. (1968) 'Learning and teaching in methods courses, parts I and II'. *Journal of teacher education*, 19, 39–46.

9 · An approach to systematic training

B. O. SMITH

Teaching is a complex activity, although to the uninformed it appears so simple that anyone can do it. Its complexity lies in its different types of techniques: material, social, intellectual and emotional. Few, if any, other occupations involve all of these. The teacher handles materials such as books, projectors and other instructional products; these require skill in thing-techniques. The teacher also relates to a large number of people: pupils, colleagues, laymen, in highly significant ways and often at crucial points in their lives. To handle these relationships skilfully one must be a master of techniques of social interaction and of empathizing. The teacher is involved in the manipulation of ideas as they relate to the growth of the pupil. He can be successful at this only if he is, in fact, skilled in linguistic, logical and psychological techniques.

To acquire skill in these techniques taxes the capacity of the most talented individual. Very few people pick up more than a small repertory of them; the average person must work for years to acquire a few of these techniques. Even then he must often rely on bits and pieces he has picked up. It is generally believed that student teaching and field experiences are the most effective ways of acquiring these skills. For current programs this assessment is perhaps correct. But the belief that direct experiences, studied and analysed in seminars and supplemented by apprentice teaching, even under the best of supervisors, are the best way to produce the skills needed in the modern school testifies to the intellectual inertia of those of us who work in the field of teacher education. Today new things are possible.

Almost all teachers are now prepared in programs that provide little or no training in teaching skills. These programs consist of

Reprinted from B. O. Smith, *Teachers for the Real World* (Washington, D.C., American Association of Colleges for Teacher Education, 1969), pp. 69–79.

courses in the sociology and philosophy of education, learning theory and human development, and in information about teaching and management of the classroom. These are taught apart from the realities that the teacher will meet and are considered preparatory to student teaching. While student teaching usually comes after the formal courses, it frequently has little relationship to them, and is ordinarily inadequate preparation for the responsibilities given the beginning teacher. The trainee studies theories that lead nowhere, then does his teaching with little theoretical understanding of the situations he meets.

More recent programs, for example, the MAT (Master of Arts in Teaching) type programs, differ little from conventional ones, except in their disregard for theory. They reduce theoretical work to almost nothing and place great emphasis upon learning on the job. Concepts and principles are discussed in seminars, along with the trainee's problems and observations. These programs suffer from lack of thoroughness and from inadequate diagnostic and remedial techniques of training. The behaviour of the student teacher in a classroom situation cannot be described except from the student's memory or the supervisor's notes. This type of information is notoriously inadequate. The fact that the trainee's memory and the supervisor's record often do not coincide threatens their rapport. Inadequate information and conflicting views on what happened are not conducive to learning. Furthermore, these more recent programs incorporate the worst features of opportunistic instruction. The supervisor of the student teacher typically works without a systematic conceptual framework to help him analyse and guide the trainee's performance.

The belief that either of these programs provides for training rests on the gratuitous assumption that first hand experience and student teaching are training. At best, student teaching is a reality from which the trainee learns by trial and error and a minimum of feedback. The situations that arise in his teaching are fleeting in tenure and can be discussed only in retrospect. He cannot 'work through' the situations again to correct his behaviour because classroom work moves rapidly from situation to situation and no situation can be reinstated for the practice of a technique.

The absence of a training component in teacher education is perhaps its principal defect. This component has not been devised because theoretical courses combined with student teaching have been considered adequate in principle and because the essentials of training have not been explicitly thought through.

A concept of training

The college training of a teacher should take cognizance of two assumptions: first, the type of community in which he is to teach is not definitely known; and, second, training beyond the beginning level will be relied upon to provide him with skills that any specialized role will require. Minimal abilities which a program of teacher education should develop are the ability to:

1 Perform stimulant operations (question, structure, probe).
2 Manipulate the different kinds of knowledge.
3 Perform reinforcement operations.
4 Negotiate interpersonal relations.
5 Diagnose student needs and learning difficulties.
6 Communicate and empathize with students, parents and others.
7 Perform in and with small and large groups.
8 Utilize technological equipment.
9 Evaluate student achievement.
10 Judge appropriateness of instructional materials.

Each of these may be exhibited in a number of ways. A consideration of all of the abilities will disclose that each can be expressed in many different behaviours.

The understanding of these abilities, as noted earlier, is to be developed in the theoretical component of the program. But skill in the performance of these abilities should be developed in the training component. The focus of study in a training program is the trainee's own behaviour, not the content of courses or some model of performance. This is in sharp contrast with the theoretical component where it is the situation that is to be examined and understood. In training, it is the trainee's performance that will be observed, analysed and modified.

To train someone is to guide him to acquire a certain skill. The trainee is put in a situation where he can perform the skill, then is stimulated to perform it. His performance is analysed and assessed. He and the trainer suggest changes in his performance. The more acceptable performance is supported through reinforcement by the trainer. Reduced to its formal structure, the training process must include the following elements:

Establishment of the practice situation.
Specification of the behaviour.
Performance of the specified behaviour.
Feedback of information about the performance.
Modification of the performance in the light of the feedback.
Performance–feedback–correction–practice schedule continued until desirable skilfulness is achieved.

In order to train new teachers and to continue the training of those in service, it is necessary to design a program and sets of training materials that will incorporate each of the above elements.

Training situations

Training always takes place in specially designed situations. The two main kinds of training situations are real and simulated. Real situations are used where it is possible to repeat the basic elements of a situation without resorting to role playing. Almost all instructional situations can be of this type. For example, the trainee can be told to teach spelling words to five or six assembled children. All the elements in this situation are genuine. No part of it has to be acted out. Situations are simulated when a real situation is not possible. It is impossible, for example, to have a discipline problem arise at will. This must be set up artificially.

Either of these two types of situations occurs in two forms: one in which the performance of the trainee is specified, and one in which the performance is suggested but not specified. The difference between specified and unspecified forms is the degree to which the trainee's behaviour is prescribed. In the specified form, the technique is prescribed as exactly as possible. In unspecified situations, the technique is left to the trainee. If the trainee is inexperienced and insecure, the technique could at first be carefully prescribed so that he learns acceptable techniques with little confusion. This highly controlled situation may also be used to develop skills that have a high incidence of success and where there is no point in letting the trainee work them out for himself.

The unspecified form of situation allows flexibility for the trainee and is more like the school situation. This sort of practice situation is more appropriate after the trainee has acquired several modes of behaviour and feels at ease in the training situation. The kind of condition with which the student is to begin cannot be specified apart from the circumstances in a particular case. A few examples will help clarify the above distinctions. Consider the following controlled simulated situation:

> A group of disadvantaged children is assembled, some half dozen. The teacher in training is told to present a given explanation to the group. One member of the group has been asked to make a drumming noise on his desk as the teacher is working with them. The specified behaviour is a task focus-technique in which the teacher recognizes the noise and directs attention to the need to complete the work.

This simulated situation could easily be converted into one with a high degree of flexibility by simply not specifying the technique.

Consider next a real situation in which the behaviour is prescribed:

> A group of disadvantaged children is assembled and the teacher is told that he is to teach a particular concept. The prescribed behaviour of the teacher is as follows. Present three characteristics that identify the concept. Then present two instances of the category and mention two or three other objects, some belonging to the category and some not. Ask the pupils which of the objects is included in the concept.

It is clear that this situation is highly structured. But it would be flexible were the trainee told to teach the particular concept and decide the procedure for himself.

A fully developed program of training requires a massive supply of situations prepared with far more care than was taken in the cases above. It is not easy to find training situations in educational literature. The following examples are taken from research literature and approximate the sort of elaboration that an instructional program would require.

Example 1

This practice situation partially develops the ability to perform stimulant operations by giving practice in four skills. These are skills in inducing pupils to clarify, in evoking critical awareness, in refocusing pupil response and in prompting.

Today you will have an opportunity to develop skills in basic classroom questioning techniques. The session is designed to help you extend the range and quality of your questioning techniques in such a way that the pupils you teach are led to think more deeply about problems raised in class.

The techniques outlined below are designed to be used in discussion, review and inductively organized lessons where active pupil participation is prerequisite to the realization of the goals of instruction. Any given technique may be appropriate in one situation but not in another. The selection of a particular technique depends upon the extent to which, in your judgement, it requires the pupil to analyse a problem critically or to justify rationally his answer. Do not use a given technique unless you feel it contributes to the educational relevance of the lesson.

Your goal is to ask penetrating and probing questions that require pupils to go beyond superficial, 'first-answer' responses.

Basic questioning techniques: There are two ways of achieving the above goal: (1) The teacher asks penetrating questions that require pupils to get at the heart of the problem. This forestalls superficial answers. Whether you are able to do this largely depends upon your knowledge of relevant content. (2) The second approach is based on specific techniques that may be used *after* the pupil has responded in some way (i.e. a question, a comment, an answer to a teacher's question). The goal here is to get the pupil to go beyond his first response. You are attempting to produce greater critical awareness and depth by *probing*. Your cue is the pupil's response – once it has occurred, don't immediately go on with the discussion yourself. *Probe* his answer by means of one of the techniques outlined below.

I *Teacher seeks further clarification by the pupil:* You may ask the pupil for more information and/or more meaning. You may respond to the pupil's responses by saying such things as:
   a 'What do you mean?'
   b 'Could you put that in other words to make clearer what you mean?'
   c 'Can you explain that further?'
   d 'What do you mean by the term . . .?'

II *Teacher seeks increased pupil critical awareness:* Here you are requiring the pupil to justify his response rationally. You may say:

a 'What are you/we assuming here?'
b 'Why do you think that is so?'
c 'Have we/you oversimplified the issue – is there more to it?'
d 'Is this one or several questions?'
e 'How would someone who took the opposite point of view respond to this?'

III *Teacher seeks to refocus the pupil's response:* If a pupil has given a high quality answer, it may seem unnecessary to *probe* it. However, you can *refocus* his or the class's attention on a related issue.
a 'Good! What are the implications of this for . . .?'
b 'How does this relate to . . .?'
c 'Can you take it from there and tie it into . . .?'

IV *Teacher prompts pupil:* In *prompting* you are giving the pupil a hint to help him go on and answer a question. Suppose a pupil has given an I-don't-know or I'm-not-sure type of response. Rather than giving him the answer or redirecting the question to another pupil, you may give the puzzled student a hint.
Teacher: 'John, define the term "polygenesis".'
John: 'I can't do it.'
Teacher (*prompting*): 'What does poly mean?' Or, 'Well, genesis means origin or birth, and poly means . . .?'
This technique allows you to *probe* even though at first it appears that the pupil can't answer the question.

V *Redirect:* This is not the *probing* technique *per se*. It helps you bring other students into the discussion quickly while still using *probing* techniques. In *redirecting*, you merely change the direction of interaction from yourself and the first pupil to yourself and the second pupil.
Teacher: 'What is the relationship between pressure and volume?'
First pupil: 'As the pressure goes up, the gas is condensed.'
Teacher: (to second pupil) 'Can you tell us what is meant by condensed?' Or, 'Can you restate that in terms of volume?'

To sum up, the techniques outlined above have two things in common:

1 They are initiated by the teacher immediately after the pupil has responded.

2 They require the pupil to go beyond the information he has already given.

Concluding remarks: Try to use the techniques as frequently as you can. Do not stay with one given technique for too long at one time. In addition, don't forget to reinforce when you *probe* – if you are not at ease you may otherwise behave like a 'Philadelphia lawyer'.

If you prefer to run through the first five-minute lesson as a warm-up, this would be fine. You may teach the same lesson over two or three times. We will focus more on *probing* than on transmitting new or complex material. The maximum amount of time for the session will be two hours (McDonald and Allen 1967).

Example 2
This situation contributes to the development of the ability to diagnose pupils' needs and errors. The skill is in identifying errors in long division and in prescribing remedial measures.

Ten examples in long division solved by a pupil in the fifth grade are given to the trainee. He is asked to study the pupil's work and to identify the errors and indicate what he would do to remedy the pupil's tendency to make these mistakes.

The trainee's prescriptions may be evaluated by the trainer as being totally relevant, moderately relevant, or not relevant (Turner 1960).

Example 3
This example may be used to develop the ability to judge appropriateness of materials. The skill is in judging the proper level of reading books for different pupils. The instructions to the trainee are:

You are the teacher of Paul, Pam, Richard and Connie. You are to select books for instruction in the classroom. You will hear each child read aloud (via video recording) the three selections which he has just finished reading silently. After each selection, decide if the material is too easy, appropriate, or too hard for that child's instruction in the classroom.

The number of words miscalled (say, one error for twenty running words) may be used as a rough criterion of difficulty in discussions with the trainee. But the cues used by the trainee should be focal points of discussion in the feedback sessions (Wade 1961).

These situations can be used with children of all cultural backgrounds and social origins. The first example is perhaps more suitable for training junior and senior high school teachers than for elementary teachers, although with appropriate modifications it could be used with teachers of the intermediate grades.

Many types of training exercises must be devised. Some are scattered through the pedagogical literature, and many have yet to be formulated. Perhaps one or two additional examples will give a rough idea of possible variations. An audio or video recording can be made of verbal exchanges in the classroom. The responses of the teacher to what pupils say can be cut out. As an illustration, consider the following excerpt from a tape recording:

Teacher: 'And crimes are classified in what way?'
Pupil: 'Well, the first one would be treason. Treason, and there is felony, and misdemeanours.'
Teacher: 'What's the meaning of treason?'
Pupil: 'There are two subdivisions – sabotage or something like that.'
Teacher: . . . .

The trainees can be asked to make the next response to the pupil. These responses will vary, and their probable effects on the pupils can be discussed. On the basis of the discussion, the trainees may devise practice exercises to find out how pupils do actually respond to what they say.

To give another instance, much of the standard instructional material is probably inadequate for disadvantaged children. The teacher-to-be must learn to distinguish the material suitable for them. Perhaps his training should begin with judging the instructional utility of visual materials such as films and slides. Assume that he has been associated with a group of deprived children in other training situations. On the basis of his knowledge of them, the trainee would be asked to select a film or set of slides to be shown to the group. If the responses of the children are good, the instructor helps the trainee identify the qualities that made the materials effective. If the materials evoke negative or indifferent responses, the trainee would then study the materials, decide what his error was, discuss his ideas with the instructor, then test them by trying other selections.

The situations should cover a wide range of social backgrounds. Here are but a few illustrations of what some of these situations might entail: There should be training situations in which the trainee learns to talk with parents who were themselves failures in school and who now see no purpose in schooling for their children. He should learn to talk with parents who have hopes for their children but cannot articulate them, or who do not see how their hopes can be realized because of the discriminations and social circumstances of their lives. The training situation should provide for the development of skills for the teacher-to-be to identify himself with children who are educationally and socially disadvantaged, and to recognize when a child feels discriminated against.

The curriculum procedure implicit in the training plan set forth here is simple and can be analysed into the following phases:

1 The job of teaching is analysed into the tasks that must be performed.
2 The abilities required for the performance of these tasks must be specified.
3 The skills or techniques through which the abilities are expressed must be clearly described.
4 Training situations and exercises for the development of each skill must be worked out in detail.
5 Training situations and exercises should be classified and indexed by tasks, abilities, skills, grade levels, fields of instruction and backgrounds of children.

The responsibility for the development of these training materials cannot be left solely to individual colleges and universities. The task is too great and the staff time and resources required are more extensive than a single institution can afford. The preparation of an adequate supply of instructional materials for the training of teachers can be done successfully – this must be emphasized – only by a massive effort supported by federal and state funds and incorporating the participation of universities, colleges, public schools and the professional organizations of teachers.

The purpose of this supply of training situations is to increase the trainer's options and to provide an orderly program in which each ability receives proper emphasis. The resourceful training instructor will often devise new situations and adapt the ready-made ones to his liking.

There is now no set of training situations available to teacher educators. There are lists of objectives, tests for assessing the cognitive achievement and attitudes of trainees, and scales for rating their teaching behaviour. There are all kinds of pretentious models for teacher education. But there are no materials to be used in actually training the teacher. As a result, the training of the teacher is carried on intuitively, haphazardly, and with little regard for the spectrum of abilities the trainee should have. If a person is poorly trained and must deal with problems by trial and error in complex and swiftly moving events, as in a classroom, he probably will be unhappy in his work. This fact, noted earlier, is perhaps related to the number of teachers who are dropouts from their profession.

Training and the principle of feedback

More is needed than just practice of a technique in a training situation if skill in its performance is to be developed. Feedback is also necessary. Many years ago Thorndike showed that not only practice but awareness of the consequences of one's behaviour is necessary to its improvement. The current term is not 'awareness of the consequences' but 'feedback', a term taken from the study of servo-mechanisms.

When the sensitive teacher observes the effects of his actions in the faces, postures, eyes and speech of the children, he is receiving feedback. What he does next is influenced by this information. When the teacher assesses an action and decides how to do it better or to try something else, he is acting in the light of feedback. The teacher who is not trained to observe the effects of his behaviour does it intuitively and crudely.

The teacher also emits cues. These cues function in teaching because they are taken by pupils as indications of the teacher's attitudes. The posture of the teacher, the look in his eyes or the frown on his face tell the pupil about his feelings and intentions. Feedback is at least a two-way track.

The trainee must be taught to analyse the teaching-learning situation as he teaches. This is too important to leave its improvement to chance. His ability to analyse the situation will largely determine the content of the feedback. He will learn how to analyse situations from his study of protocol materials involving diagnosis and reinforcement in the theoretical component of his training. This will be developed further in the training situations worked out for techniques of analysis and reinforcement.

This sort of feedback might be called primary feedback. It is what the teacher tells himself from his observations of what is going on about him. But there is another kind of feedback – a secondary kind. It comes from others and, in the training situation, from the teacher trainer. The instructor encourages, approves and criticizes the trainee's performance. He uses the principle of feedback to shape the trainee's behaviour to the specifications of the technique.

The kinds of feedback discussed above cannot be planned in advance as can the training situations. Neither trainees nor pupils will respond in the same way from one performance to another. Therefore, the information that can be fed back to the trainee cannot be predetermined. How, then, can the training instructor use the principle of feedback to help him shape the trainee's performance (McDonald and Allen 1967)? He can use this principle only if he has a record of the trainee's practice sessions. The teacher trainer must see that audio and video recordings of the trainee's behaviour are made for more careful study. By analysing the recorded material, the trainer can decide what aspects of the trainee's behaviour are to be reinforced and how to do this. The teacher trainer would need to analyse the behaviour of the trainee and pupils as it occurred on the recording before he begins to help the trainee improve his performance. From his study of the materials, the trainer would be able to raise questions that would help the trainee reflect upon his behaviour. The trainer could also reinforce or extinguish the way certain questions were asked or the way the trainee responded to the behaviour of the pupil.

Another way the consequences of the trainee's behaviour could be fed back to him is by use of video tapes and films that present a high degree of skill in the performance of the technique. Viewing his own video recordings and comparing them with the more skilled performance, the trainee could modify his own teaching behaviour (McDonald and Allen 1967). The trainee should not imitate a model, nor study *it* instead of his own behaviour, but gather information from it that will help him examine and change his behaviour.

It has been shown in a number of studies that immediate feedback is more effective than delayed feedback. But this principle does not hold when the performance of the trainee can be replayed through tape and film. If a practice session is video taped and played back to the trainee several days or weeks later, the effects are as great as if the feedback had immediately followed the original performance (McDonald and Allen 1967). The video recording is able to recreate the situation so vividly that the trainee can relive it and profit from the feedback. This allows the trainer to study the behaviour of the trainee before discussing it with him. Feedback is only as good as the monitoring.

Moreover, successive practice sessions are a source of primary feedback for the teacher trainer. They give him an opportunity to assess the effectiveness of his training techniques.

Objections and answers

At least three objections may be raised against the view of teacher training presented here. The first is that the term 'training' is a bad word. To those who suffer from semantic afflictions, it is an insult to human intelligence because training is used to teach tricks to animals. To others 'training' means a mechanical performance without a strong basis in theory. Training a teacher supposedly violates his individuality and makes him incapable of operating as a self-determining agent; it cripples his innovative capacity. This is a strange position because it is contradicted by everything known about training in other occupations. The trained surgeon or aeroplane pilot will perform his duties more successfully in an emergency than anyone else. A trained individual has relaxed control which frees him from preoccupation with immediate acts so he can scan the new situation and respond to it constructively. Training and resourcefulness are complementary, not antithetical, elements of behaviour.

The second objection is that there are not enough tested techniques to form the basis of an explicit program. No one can deny that the effectiveness of most teaching skills has yet to be proved. These skills have been distilled from practical experience, enriched by research in psychology and philosophy; but only a few, such as techniques of teaching reading, spelling and typing, have been developed by research. The least dependable techniques can be weeded out with practical experience and theoretical knowledge. The remainder will be the initial stock of a viable store of pedagogical techniques. Research workers can test the effects of these techniques when there is a dependable way of training teachers. The effectiveness of skills cannot be established experimentally until teachers can be trained to perform them. Objecting to a training program because of lack of tested techniques is the same as denying the efficacy of any training program at all.

In the third place, it can be objected that the program of training proposed here has not been shown to be empirically superior to other ways of producing teachers. Of course this point is readily admitted. But this is a defeatist argument that carries little weight except in the field of education where it is the refuge of the 'stand-patter'. Had it been listened to in other fields, progress would have been impeded just as it will be in teacher education. Nevertheless, some aspects of this program do have experimental support. It has been shown that feedback affects what the teacher and trainee do and that it is most effective when the trainee is aware of the behaviour to which it is relevant (McDonald and Allen 1967). It is also evident from research and practical experience that the abilities listed in the early part of this chapter are in fact those that teachers use as they teach, however crudely they may be performed.

But there is no conclusive evidence that any program of teacher training is superior to another, just as there is no conclusive evidence of a superior way to train physicians or engineers. So it is the better part of wisdom to provide explicit programs and carefully designed training materials, and to rely as little as possible upon haphazard instruction and incidental learning. Systematic instruction is a far better basis for subsequent self-correction and growth in skills.

References

McDonald, F. J. and Allen, D. W. (1967) *Training effects of feedback and modeling procedures on teaching performance*. Stanford University.

Turner, R. L. (1960) *Problem solving proficiency among elementary school teachers II: teachers of arithmetic, grades 3–6*, Indiana University.

Wade, E. W. (1961) *Problem solving proficiency among elementary school teachers III: reading, grades 2–5*, Indiana University.

10 · The teacher education centre: a unified approach to teacher training

UNIVERSITY OF MARYLAND

The teacher education centre concept is a unified approach to the study of teaching and supervision. It is a coordinated program of pre-service and in-service experiences planned and administered cooperatively by the University of Maryland and the public school system. The program is designed so as to serve the needs and interests of the experienced professional as well as those of the inexperienced undergraduate student. An individualized approach makes it possible for each to become a *student of teaching* in accordance with his own particular stage of professional development. Organizationally, a teacher education centre is a cluster of two or three geographically contiguous elementary schools or a cluster of one or two junior high schools and a senior high school.

Coordinating the continuing career development program in each centre is a full-time teacher education centre coordinator who is jointly selected and employed by the University and the public school. Generally, his role is to plan an effective program of laboratory experiences for the University students assigned to the centre schools and to coordinate an in-service program for the centre staff who work with these students.

Development

The teacher education centre concept began with conversations between the University of Maryland and the adjoining public school systems. The impetus came from a mutual desire on the part of the

Reprinted from *The Teacher Education Center: A Unifying Approach to Teacher Education*, edited by J. F. Collins (Office of Laboratory Experiences, College of Education, University of Maryland, undated, mimeo).

University and the public schools to develop a more effective teacher education program, a program that would articulate, and in fact integrate, theory with practice and bring together the pre-service and the in-service components in such a way that a unified and continuous teacher education program evolves. It was recognized from the beginning that, if this was to be accomplished, the public school must assume earlier and increased responsibility for the pre-service aspects of teacher education and the University must assume an increased and continuing responsibility for the in-service aspects.

In the numerous planning and policy forming sessions that preceded the opening of these centres, it was agreed that the school system would provide the facilities, the instructional staff and half the salary of the centre coordinators. The University agreed to provide resource consultants, a tuition-free sequence of courses designed to develop a resident staff of *teacher education associates*, and half the salary of the centre coordinators.

Procedures and organizational patterns were also established for the joint identification and selection of centre schools and centre coordinators.

In the fall of 1966 five teacher education centres, two secondary and three elementary, were opened in Montgomery County. One of these centres, Kemp Mill Elementary School, also had the distinction of becoming a part of the Multi-State Teacher Education Project.

In each centre a full-time person who qualified by virtue of exceptional training and experience was jointly employed to coordinate the continuous teacher education program. Although coordinators can be selected from the school system or the University or from outside the public school or the University, all of the initial appointments were selected from public school personnel.

Program

The teacher education centre concept encompasses both pre-service and in-service staff development. The pre-service component consists of *intensive* and *extensive* experiences.

Student teachers have intensive ongoing experiences wherein they gradually assume major instructional responsibilities. These experiences vary in number, duration, subject matter, grade level and ability groupings depending upon needs, interests and developmental patterns of the individual student. Interspersed between these intensive experiences are a number of extensive experiences designed to give the student a broad and comprehensive view of teaching. The extensive experiences can vary from short observations to longer periods involving limited participation. These are carefully planned as to the needs, the interests and the strengths of the individual and the resources of the centre. With careful scheduling and planning, the resources of the centre, the school system and the University are unified into a meaningful pattern of developmental experiences.

By providing the student teacher with the opportunity to associate and work with many faculty members, he is exposed to a variety of models as opposed to a single model. For example, student teachers may teach specific lessons in fields other than their area of specialization, teach at other grade levels and devote substantial time to 'focused' observation in order that they may discover the variety of teaching strategies employed by the teachers in the centre. The extensive phase may also include microteaching sequences for skill development, video tape feedback of classroom teaching and inter-school and inter-centre exchanges of student teachers.

The centre coordinator coordinates the development of an in-service program reflecting the needs and interests of the faculty. Both the resources of the University and of the school district are utilized by the centre coordinator as he develops this program. The in-service component encompasses both a 'formal' instructional program and 'informal' conferences with resource consultants from the University who assist in the development of curriculum and supervisory procedures.

The 'formal' program is specifically designed to assist the teacher in his efforts to become a better and more effective teacher as well as a better and more effective teacher of teachers. A sequence of instruction is offered which has as its goal establishing the staff of the teacher education centre as *associates* in teacher education. This sequence emphasizes the analysis and modification of teacher behaviour, an examination of the research in teacher education and allied fields, the use of multi-media and educational technology, assessment of behavioural change and the general skills required in conferencing with student teachers.

I

Objectives

The ultimate objective is a joint sovereignty for teacher education between the University of Maryland and the public school systems. The specific objectives which have been accomplished are listed below:

1 Eleven centres have been established in four school systems with a jointly appointed full-time coordinator in each centre.
2 The first three courses of a sequence preparing teacher education associates have been organized.
3 The Teacher Education Centre staff is assuming increasing responsibility for the supervision of pre-service students.
4 Individualized student teaching programs are providing a wide variety of models and experiences for University students.
5 The professional sequence for preparing teacher education associates is being expanded into a sixth-year program.
6 Media to record, analyse and modify teaching and supervisory behaviour is being developed for regular use by teachers.
7 Microteaching is being utilized.
8 A school–university coordinating committee has been established.
9 The teaching of undergraduate methods courses as an integrated part of the field experience is being tried experimentally.
10 The recognition of supervising teachers in released time and loads is being seriously considered with some minimal progress.

Personnel

The development of the teacher education centre concept has created new roles and necessitated a redefinition of existing roles of both the University and the public school.

The *Centre Coordinator* is equally and simultaneously a staff member of both the University and the public school. In coordinating the pre-service and in-service program, he unifies the interests, the resources and the ambitions of both institutions and enhances the attainment of mutual objectives. A more detailed description of his role appears in the exhibits.

Supervising Teachers include all teachers who are involved in guiding intensive experiences and/or extensive experiences. Their role is greatly expanded beyond that of the conventional supervising teacher. Since the entire centre is a 'classroom', the strengths of every teacher become available in some manner for the development of the prospective teacher. Supervision becomes a team effort in a very real sense.

The term *University Resource-Consultant Supervisor* represents an extension of the role of the conventional University supervisor. He serves as a curriculum and subject matter consultant, as well as a teacher education specialist to the centre staff.

Budget

Teacher education centres have been established without additional funding. The customary honorarium paid to cooperating teachers has been diverted to staff development. These monies are used to recognize supervising teachers by providing University courses and workshop credit, consultant services to the in-service program, and sending selected centre staff members to professional meetings and conferences.

Evaluation and research

Preliminary research indicates that student teachers placed in teacher education centres hold more socially desirable attitudes towards supervision from University faculty members than students in non-centre schools. Centre student teachers also rate the evaluative criteria used by college supervisors as clearer and more adequately communicated than do non-centre students.

Centre students participate more widely in the total school program and become involved in a greater diversity of experiences. Student teachers in centres also use a greater variety of instructional approaches than students in non-centre schools.

Student teachers are being randomly assigned to centres and non-centres in order to compare their teaching performance and attitudes.

Although student teachers typically become more closed minded, apathetic and resistant to change, students in teacher education centres do not. They seem to maintain the same general attitudes at the close of student teaching as they possessed at the beginning.

An analysis of the teaching performance data of the two groups indicates that student teachers in centres teach differently (statistically significant) from the non-centre group.

Centre student teachers talk less, elicit more pupil responses and extended pupil initiated responses, use, summarize and accept more pupil responses, and have a higher indirect–direct ratio as indicated by Flanders's Interaction Analysis. They also ask more divergent and elaborating questions as indicated by the OScAR 5V.

The teacher education centre also provides a site for the study of teaching and supervision. Research is being conducted to test the efficacy of various procedures (modelling, video tape feedback, etc.) for modifying both teacher and supervisory behaviour using the classroom and/or microteaching format.

In addition to the above formal studies, an ongoing evaluation program is being conducted jointly by the University of Maryland and the public school system.

Contributions to teacher education

Full implementation of the ideas embodied in the centre concept will ultimately establish a new kind of joint sovereignty for teacher education shared by colleges, state departments of education, public schools and professional associations.

A list of the implications of the University of Maryland teacher education centre concept can be found below:

1 An integration of the on-campus and the off-campus aspects of teacher education programs.
2 The assumption of greater responsibility for the pre-service component of teacher education by the public schools, and for the in-service component by the University.
3 A new position shared equally between the public schools and the University of Maryland.
4 The emergence of a new role for the college supervisor.
5 The assumption of greater direct financial responsibility for the preparation of teachers by state departments of education in the form of adjusted state-aid programs.
6 The abolishment of honoraria to cooperating teachers with the subsequent adjustment of regular salaries and/or faculty loads.
7 An increasing concern for teacher education skills in the employment of public school teachers.
8 The emergence of levels of pre-professional status and de-lineation and a clarification of the levels of professional status.

9 The strengthening of in-service teacher education programs.
10 The emergence of the supervised teaching internship as the usual practice rather than the exception.
11 Teacher certification will come after the successful completion of a supervised intern experience.
12 An uninterrupted, carefully planned, sequential transition from entry into the profession to full advanced professional status.
13 The emergence of standards for off-campus clinical teacher education centres.

University of Maryland Summer School, 1969

(The University also runs summer schools for college and school personnel engaged in pre-service or in-service teacher education. The programme for the school of 1969 will give an idea of the type of activity that the University is engaged in.)

Microteaching	The focusing on specific teaching behaviours via a scaled down teaching encounter utilizing a teach–reteach cycle sequence with an intervening supervisory session.
Interaction analysis	The analysis of audio and video taped teaching performance using verbal and non-verbal interaction analysis systems, e.g. Flanders, Withall, Hough, Gallagher–Aschner.
Specific teaching and supervisory behaviour	The identification of specific teaching and supervisory behaviour and development of performance criteria for those behaviours applicable to the participant's situation.
Micro-supervision	The development of specific supervisory strategies in a microteaching setting.
Self-instructional models	The preparation of model video and/or audio tapes featuring a specific teaching or supervisory behaviour.
Media in teacher education	The assessment of a multi-media approach to supervision.
Simulation	The utilization of simulated teaching and supervisory experiences.
Research	The review of research on teaching and teacher education.

12

11 · The Stanford Teacher Competence Appraisal Guide

STANFORD UNIVERSITY

This Appraisal Guide defines the major teacher competences which the program of secondary teacher education at Stanford aims to develop. The total program of teacher education focuses on growth towards these standards as the common target.

To determine whether the program produces the desired growth, levels of competence must be appraised. Evidence for such appraisals may come from the trainee himself, from experienced teachers and administrators who supervise in the schools, from University teachers who instruct the trainees, and from the pupils taught.

This Appraisal Guide has been designed to assist in a cooperative effort to assess and to improve levels of competence in teaching. The basic sources of evidence are direct observations of the teacher followed by conferences and discussions related to observations. Secondary sources are communications with others who are in a position to observe and to know the teacher's work. The guide encourages the teacher (1) to accept with confidence his proper responsibility for continual self-improvement as a practising professional in his specialty, and (2) to contribute to the ongoing enquiry and the guiding body of theory by which he and his peers seek excellence in their area or specialty subject matter.

Purposely the guide avoids a rigid formula by defining thirteen general practitioner competences, around which departmental specialists may build specific standards of expert practices appropriate to subject matter, grade levels and groupings of pupils. The teacher being appraised is a most important one of these specialists and should be encouraged to participate in defining and improving standards for his specialty. Self-appraisals followed by observation

Reprinted from the *Stanford Teacher Competence Appraisal Guide*, by the School of Education, Stanford University.

and conferences with fellow teachers within a department will be useful to teachers as they accept increasing responsibility for self-improvement.

The conference following each observation stresses cooperative sharing of perceptions and ideas between professional teachers focused on the target of improving teaching, supervising and learning. To facilitate this communication, the conference record is provided in duplicate so both participants may have copies for future use.

Aims	**1**	**Clarity of aims**	The purposes of the lesson are clear.
	2	**Appropriateness of aims**	The aims are neither too easy nor too difficult for the pupils. They are appropriate, and are accepted by the pupils.
Planning	**3**	**Organization of the lesson**	The individual parts of the lesson are clearly related to each other in an appropriate way. The total organization facilitates what is to be learned.
	4	**Selection of content**	The content is appropriate for the aims of the lesson, the level of the class, and the teaching method.
	5	**Selection of materials**	The specific instructional materials and human resources used are clearly related to the content of the lesson and complement the selected method of instruction.
Performance	**6**	**Beginning the lesson**	Pupils come quickly to attention. They direct themselves to the tasks to be accomplished.
	7	**Clarity of presentation**	The content of the lesson is presented so that it is understandable to the pupils. Different points of view and specific illustrations are used when appropriate.
	8	**Pacing of the lesson**	The movement from one part of the lesson to the next is governed by the pupils' achievement. The teacher 'stays with the class' and adjusts the tempo accordingly.
	9	**Pupil participation and attention**	The class is attentive. When appropriate the pupils actively participate in the lesson.
	10	**Ending the lesson**	The lesson is ended when the pupils have achieved the aims of instruction. There is a deliberate attempt to tie together the planned and chance events of the lesson and relate them to the immediate and long range aims of instruction.
	11	**Teacher-pupil rapport**	The personal relationships between pupils and the teacher are harmonious.
Evaluation	**12**	**Variety of evaluative procedures**	The teacher devises and uses an adequate variety of procedures, both formal and informal, to evaluate progress in all of the aims of instruction.
	13	**Use of evaluation to improve teaching and learning**	The results of evaluation are carefully reviewed by teacher and pupils for the purpose of improving teaching and learning.
Community & professional	**14**	**Concern for professional standards and growth**	The teacher helps, particularly in his specialty, to define and to enforce standards (1) for selecting, training and licensing of teachers and (2) for working conditions, tools and equipment necessary for efficient and effective practice.
	15	**Effectiveness in school staff relationships**	The teacher is respectful and considerate of his colleagues. He demonstrates awareness of their personal concerns and professional development.
	16	**Concern for the total school program**	The teacher's concern is not simply for his courses and his students. He sees himself as part of the total school endeavour and actively works with other teachers, students and administrators to bring about the success of the program.
	17	**Constructive participation in community affairs**	The teacher understands the particular community context in which he works and helps to translate the purposes of the school's program to the community. He is a responsible member of the community.

	30%	15%	15%	15%	15%	10%	
0	1	2	3	4	5	6	7
Unable to observe	Weak	Below average	Average	Strong	Superior	Outstanding	Truly exceptional

Name _____

Date _____

Class observed _____

Length of observation _____

Observer _____

□	1 □	2 □	3 □	4 □	5 □	6 □	7 □	**1**	Aims
□	1 □	2 □	3 □	4 □	5 □	6 □	7 □	**2**	
□	1 □	2 □	3 □	4 □	5 □	6 □	7 □	**3**	Planning
□	1 □	2 □	3 □	4 □	5 □	6 □	7 □	**4**	
□	1 □	2 □	3 □	4 □	5 □	6. □	7 □	**5**	
□	1 □	2 □	3 □	4 □	5 □	6 □	7 □	**6**	Performance
□	1 □	2 □	3 □	4 □	5 □	6 □	7 □	**7**	
□	1 □	2 □	3 □	4 □	5 □	6 □	7 □	**8**	
□	1 □	2 □	3 □	4 □	5 □	6 □	7 □	**9**	
□	1 □	2 □	3 □	4 □	5 □	6 □	7 □	**10**	
□	1 □	2 □	3 □	4 □	5 □	6 □	7 □	**11**	
□	1 □	2 □	3 □	4 □	5 □	6 □	7 □	**12**	Evaluation
□	1 □	2 □	3 □	4 □	5 □	6 □	7 □	**13**	
□	1 □	2 □	3 □	4 □	5 □	6 □	7 □	**14**	Community & professional
□	1 □	2 □	3 □	4 □	5 □	6 □	7 □	**15**	
□	1 □	2 □	3 □	4 □	5 □	6 □	7 □	**16**	
□	1 □	2 □	3 □	4 □	5 □	6 □	7 □	**17**	

CONFERENCE RECORD

I. Summarize notes relevant to the class setting.

II. Summarize interpretations of observation data: related to aims, planning, performance and evaluation.

III. Summarize suggestions, possible resources and procedures for improvement of the teaching and learning. What should be retained, discarded, improved? How might this be done? What hypotheses for achieving more effective and efficient teaching and learning were discussed?

Date of Conference _____

Tentative plans for next observation _____

Bibliography

Adams, R. S. and Biddle, B. J. (1970) *Realities of teaching*. New York: Holt, Rinehart & Winston.

Allen, D. W., Berliner, D. C., McDonald, F. J. and Sobol, F. T. (1967) *A comparison of different modeling procedures in the acquisition of a teaching skill*. Paper presented to the annual conference of the American Educational Research Association (mimeo).

Allen, D. and Ryan, K. (1969) *Microteaching*. Reading, Mass.: Addison-Wesley.

Allen, E. A. (1961) 'Attitudes to school and teachers in a secondary modern school'. *British journal of educational psychology*, 31, 1, 106-9.

Allen, E. A. (1963) 'The professional training of teachers: a review of research'. *Educational research*, 5, 3, 200-15.

Amidon, E. J. (1966) *Using interaction analysis at Temple University*. Paper presented to the annual conference of the American Educational Research Association (mimeo).

Amidon, E. J. (1968) 'Interaction analysis'. *Theory into practice*, 7, 5, 159-67.

Amidon, E. J. and Flanders, N. A. (1963) *The role of the teacher in the classroom*. Minneapolis: Paul S. Amidon & Associates.

Amidon, E. J. and Flanders, N. A. (1967) *The role of the teacher in the classroom*. Association for Productive Teaching Inc.

Amidon, E. J., Furst, N. and Mickelson, J. (1967) *The effects of teaching interaction analysis to student teachers*. Paper presented to the annual conference of the American Educational Research Association (mimeo).

Amidon, E. J. and Hough, J. B. (1967) *Interaction analysis: theory, research and application*. Reading, Mass.: Addison-Wesley.

Amidon, E. J. and Hunter, E. (1966) *Improving teaching: the analysis of classroom verbal interaction*. New York: Holt, Rinehart & Winston.

Amidon, E. J. and Powell, E. (1966) 'Interaction analysis as a feedback system in teacher preparation'. In Raths, J. and Leeper, R. R. (eds.) *The supervisor: agent for change in teaching*. Washington, D.C.: Association for Supervision and Curriculum Development. 44–56.

Ammons, M. (1964) 'An empirical study of process and product in curriculum development'. *Journal of educational research*, 57, 9, 451–7.

Anderson, C. C. and Hunka, S. M. (1963) 'Teacher evaluation: some problems and a proposal'. *Harvard educational review*, 33, 1, 74–95.

Anderson, R. C., Faust, G. W., Roderick, M. C., Cunningham, D. J. and Andre, T. (eds.) (1969) *Current research in instruction*. Englewood Cliffs, N.J.: Prentice-Hall.

Anders-Richards, D. (1969) 'Teaching practice assessment procedures'. *Education for teaching*, 80, 71–2.

Association of Teachers in Colleges and Departments of Education (1969) *Relations between colleges of education and schools: practical work with children: school practice*. London.

Ausubel, D. P. (1968) *Educational psychology, a cognitive view*. New York: Holt, Rinehart & Winston.

Ausubel, D. P. (1969) 'Is there a discipline of educational psychology?' In Herbert, J. and Ausubel, D. P., *Psychology in teacher preparation*. Ontario Institute for Studies in Education monograph 5.

Bach, J. O. (1952) 'Practice teaching success in relation to other measures of teaching ability'. *Journal of experimental education*, 21, 1, 57–80.

Baird, J. H., Belt, W. D. and Webb, C. D. (n.d.) *Microteaching at Brigham Young University*. Department of Teacher Education, Brigham Young University (mimeo).

Baker, E. L. (1969) 'Relationship between learner achievement and instructional principles stressed during teacher preparation'. *Journal of educational research*, 63, 3, 99–102.

Baker, J. R. (1967) 'A teacher-co-tutor scheme'. *Education for teaching*, 73, 25–30.

Bales, R. F. (1955) 'How people react in conferences'. *Scientific American*, 192, 31–5.

Bamford, T. W. (1964) 'Students, teachers and teacher shortages'. *Aspects of education*, 1, 86–9.

Bandura, A., Ross, D. and Ross, S. O. (1963) 'Imitation of film-mediated aggressive models'. *Journal of abnormal social psychology*, 66, 3–11.

Bandura, A. and Walters, R. H. (1963) *Social learning and personality development*. New York: Holt, Rinehart & Winston.

Banfield, J. (1968) 'Time-tables, teaching practice and education tutors in colleges of education, I', *Educational research*, 10, 2, 152–3. 'Time-tables, teaching practice and organisation in colleges of education, II', *Educational research*, 11, 3, 238–9.

Barnes, D. (1969) 'Language in the secondary classroom'. In Barnes *et al.* (1969), 9–77.

Barnes, D., Britton, J. and Rosen, H. (1969) *Language: the learner and the school*. Harmondsworth: Penguin.

Barnes, M. W. (1967) 'Building school-university relations in teacher education'. In Elam, S. (ed.) *Improving teacher education in the U.S.A*. Stanford University: Phi Delta Kappa. 137–63.

Barr, A. S. (1948) 'The measurement and prediction of teacher efficiency: a summary of investigations'. *Journal of experimental education*, 16, 203–83.

Barr, A. S., Eustice, D. E. and Noe, E. J. (1955) 'The measurement and prediction of teacher efficiency'. *Review of educational research*, 25, 3, 261–9.

Barr, A. S. and Jones, R. E. (1958) 'The measurement and prediction of teacher efficiency'. *Review of educational research*, 28, 3, 256–64.

Bayles, E. E. (1966) 'Theories of learning and classroom methods'. *Theory into practice*, 5, 71–6.

Becker, H. S. and Carper, J. W. (1956) 'The development of identification with an occupation'. *American journal of sociology*, 61, 4, 289–98.

Bell, J. K. and Mundy, P. G. (1966) 'Learning their job in a comprehensive'. *Times educational supplement*, 2682, p. 849.

Bellack, A. A. (ed.) (1967) *Theory and research in teaching*. New York: Teachers College Press, Columbia University.

Bellack, A. A. and Davitz, J. R., in collaboration with Kliebard, H. M., Herbert, M. and Hyman, R. T. (1963) *The language of the classroom*. New York: Institute of psychological research, Columbia University.

Bellack, A. A., Kliebard, H. M., Hyman, R. T. and Smith, F. L. (1966) *The language of the classroom*. New York: Teachers College Press, Columbia University.

Belt, W. D. (1967) *Microteaching: observed and critiqued by a group of trainees*. Department of Teacher Education, Brigham Young University.

Berliner, D. C. (1969) *Microteaching and the technical skills approach to teacher training*. Technical Report No. 8, Stanford Center for Research and Development in Teaching, School of Education, Stanford University (mimeo).

Bewsher, L. G. (1966) *A study of attitudes and incentives among a group of students training to be teachers*. Unpublished M.A. thesis, University of London.

Biddle, B. J. and Ellena, W. J. (1964) *Contemporary research on teacher effectiveness*. New York: Holt, Rinehart & Winston.

Biddle, B. J. and Thomas, E. J. (1966) *Role theory: concepts and research*. New York: Wiley.

Birmingham University School of Education (1971) *Postgraduate Certificate in Education students' questionnaire on school practice* (mimeo).

Bishop, A. J. and Levy, L. B. (1968) 'Analysis of teaching behaviours'. *Education for teaching*, 76, 61–5.

Bjersted, A. (1967) 'Tele-observation: closed circuit television and video-recording in teacher training'. *Didakometry*, May 1967. Department of Educational and Psychological Research, School of Education, Malmo, Sweden.

Blanchard, W. J. and Goodkind, T. B. (1967) *The university 'clinical professor' as a change agent in public schools*. Paper presented to the annual conference of the American Educational Research Association (mimeo).

Bloom, B. S. (ed.), Engelhart, M. D., Furst, E. J., Hill, W. H. and Krathwohl, D. R. (1956) *Taxonomy of educational objectives: the classification of educational goals. Handbook I: the cognitive domain*. New York: Longmans Green.

Bolam, R. (1970) *The teacher/tutor relationship*. Conference Report, Cambridge Institute of Education (mimeo). 64–77.

Bondi, J. C. and Ober, R. L. (1969) *The effects of interaction analysis feedback on the verbal behaviour of student teachers*. Paper presented at the annual conference of the American Educational Research Association (mimeo).

Borg, W. R. (1968) *The three tests in the minicourse development cycle.* California: Far West Laboratory for Research and Development (mimeo).

Borg, W. R. (1969a) *The minicourse as a vehicle for changing teacher behaviour: the research evidence.* Paper presented to the annual meeting of the American Educational Research Association.

Borg, W. R. (1969b) *Overview of the teacher education programme.* Far West Laboratory for Educational Research and Development, California (mimeo).

Borg, W. R., Kelley, M. L. and Langer, P. (1970) *Minicourse: effective questioning, teachers handbook.* New York: Macmillan Educational Services Inc.

Borg, W. R., Langer, P. and Kelley, M. (1969) 'The minicourse: a new tool for the education of teachers'. *Education*, February–March 1970, 1–7. Reprinted on pp. 220–30 of this volume.

Brain, P. B. (1967) *An enquiry into the way in which a college of education prepares its students for the role of technical college teacher.* Unpublished M.A. thesis, University of London.

Brode, L. E. N. (1967) *Imitation of supervisors as a factor in teachers' classroom behavior.* Paper presented at the annual conference of the American Educational Research Association (mimeo).

Broudy, H. S. (1969) 'Can we define good teaching?' *Record*, 70, 583–92.

Brown, A. F. (1966) 'A perceptual taxonomy of the effective-rated teacher'. *Journal of experimental education*, 35, 1, 1–10.

Brown, B. B. and McClave, J. T. (n.d.) *Observation and evaluation of the classroom behaviour of student teachers.* University of Florida (mimeo).

Brown, B. B. and Stoffel, W. N. (n.d.) *Some effects of observers' beliefs on classroom observations of teachers' behaviour.* University of Florida (mimeo).

Bruner, J. S. (1964) 'Some theorems on instruction illustrated with reference to mathematics'. In Hilgard, E. R. (ed.) *Theories of learning and instruction.* Chicago: National Society for the Study of Education. 306–35.

Bruner, J. S. (1966) *Toward a theory of instruction.* Cambridge, Mass.: The Belknap Press.

Burkhart, R. C. (ed.) (1969) 'The assessment revolution: new viewpoints for teacher evaluation'. New York State Department of

Education Division of Teacher Education and Certification, and Buffalo State University Teacher Learning Center. Reviewed in *Journal of teacher education*, 21, 3 (1970), 434–5.

Burnham, P. (1969) 'Commentary on "The role of the teacher in advanced society" '. In Taylor, W. (ed.) *Towards a policy for the education of teachers*. Colston Papers No. 20. London: Butterworth. 23–31.

Bush, R. (1968) 'Redefining the role of the teacher'. *Theory into practice*, 6, 246–51.

Butcher, H. J. (1965) 'The attitudes of student teachers to education: a comparison with the attitudes of experienced teachers and a study of changes during the training course'. *British journal of social and clinical psychology*, 4, 17–24.

Cambridge University Institute of Education (1970) *Conference on school experience in a college of education course* (mimeo).

Cane, B. (1967) 'Research on teachers and teacher education'. In *Educational research in colleges of education*. London: Society for Research in Higher Education. 10–19.

Carroll, B. J. (1961) 'Barren ground? Training the teacher'. *Times educational supplement*, 2423, p. 569.

Carroll, B. J. (1962) 'Baptism of fire'. *Times educational supplement*, 2445, p, 614.

Cartmell, A. F. (1971) 'The use of closed circuit television in the assessment of teacher effectiveness'. *Programmed learning and educational technology*, 8, 3, 173–85.

Caspari, I. and Eggleston, J. (1965) 'A new approach to supervision of teaching practice'. *Education for teaching*, 68, 47–52.

Cattell, R. B. (1931) 'The assessment of teaching ability'. *British journal of educational psychology*, 1, 1, 48–71.

Chabassol, D. J. (1968) 'The possession of certain attitudes as predictors of success in practice teaching'. *Journal of educational research*, 61, 7, 304–6.

Chambers, P. (1962) *A study of students' attitudes towards some aspects of teacher training with special reference to changes in attitudes in the course of training*. Unpublished M.Ed. thesis, Leicester University.

Charlton, K., Stewart, W. A. C. and Paffard, M. K. (1958) 'Students' attitudes to courses in departments of education in universities'. *British journal of educational psychology*, 28, 3, 243–52.

Charlton, K., Stewart, W. A. C. and Paffard, M. K. (1960) 'Students' attitudes to courses of education'. *British journal of educational studies*, 8, 2, 148–64.

Charters, W. W. (1963) 'The social background of teaching'. In Gage, N. L. (ed.) *Handbook of research on teaching*. Chicago: Rand McNally. 715–813.

Checketts, H., Davies, G. and Horton, K. (1970) 'A problem-based examination in education'. In Stones, E., *Towards evaluation: some thoughts on tests and teacher education*. Occasional publication No. 4, *Educational review*, 47–58.

Clark, J. M. (1967) 'Supervision of teaching practice'. *Education for teaching*, 74, 44–50.

Clark, R. P. and Nisbet, J. D. (1963) *The first two years of teaching*. Aberdeen College of Education (mimeo).

Clarke, S. C. T. (1970) 'General teaching theory'. *Journal of teacher education*, 21, 3, 403–16.

Claus, K. E. (1969) *Effects of modeling and feedback treatments on the development of teachers' questioning skills*. Technical report No. 6, Stanford Center for Research and Development in Teaching, School of Education, Stanford University (mimeo).

Cohen, L. (1965) *An exploratory study of the teacher's role as perceived by headteachers, tutors and students in a training college*. Unpublished M.Ed. thesis, Liverpool University.

Cohen, L. (1968) 'College and the training of teachers'. *Educational research*, 2, 1, 14–22.

Cohen, L. (1969a) 'Functional dependence, exchanges and power of influence'. *Educational sciences*, 3, 1, 47–51.

Cohen, L. (1969b) 'Students' perceptions of the school practice period'. *Research in education*, 2, 52–8.

Collier, K. G. (1957) 'The study of students' attitudes'. *Education for teaching*, 42, 34–41.

Collier, K. G. (1959) 'The criteria of assessment of practical teaching'. *Education for teaching*, 48, 36–40.

Collier, K. G. (1962) 'Group practice', *Times educational supplement*, 2433, p. 10.

Collier, K. G. (1969) 'The place of observation in professional preparation'. *Education for teaching*, 79, 35–7.

Collier, K. G. (1970) 'Colleges and teachers'. *Trends in education*, 18, 41–4.

Collins, M. (1959a) *Some correlates of inadequate teaching ability.* Unpublished Ph.D. thesis, University of London.

Collins, M. (1959b) 'A follow-up study of some former graduate student teachers'. *British journal of educational psychology*, 29, 3, 187–97.

Collins, M. (1964) 'Untrained and trained graduate teachers: a comparison of their experiences during the probationary year'. *British journal of educational psychology*, 34, 1, 75–84.

Coltham, J. B. (1966) 'An experiment in school practice'. *Education for teaching*, 69, 71–6.

Cooper, J. M. and Allen, A. W. (1970) *Microteaching: history and present status.* Washington, D.C.: Educational Resources Information Center Clearinghouse on Teacher Education.

Cope, E. (1968) *The functions of school practice in courses of teacher education.* University of Bristol Institute of Education (mimeo).

Cope, E. (1969a) *British research on the training of teachers with special reference to school practice.* University of Bristol Institute of Education (mimeo).

Cope, E. (1969b) 'Students and school practice'. *Education for teaching*, 80, 25–35.

Cope, E. (1969c) 'School practice: the concept of role'. *Trends in education*, 16, 34–8.

Cope, E. (1970a) 'Discussions with college and school staff on the subject of "school practice" '. *Education for teaching*, 81, 30–7.

Cope, E. (1970b) 'Teacher training and student practice'. *Educational research*, 12, 2, 87–98.

Cope, E. (1971) *School experience in teacher education.* Research Unit, School of Education, Bristol University.

Corrigan, D. and Griswold, K. (1963) 'Attitude changes of student teachers'. *Journal of educational research*, 57, 2, 93–5.

Cortis, G. A. (1968) 'Predicting student performance in the teaching profession'. *British journal of educational psychology*, 38, 2, 115–22.

Cortis, G. A. and Dean, A. J. (1970) 'Teaching skills of probationary primary teachers'. *Educational research*, 12, 3, 230–4.

Craft, M. (1969) 'Teaching, social work and interprofessional training'. In Bulman, I., Craft, M. and Milson, F. (eds.) *Youth service and interprofessional studies.* Oxford: Pergamon. 121–40.

Cruickshank, D. R. (1968) 'Simulation'. *Theory into practice*, 7, 5, 190–3.

Cruickshank, D. R. and Broadbent, F. W. (1970) *Simulation in preparing school personnel*. Washington, D.C.: Educational Resources Information Center Clearinghouse on Teacher Education.

Dale, R. R. (1965) 'An enquiry into the relationship between academic attainment and teaching ability among student teachers'. *University College of Swansea Collegiate Faculty of Education journal*, 23–5.

Davies, D. (1969) 'Student teaching'. In Ebel, R. L. (ed.) *Encyclopedia of educational research* (4th ed.). London: Macmillan. 1376–87.

Davis, O. L. Jr and Drew, C. T. (1967) *Cognitive objectives revealed by classroom questions asked by social studies student teachers*. Paper presented to the annual conference of the American Educational Research Association (mimeo).

Davis, T. N. and Satterly, D. J. (1969) 'Personality profiles of student teachers'. *British journal of educational psychology*, 39, 2, 183–7.

Denemark, G. (1967) 'Preparing tomorrow's teachers'. *Theory into practice*, 6, 252–9.

Department of Education and Science (1966) *Relations between colleges of education and schools*. Circular 24/66. London: H.M.S.O.

Department of Education and Science (1967a) 'Switched-on education'. *Trends in education*, 8, 37–45.

Department of Education and Science (1967b) *Children and their primary schools (The Plowden Report)*. London: H.M.S.O.

Department of Education and Science (1969) *Country school teachers*. Reports on Education, 55.

Dewey, J. (1904) *The relation of theory to practice in education*. Third Yearbook of the National Society for the Scientific Study of Education, Part I, 9–30.

Dickson, G. E. and Wiersma, W. (1966) 'Student teachers – American and British'. *New society*, 201, 187–9.

Domas, S. J. and Tiedman, D. V. (1950) 'Teacher competence: an annotated bibliography'. *Journal of experimental psychology*, 19, 101–218.

Downes, L. W. and Shaw, K. E. (1968) 'Innovation in teaching practice'. *Trends in education*, 12, 42–5.

Drabick, L. W. (1967) 'Perceivers of the teacher's role: the teacher educator'. *Journal of teacher education*, 18, 1, 51–7.

Dubin, R. (1969) *Theory building*. New York: The Free Press.

Dumas, W. W. (1966) 'Strengths and weaknesses of student teachers in English'. *Journal of experimental education*, 35, 1, 19–27.

Dumas, W. (1969) 'Factors associated with self-concept change in student teachers'. *Journal of educational research*, 62, 6, 275–8.

Emans, R. (1969) 'Teacher attitudes as a function of values'. *Journal of educational research*, 62, 10, 459–63.

Emmett, R. (1965) 'School practice re-appraised: towards a closer partnership'. *Times educational supplement*, 2621, p. 266.

Evans, K. M. (1951) 'A critical survey of methods of assessing teaching ability'. *British journal of educational psychology*, 21, 2, 89–95.

Evans, K. M. (1952) *A study of teaching ability at the training college stage in relation to the personality and attitudes of the students.* Unpublished Ph.D. thesis, University of London.

Evans, K. M. (1959) 'Research on teaching ability'. *Educational research*, 1, 3, 22–36.

Evans, K. M. (1961) 'An annotated bibliography of British research on teaching and teaching ability'. *Educational research*, 4, 1, 67–80.

Evans, K. M. (1966) 'The Minnesota teacher attitude inventory'. *Educational research*, 8, 2, 134–41.

Evans, K. M. (1967) 'Teacher training courses and students' personal qualities'. *Educational research*, 10, 1, 72–7.

Evans, K. M. (1969) 'Teachers and some others: a comparative study'. *Educational research*, 11, 2, 153–6.

Finlayson, D. S. and Cohen, L. (1967) 'The teacher's role: a comparative study of the conceptions of college of education students and headteachers'. *British journal of educational psychology*, 37, 1, 22–31.

Flanders, N. A. (1960) *Teacher influence, pupil attitudes and achievement.* Quoted in Amidon and Flanders (1967).

Flanders, N. (1961) *Interaction analysis: a technique for quantifying teacher influence.* Paper presented to the A.E.R.A. (mimeo).

Flanders, N. (1969) 'Teacher effectiveness'. In Ebel, R. L. (ed.) *Encyclopedia of educational research*. London: Macmillan. 1423–37.

Fletcher, C. (1958) 'Supervision and assessment of practical teaching'. *Education for teaching*, 47, 17–23.

Flynn, J. M. *et al.* (1970) 'The changing role of the teacher'. *Educational technology*, 10, 2 (whole volume).

Fortune, J. C., Cooper, J. M. and Allen, D. W. (1967) 'The Stanford summer microteaching clinic, 1965'. *The journal of teacher education*, 18, 4, 389–93.

Gage, N. L. (1967) 'Psychological conceptions of teaching'. *International journal of educational science*, 1, 151–61.

Gage, N. L., Belgard, M., Dell, D., Hiller, J. E., Rosenshine, B. and Unruh, W. R. (1968) *Explorations of the teacher's effectiveness in explaining.* Technical Report 4, Stanford Center for Research and Development in Teaching (mimeo).

Gagné, R. M. (1965) 'Educational objectives and human performance'. In Krumboltz, J. D. (ed.) *Learning and the educational process.* Chicago: Rand McNally. 1–24.

Gall, M. D., Dunning, B. and Galassi, J. (1971) *Minicourse: individualizing instruction in mathematics.* Macmillan Educational Services Inc.

Gallagher, J. J. and Aschner, M. J. M. (1963) 'A preliminary report: analysis of classroom interaction'. *Merrill-Palmer Quarterly of behaviour and development*, 9, 2, 183–94.

Galloway, C. (1968) 'Nonverbal communication'. *Theory into practice*, 7, 5, 172–5.

Getzels, J. W. and Jackson, P. W. (1963) 'The teacher's personality and characteristics'. In Gage, N. L. (ed.) *Handbook of research on teaching.* Chicago: Rand McNally. 506–82.

Gibb, G. (1970) 'C.C.T.V.: some guidelines for the future use of video-tapes in professional training'. *Education for teaching*, 81, 51–6.

Gibson, D. R. (1970) 'The role of the primary and secondary school teacher'. *Educational research*, 73, 1, 20–7.

Gibson, T. (1970) 'The camera as the student's eye'. In University of Exeter Institute of Education, *Innovations in teaching practice* (mimeo). 11–14.

Glaser, R. (1963) 'Instructional technology and the measurement of learning outcomes: some questions'. *American psychologist*, 18, 8, 519–21.

Glaser, R. (1969): 'Learning'. In Ebel, R. L. (ed.) *Encyclopedia of educational research.* London: Macmillan. 706–33.

Goldman, R. J. (1966) 'Creative methods in the education of teachers'. *Education for teaching*, 71, 5–10.

Good, T. L. and Brophy, J. E. (1969) *Analyzing classroom inter-action: a more powerful alternative.* Report series No. 26, The Research and Development Center for Teacher Education, University of Texas (mimeo).

Goodkind, T. B. (1968) *An evaluation of the effectiveness of the micro-teaching technique in the training of elementary school teachers.* Paper presented at the annual conference of the American Educational Research Association.

Gordon, J. (1968) *Systems for evaluating videotaped instruction.* Paper presented at the annual conference of the American Educational Research Association, Oregon State System of Higher Education (mimeo).

Gorman, G. H. (1969) *Teachers and the interactive process of educa-tion.* Boston, Mass.: Allyn and Bacon.

Gough, H. G., Durflinger, G. W., and Hill, R. E. (1968) 'Predicting performance in student teaching from the California Psycho-logical Inventory'. *Journal of educational psychology,* 59, 2, 119–27.

Greenberg, S. (1967) *Comparative studies of systems for analyzing classroom interaction.* Paper presented at the annual conference of the American Educational Research Association (mimeo).

Griffiths, A. and Moore, A. H. (1967) 'Schools and teaching practice'. *Education for teaching,* 74, 33–9.

Hallworth, H. J. (1957) 'Group discussion in its relevance to teacher training'. *Educational review,* 10, 41–53.

Hannam, C. L., Smyth, P. and Stephenson, N. (1967) 'Supple-mentary teaching practice: the student and the small group'. *Education for teaching,* 72, 68–74.

Harrison, A. (1968) 'Teacher education objectives – a lack of con-gruence'. *Journal of teacher education,* 19, 3, 357–64.

Headmasters' Association (1965) *Report of the working party on the training of teachers.*

Herbert, J. and Ausubel, D. P. (1969) *Psychology in teacher prepara-tion.* Monograph No. 5, Ontario Institute for Studies in Education.

Herbert, N. and Turnbull, G. H. (1963) 'Personality factors and effective progress in teaching'. *Educational review,* 16, 24–31.

Hill, R. A. and Medley, D. M. (1968) *Change in behaviors of first year interim teachers.* Paper presented to the annual conference of the American Educational Research Association (mimeo).

BIBLIOGRAPHY · 269

Hill, R. A. and Medley, D. M. (1969) *Goal oriented teaching exercise (G.O.T.E.): a methodology for measuring the effects of teaching strategies.* Paper presented to the annual conference of the American Educational Research Association (mimeo).

Hinley, R. T., Galloway, C. M., Coody, B. R. and Sandefur, W. S. (1966) 'An exploratory study of teaching styles among student teachers'. *Journal of experimental education*, 35, 2, 30–5.

Hughes, M. M. (1959) *Development of the means for the assessment of the quality of teaching in elementary schools.* University of Utah (mimeo).

Hughes, M. M. (1963) 'Utah study of the assessment of teaching'. In Bellack, A. A. (ed.) *Theory and research in teaching.* New York: Teachers College, Columbia University. 25–36.

Hyman, R. (1970) *Ways of teaching.* Philadelphia: Lippincott.

Inlow, G. (1952) 'Evaluating student-teacher experiences'. *Journal of educational research*, 45, 9, 705–14.

James, H. H. (1970) *Differential efficacy of three supervisory methods for development of a teaching strategy.* Paper presented to the annual conference of the American Educational Research Association (mimeo).

Jeffreys, M. V. C. (1961) *Revolution in teacher education.* London: Pitman.

Jenkins, T. R. (1968) 'Group practice in four selected schools . . . a draft report on the experiment'. *Swansea Collegiate Faculty of Education journal.*

Jervis, F. M. and Congdon, R. G. (1958) 'Student and faculty perceptions of educational values'. *American psychologist*, 13, 7, 464–6.

Johnson, J. S. (1968) 'Change in student teacher dogmatism'. *Journal of educational research*, 62, 5, 224–6.

Johnson, M. E. B. (1966) 'Teachers' attitudes to educational research'. *Educational research*, 9, 1, 74–9.

Johnson, W. D. and Knaupp, J. E. (1970) 'Trainee role expectations of the microteaching supervisor'. *Journal of teacher education*, 21, 3, 396–401.

Jones, M. H. (1969) *Reliability of coding of the system for the analysis of classroom communication.* Center for the Study of Evaluation, University of California at Los Angeles Graduate School of Education (mimeo).

Kallenbach, W. (1967) *The effectiveness of video-taped practice teaching sessions in the preparation of elementary intern teachers.* San Jose State College, San Jose, California (mimeo).

Kallenbach, W. (1968) *The effectiveness of microteaching in the preparation of elementary intern teachers.* Paper presented to the annual conference of the American Educational Research Association (mimeo).

Kallenbach, W. (1969) *Results of preservice field tests of minicourse 1.* Paper presented to the annual conference of the American Educational Research Association (mimeo).

Kallenbach, W. W. and Gall, M. D. (1969) 'Micro-teaching versus conventional methods in training elementary intern teachers'. *Journal of educational research,* 63, 3, 136–41.

Kaltsounis, T. and Nelson, J. L. (1968) 'The mythology of student teaching'. *Journal of teacher education,* 19, 3, 277–81.

Katz, F. M. (1959) 'Some problems in teacher training'. *Education for teaching,* 48, 30–5.

Kelsall, H. M. and Kelsall, R. K. (1968) 'Basic types of incompatibility inherent in teacher role'. *Education for teaching,* 76, 28–36.

Kerlinger, F. N. (1965) *Foundations of behavioural research.* New York: Holt, Rinehart & Winston.

Kersh, B. Y. (1962) 'The classroom simulator'. *Journal of teacher education,* 13, 1, 109–10.

Kirwan, M. and Shaw, K. (1966) 'School and college co-operation in teaching practice'. *Education for teaching,* 70, 44–8.

Kitchen, R. D. (1966) 'Measuring students' attitudes'. *Education for teaching,* 71, 75–9.

Kohl, H. R. (1969) *The open classroom.* New York: Vintage Books (London: Methuen, 1970).

Komisar, N. P. (1966) 'Conceptual analysis of teaching'. *High schoo journal,* 50, 14–21.

Koran, M. L., McDonald, F. J. and Snow, R. E. (1969) *The effects of individual differences on observational learning in the acquisition of a teaching skill.* Paper presented to the annual conference of the American Educational Research Association (mimeo).

Kounin, J. S. (1970) *Discipline and group management in classrooms.* New York: Holt, Rinehart & Winston.

Krasno, R. M. and Allen, D. W. (1968) *The development of a data bank of diagnostic teacher training information.* Paper presented to the annual conference of the American Educational Research Association (mimeo).

Krathwohl, D. R., Bloom, B. S. and Masia, B. (1964) *Taxonomy of educational objectives: the classification of educational goals. Handbook II: the affective domain.* New York: David McKay.

Lail, S. S. (1968) 'The model in use (non-verbal communication)'. *Theory into practice,* 7, 5, 172–5.

Langer, P. and Allen, G. E. (1970) *The minicourse as a tool for training teachers in interaction analysis.* Paper presented to the annual conference of the American Educational Research Association (mimeo).

Lantz, D. L. (1967) 'The relationship of university supervisors' and supervising teachers' ratings to observed student teachers' behavior'. *American educational research journal,* 4, 3, 279–88.

La Shier, W. S. and Westmeyer, P. (1967) 'The use of interaction analysis in Biological Sciences Study Committee laboratory block classrooms'. *Journal of teacher education,* 17, 4, 439–46.

Levin, H. (1954) 'A new perspective on teacher competence research'. *Harvard educational review,* 24, 98–105.

Lewis, E. A. (1968) 'Experiments in pairing students on specialist secondary school practice'. *Swansea Collegiate Faculty of Education journal,* 17–20.

Lovegrove, W. R. (1968) 'Links between a college of education and the local teaching community'. *Education for teaching,* 77, 75–7.

Lundy P. R. and Hale, J. R. (1967) 'Episode teaching: a rationale for inducting student teachers into the teaching act'. *Journal of teacher education,* 18, 4, 395–8.

Lynch, J. and Preen, D. W. (1967) 'The flexible college'. *Education for teaching,* 74, 4–10.

McAleese, W. R. and Unwin, D. (1971) 'A selective survey of microteaching'. *Programmed learning and educational technology,* 8, 1, 10–21.

McAulay, J. B. (1960) 'How much influence has a co-operating teacher?' *Journal of teacher education,* 11, 1, 79–83.

McDonald, F. J. and Allen, D. W. (1967) *Training effects of feedback and modeling procedures on teaching performance.* Stanford University, Stanford Center for Research and Development in Teaching technical report no. 3.

McIntyre, D. and Morrison, A. (1967) 'The educational opinions of
K

teachers in training'. *British journal of social and clinical psychology*, 6, 1, 32–7.

McKnight, P. C. and Baral, D. P. (1969) *Microteaching and the technical skills of teaching: a bibliography of research and development at Stanford University*, 1963–9. Research and development memorandum No. 48, School of Education, Stanford University, Stanford, California (mimeo).

McLain, E. W. (1968) '16 PF scores and success in student teaching'. *Journal of teacher education*, 19, 1, 25–32.

McLeish, J. (1970) *Students' attitudes and college environments*. Cambridge Institute of Education.

McNaught, P. (1968) 'Plowden's "long practice" proposals must go through'. *Times educational supplement*, 2769, p. 1963.

McNaughton, A. H., Wallen, N. W., Ho, S. K. and Crawford, W. R. (1967) 'The use of teaching modules to study high-level thinking in social science'. *Journal of teacher education*, 18, 4, 495–502.

Maddox, H. (1968) 'A descriptive study of teaching practice'. *Educational review*, 20, 3, 177–90.

Mager, R. F. (1962) *Preparing instructional objectives*. Palo Alto, Calif.: Fearon.

Manchester University School of Education (1968) *The organisation and use of teaching practice places in the Manchester A.T.O.*

Martin, N. B., Hagestadt, M., Thompson, V. and Newsome, B. (1965) *Two in a classroom – new forms of co-operation*. Bulletin of London University Institute of Education, new series, 7, 14–17.

Medley, D. M. (1969) *Assessing the learning environment in the classroom: a manual for users of OScAR 5V*. Educational Testing Service, Princeton (quoted by Hill and Medley, 1969).

Medley, D. M. and Mitzel, H. E. (1963a) 'The scientific study of teacher behavior'. In Bellack, A. A. (ed.) *Theory and research in teaching*. New York: Teachers College Press, Columbia University. 79–90.

Medley, D. M. and Mitzel, H. E. (1963b) 'Measuring classroom behavior by systematic observation'. In Gage, N. L. (ed.) *Handbook of research on teaching*. Chicago: Rand McNally. 247–328.

Meier, J. H. (1968) 'Rationale for and application of microtraining to improve teaching'. *Journal of teacher education*, 19, 2, 145–57.

Meldon, R. P. (1966) *A development study of insight as a related factor in teaching efficiency with special reference to mature students*. Society for Research in Higher Education Register of Research.

Meux, M. O. (1967) 'Studies of learning in the school setting'. *Review of educational research*, 37, 5, 539–62.

Miller, L. K., Witty, D. S. and Comas, J. D. M. (1965) 'A suggested research model for the investigation of classroom teacher effectiveness'. *Journal of education research*, 58, 9, 405–8.

Ministry of Education (1957) *The training of teachers, professional studies and teaching practice*. Pamphlet No. 34. London: H.M.S.O.

Minnis, D. L. and Shrable, K. (1968) 'Interaction analysis: the model in use'. *Theory into practice*, 7, 5, 168–71.

Mitchell, F. W. (1966) 'Some notes on the concept of teaching'. *Journal of teacher education*, 17, 2, 162–71.

Morgan, J. C. and Woerdehoff, F. J. (1969) 'Stability of student teacher behaviors and their relationship to personality and creativity factors'. *Journal of educational research*, 62, 6, 251–4.

Morris, B. and Cock, M. (1969) 'Theory and practice'. *Trends in education*, 16, 39–42.

Morris, J. N. (1967) 'The case against Plowden's "long practice" for student teachers'. *Times educational supplement*, 2740, p. 1195.

Morris, S. (1969) 'Teaching practice: objectives and conflicts'. *Educational review*, 21, 2, 120–9.

Morris, S. (1970) 'The assessment and evaluation of teaching practice'. In Stones, E. (ed.) *Towards evaluation: some thoughts on tests and teacher education*. Occasional publication No. 4, *Educational review*. 64–70.

Morrison, A. and McIntyre, D. (1967) 'Changes in the opinions about education during the first year of teaching'. *British journal of social and clinical psychology*, 6, 3, 161–3.

Morrison, A. and McIntyre, D. (1969) *Teachers and teaching*. Harmondsworth: Penguin.

Morse, K. R. and Davis, O. L. (1970) *The effectiveness of teaching laboratory instruction on the questioning behaviours of beginning teacher candidates*. Paper presented to the annual conference of the American Educational Research Association (mimeo).

Morsh, J. E., Burgess, G. C. and Smith, P. N. (1956) 'Student achievement as a measure of instructor effectiveness'. *Journal of educational psychology*, 47, 2, 79–88.

Moskowitz, G. (1968a) 'The effects of training foreign language teachers in interaction analysis'. *Foreign language annals*, 1, 3. 281–35.

Moskowitz, G. (1968b) *A comparison of foreign language student teachers trained and not trained in interaction analysis*. Paper presented to the annual conference of the A.E.R.A. (mimeo).

Musella, D. (1970) 'Improving teacher education'. *Journal of teacher education*, 21, 1, 15–21.

National Association of Schoolmasters (1964) *Teaching practice in primary and secondary schools, some suggestions for a new pattern*. London.

National Union of Students (1964) *Report of conference on teaching practice*. London (mimeo).

National Union of Students (1966) *Colleges of education – the three year course*. London.

National Union of Teachers (1963) *Aims and principles of the three year course*. London.

National Union of Teachers (1964) *Teaching practice in the '60s*. London.

National Union of Teachers (1970) *Teacher education: the way ahead*. London.

Neal, C. D., Kraft, L. E. and Kracht, C. R. (1967) 'Reasons for college supervision of the student teaching program'. *Journal of teacher education*, 18, 1, 24–7.

Nicholson, C. (1965) 'A kind of guidance'. *The new era*, 46, 3, 77–8; 4, 93–5; 5, 128–30.

Ober, R. L., Wood, S. and Roberts, A. (1968) *A study of the development of a reciprocal category system for assessing teacher-student classroom verbal interaction*. Paper presented to the annual conference of the A.E.R.A. (mimeo).

Oelke, M. C. (1956) 'A study of student teachers' attitudes towards children'. *Journal of educational psychology*, 47, 4, 193–8.

Oliver, R. A. C. and Butcher, H. J. (1962) 'Teachers' attitudes to education: the structure of educational attitudes'. *British journal of social and clinical psychology*, 1, 1, 56–9.

Oliver, W. A. (1953) 'Teachers' educational beliefs versus their classroom practice'. *Journal of educational research*, 47, 1, 47–56.

Olivero, J. L. (1970) Microteaching: medium for improving instruction. Merrill (Foundations of Education).

Ort, U. K. (1964) 'A study of some techniques used for predicting the success of teachers'. *Journal of teacher education*, 15, 67–71.

Ottoway, A. K. C. (1952) 'Mental health in the training of teachers'. *Bulletin of education*, 27, 7–11.

Owens, G. (1970) 'The module: an alternative to the present pattern of teacher education'. *Universities quarterly*, 25, 1, 20–7.

Panton, J. H. (1934) *The assessment of teaching ability with special reference to men students in training.* Unpublished M.A. thesis, University of London.

Pearce, W. M. (1959) 'A follow-up study of training college students'. *Education for teaching*, 48, 41–8.

Pedley, R. (1965) 'Teacher training: a new approach'. *Education*, 125, 1151–2.

Pedley, R. (1969) 'Teaching practice'. University of Exeter Institute of Education (1970). *Innovations in teaching practice*, 5–8 (mimeo).

Penfold, D. M. and Meldon, R. P. (1969) 'Social sensitivity in relation to teaching competence'. *Educational research*, 12, 1, 64–8.

Perlberg, A. (1969) *Microteaching studies in vocational-technical education.* Paper presented to the annual conference of the American Educational Research Association (mimeo).

Perrott, E. and Duthie, J. H. (1970) 'Television as a feedback device: microteaching'. *Educational television international*, 4, 4, 258–61.

Perry, L. R. (1969) 'Training'. *Education for teaching*, 79, 4–10.

Peters, R. S. (1968) 'Theory and practice in teacher training'. *Trends in Education*, 9, 3–9.

Phillips, A. S. (1963) 'The self-concepts of teacher trainees in two cultures'. *British journal of educational psychology*, 33, 2, 154–61.

Phillips, M. (1931–2) 'Professional courses in the training of teachers'. *British journal of educational psychology*, 1, 3, 225–45; 2, 1, 1–24.

Pinney, R. H. and Miltz, R. J. (n.d.) *Television recordings and teacher education: new directions.* Television and Audio Visual Center, Center for Research and Development in Teaching, School of Education, Stanford University, California (mimeo).

Pinsent, A. (1933) 'Pre-college teaching experience and other factors in the teaching success of university students'. *British journal of educational psychology*, 3, 2, 109–25 and 3, 201–20.

Plaskow, M. (1969) 'Sitting with Nellie'. *Times educational supplement*, 2841, p. 2.

Pollock, J. (1964) *The opinions of science teachers on the objectives of teaching science*. Unpublished M.Ed. thesis, Manchester University.

Popham, W. J. (1965) 'Student teachers' classroom performance and recency of instructional methods course work'. *Journal of experimental education*, 34, 1, 85–8.

Popham, W. J. (1967) *Development of a performance test of teacher efficiency*. Washington, D.C.: Department of Health, Education and Welfare.

Popham, W. J. (1969) *Validation results: performance tests of teaching proficiency in vocational education*. Paper presented to the annual conference of the American Educational Research Association (mimeo).

Popham, W. J. and Baker, E. L. (1967) *Development of instructional competency tests for vocational education teachers: a status report*. Paper presented at the annual conference of the American Educational Research Association (mimeo).

Popham, W. J. and Baker, E. L. (1968) *Validation results: a performance test of teaching proficiency*. Paper presented at the annual conference of the American Educational Research Association (mimeo).

Popham, W. J., Eisner, E. W., Sullivan, H. J. and Tyler, L. L. (1969) *Instructional objectives*. American Educational Research Association. Chicago: Rand McNally.

Popper, K. R. (1959) *The logic of scientific discovery*. London: Hutchinson. Quoted by Dubin (1969).

Poppleton, P. K. (1968) 'The assessment of teaching practice: what criteria do we use?' *Education for teaching*, 75, 59–64.

Pounds, R. L. (1966) 'Educational values and classroom methods'. *Theory into practice*, 5, 63–6.

Price, G. (1964) 'Crisis in school practice'. *Education for teaching*, 65, 36–40.

Purpel, D. E. (1967) 'Student teaching'. *Journal of teacher education*, 18, 1, 20–3.

Raths, J. and Leeper, R. R. (eds.) (1966) *The supervisor: agent for change in teaching*. Washington, D.C.: Association for Supervision and Curriculum Development.

Ree, H. (1968) 'Wanted – a Royal Commission'. *Higher education review*, 1, 1, 55–62.

Resnick, L. B. and Kiss, L. E. (1970) *Discrimination training and feedback in shaping teacher behaviour*. Paper presented to the annual conference of the American Educational Research Association (mimeo).

Richardson, E. (1965) 'Personal relations and formal assessment in a graduate course in education'. *Education for teaching*, 67, 43–56.

Richardson, J. E. (1967a) *The environment of learning*. London: Nelson.

Richardson, J. E. (1967b) 'Projects, pupils and teachers: reflections on a school practice term'. *New era*, 48, 159–66.

Robbins Committee (1963) *Report on Higher Education*. London: H.M.S.O.

Robertson, J. D. C. (1957) 'An analysis of the views of supervisors on the attributes of successful graduate student teachers'. *British journal of educational psychology*, 27, 2, 115–26.

Rosenfeld, V. M. (1969) 'Possible influences of student teachers on their co-operating teachers'. *Journal of teacher education*, 20, 1, 40–3.

Rousseau, H. J. (1968) 'The impact of educational theory on teachers'. *British journal of educational studies*, 16, 60–71.

Rowell, G. (1968) 'The model in use' (simulation). *Theory into practice*, 7, 5, 194–6.

Rudd, W. G. A. and Wiseman, S. (1962) 'Sources of dissatisfaction among a group of teachers'. *British journal of educational psychology*, 32, 3, 275–91.

Ryans, D. G. (1960a) *Characteristics of teachers*. Washington, D.C.: American Council on Education.

Ryans, D. G. (1960b) 'Research on teacher behavior in the context of the teacher characteristics study'. In Biddle, B. J. and Ellena, W. J. (eds.) *Contemporary research on teacher effectiveness*. New York: Holt, Rinehart & Winston. 67–101.

Ryans, D. G. (1961) 'Some relationships between pupil behavior and certain teacher characteristics'. *Journal of educational psychology*, 52, 2, 82–90.

Saadeh, I. Q. (1970) 'Teacher effectiveness or classroom efficiency: a new direction in the evaluation of teaching'. *Journal of teacher education*, 21, 1, 73–91.

Saer, H. (1941) 'A further investigation of pre-college teaching experience and other factors in the teaching success of university students'. *British journal of educational psychology*, 11, 3, 183–96.

Salt, J. (1969) 'Interaction between school and college of education: a case study'. *Education for teaching*, 80, 64–70.

Sand, O. and Bishop, L. J. (eds.) (1966) *The way teaching is*. Washington, D.C.: Association for supervision and curriculum development.

Sandgren, D. L. and Schmidt, L. G. (1956) 'Does teaching practice change attitudes towards teaching?' *Journal of educational research*, 49, 9, 673–80.

Sangster, P. (1969) 'Ending the practice nightmare'. *Times educational supplement*, 2832, p. 11.

Sarason, S. B., Davidson, K. and Blatt, B. (1962) *The preparation of teachers*. New York: Wiley.

Scandura, J. (1970) 'A research basis for teacher education'. *Journal of structural learning*, 2, 3, 1–18.

Schueler, H. and Lesser, G. S. (1967) *Teacher education and the new media*. Washington, D.C.: American Association of Colleges for Teacher Education.

Scott, O. and Brinkley, S. G. (1960) 'Attitude changes of student teachers and the validity of the M.T.A.I.' *Journal of educational psychology*, 51, 2, 76–81.

Selakovich, D. (1961) 'Self-evaluation by student teachers'. *Journal of teacher education*, 12, 2, 225–8.

Shaplin, J. T. (1962) 'Practice in teaching'. In Smith, E. R. (ed.) *Teacher education: a re-appraisal*. New York: Harper. 80–124.

Sharpe, D. M. (1956) 'Professional laboratory experiences'. In Cottrell, D. P. (ed.) *Teacher education for a free people*. Washington, D.C.: American Association of Colleges of Teacher Education. 183–230.

Shaw, K. E. (1962) 'Using the approved schools for teaching practice – an opportunity'. *Education for teaching*, 58, 43–7.

Shipman, M. D. (1965) *Personal and social influences on the work of a teacher training college*. Unpublished Ph.D. thesis, University of London.

Shipman, M. D. (1966) 'The assessment of teaching practice'. *Education for teaching*, 70, 28–31.

Shipman, M. D. (1967a) 'Theory and practice in the education of teachers'. *Educational research*, 9, 3, 208–12.

Shipman, M. D. (1967b) 'Education and college culture'. *British journal of sociology*, 18, 4, 425–34.

Shumsky, A. (1962) 'The personal interpretation of subject matter: a study of student teachers'. *New era*, 43, 8, 151–4.

Simon, A. and Boyer, E. G. (1967) *Mirrors for behavior: an anthology of classroom observation instruments* (6 volumes). Research for Better Schools.

Simpson, R. H. (1966) *Teacher self-evaluation*. New York: Macmillan.

Smith, B. O. (1961) 'A concept of teaching'. In Smith, B. O. and Ennis, R. H. (eds.) *Language and concepts in education*. Chicago: Rand McNally. 86–101.

Smith, B. O. (1963) 'Toward a theory of teaching'. In Bellack, A. A. (ed.) *Theory and research in teaching*. New York: Teachers College Press, Columbia University. 1–10.

Smith, B. O. (1964) 'The need for logic in methods courses'. *Theory into practice*, 3, 1, 5–8.

Smith, B. O., in collaboration with Cohen, S. B. and Perl, A. (1969) *Teachers for the real world*. Washington, D.C.: American Association of Colleges for Teacher Education.

Smith, B. O. and Meux, M. O. (1962) *A study of the logic of teaching*. University of Illinois.

Smith, E. B. (1969) 'Needed: a new order in student teaching that brings joint accountability for professional development'. *Journal of teacher education*, 20, 1, 27–36.

Smith, E. B., Kerber, J. E., Olberg, R. and Protheroe, D. (1968) 'Toward real teaching: a team internship proposal'. *Journal of teacher education*, 19, 1, 7–16.

Snow, R. E. (1967) *Brunswikian approaches to research on teaching*. Stanford Center for Research and Development in Teaching research memorandum No. 4. School of Education, Stanford University (mimeo).

Sorenson, G. (1967) 'What is learned in practice teaching?' *Journal of teacher education*, 18, 2, 173–8.

Sorenson, G. and Halpert, R. (1968) 'Stress in student teaching'. *California journal of educational research*, 19, 1, 28–33.

Southworth, H. C. (1968) 'Teacher education for the middle school: a framework'. *Theory into practice*, 7, 3, 123–8.

Start, K. B. (1966) 'The relation of teaching ability to measures of personality'. *British journal of educational psychology*, 36, 2, 158–65.

Start, K. B. (1967a) *A follow-up of the 1961 group of teachers: a report on one group of teachers in the on-going study of teachers.* Manchester University School of Education.

Start, K. B. (1967b) 'How they got on'. *Times educational supplement*, 2728, p. 355.

Start, K. B. (1967c) *Teachers from different colleges of education.* Manchester University School of Education (mimeo).

Start, K. B. (1967d) *Personality, motivation and educational opinions of final year students in colleges of education.* Register of Research into Higher Education.

Start, K. B. (1968a) 'Rater-ratee personality in the assessment of teacher ability'. *British journal of educational psychology*, 38, 1, 14–20.

Start, K. B. (1968b) 'The frequency with which teachers teach the subject for which they received special training'. *Education for teaching*, 75, 54–8.

Steele, P. M. (1958) *Changes in attitudes amongst training college students towards education in junior schools.* Unpublished M.Ed. thesis, Manchester University.

Stern, G. G. (1963) 'Measuring noncognitive variables in research on teaching'. In Gage, N. L. (ed.) *Handbook of research on teaching.* Chicago: Rand McNally. 398–447.

Stewart, L. H. (1956) 'A study of critical training requirements for teaching success'. *Journal of educational research*, 49, 9, 651–62.

Stolurow, L. M. (1965) 'Model the master teacher or master the teaching model'. In Krumboltz, J. D. (ed.) *Learning and the educational process.* Chicago: Rand McNally. 223–47. Reprinted on pp. 165–71 of this volume.

Stolurow, L. M. and Davis, D. J. (1965) 'Teaching machines and computer based systems'. In Glaser, R. (ed.) *Teaching machines and programmed learning: data and directions.* Washington, D.C.: National Educational Association. 162–212.

Stones, E. (1966) *Task analysis.* School of Education, University of Birmingham (mimeo).

Stones, E. (1970a) 'Evaluation and the colleges'. In Stones, E. (ed.) *Towards evaluation: some thoughts on tests and teacher education.* Occasional publication No. 4, *Educational Review* 13–29.

Stones, E. (1970b) 'Co-operative research in colleges of education'.

In Stones, E., *Towards evaluation: some thoughts on tests and teacher education*. Occasional publication No. 4, *Educational review* 71–5.

Stones, E. (1972) (in collaboration with Anderson, D.) *Educational objectives and the teaching of educational psychology*. London: Methuen.

Stones, E. and Morris, S. (1972) 'The assessment of practical teaching'. *Educational research*, 14, 2. Reprinted on pp. 145–64 of this volume.

Strasser, B. (1967) 'A conceptual model of instruction'. *Journal of teacher education*, 18, 1, 63–74. Reprinted on pp. 172–86 of this volume.

Swineford, E. J. (1964) 'An analysis of teaching improvement suggestions to student teachers'. *Journal of experimental education*, 32, 3, 299–303.

Taba, H. (1965) *Teaching strategies and cognitive functioning in elementary school children*. San Francisco: San Francisco State College.

Taba, H. and Elzey, F. F. (1964) 'Teaching strategies and thought processes'. *Teachers College Record*, 65, 6, 524–34.

Taba, H., Levine, S. and Elzey, F. (1964) *Thinking in elementary school children*. San Francisco: San Francisco State College.

Tansey, P. J. (1969) 'Teacher training in England: a suggestion for integration'. *Educational sciences*, 3, 2, 109–15.

Tansey, P. J. and Unwin, D. (1969) *Simulation and gaming in education*. London: Methuen.

Taylor, P. H. (1962) 'Children's evaluations of the characteristics of the good teacher'. *British journal of educational psychology*, 32, 3, 258–66.

Taylor, P. H. (1971) 'Are colleges of education ready to change?' *Higher education review*, 3, 2, 46–52.

Taylor, P. H., Christie, T. and Platts, C. V. (1970) 'An exploratory study of science teachers' perceptions of effective teaching'. *Educational review*, 23, 1, 19–32.

Taylor, W. (1964) 'The training college principal'. *Sociological review*, 12, 2, 185–201.

Taylor, W. (1965a) 'The university teacher of education'. *Comparative education*, 1, 3, 193–201.

Taylor, W. (1965b) 'Who teaches education?' *Universities quarterly*, 20, 1, 48–55.

Taylor, W. (1966) *The staff of the colleges of education*. University of Oxford Department of Education (mimeo).

Taylor, W. (1969a) *Society and the education of teachers*. London: Faber and Faber.

Taylor, W. (1969b) 'Recent research on the education of teachers'. In Taylor, W. (ed.) Colston papers No. 20 *Towards a policy for the education of teachers*. London: Butterworth. 223–55.

Teaching, No. 1, April 1970. Stanford Center for Research and Development in Teaching.

Thelen, H. D. (1967) *Classroom grouping for teachability*. New York: Wiley.

Thimme-Gowda, T. V. (1948) *A study of the attitudes of teachers in England towards their courses of training*. Unpublished M.A. thesis, University of London.

Thomas, A. M. (1967) 'Studentship and membership: a study of roles in learning'. *Journal of educational thought*, 1, 2, 65–76. (Society for Research into Higher Education abstracts, 2, 2).

Tibble, J. W. (1959) 'Problems in the training of teachers and social workers'. *Sociological review* Monograph No. 2 (University of N. Staffordshire), 47–57.

Tibble, J. W. (1966) 'Practical work training in the education of teachers'. *Education for teaching*, 70, 49–54.

Tibble, J. W. (1967) 'Interprofessional training'. In Craft, M., Raynor, J. and Cohen, L. (eds.) *Linking home and school*. London: Longmans. 219–24.

Travers, R. M. (1962) 'A study of the relationship of psychological research to educational practice'. In Glaser, R. (ed.) *Training, research and education*. University of Pittsburgh Press. 525–58.

Tuckman, B. W. (1968) *The development and evaluation of techniques to assess teacher directiveness*. Paper presented to the annual conference of the American Educational Research Association (mimeo).

Tudhope, W. B. (1942, 1943) 'A study of the training college final teaching mark as a criterion of future success in the teaching profession, I and II'. *British journal of educational psychology*, 12, 3, 167–71; 13, 1, 16–23.

Tuppen, C. J. S. (1966) 'The measurement of teachers' attitudes'. *Educational research*, 8, 2, 142–5.

Turnbull, G. H. (1934) 'The influence of previous teaching experience on results obtained by students in a university department of education'. *British journal of educational psychology*, 4, 1, 1–10.

Turney, C. (1970) 'Microteaching – a promising innovation in teacher education'. *The Australian journal of education*, 14, 2, 123–41.

University of Exeter Institute of Education (1969) *Innovations in teaching practice* (mimeo).

University of Maryland (n.d.) *The teacher education center – a unifying approach to teacher education* (mimeo). Reprinted on pp. 245–51 of this volume.

Unwin, D. and McAleese, W. R. (1971) 'The New University of Ulster microteaching system'. *Times educational supplement*, 2905, pp. 34–5.

Urwin, G. G. (1961) 'Teacher training in schools'. *Universities quarterly*, 15, 271–5.

Van Mondfrans, A. P., Smith, T. H., Feldhusen, J. F. and Stafford, C. W. (1969) *Student attitudes and achievement in an educational psychology course after microteaching*. Paper presented to the annual conference of the American Educational Research Association (mimeo).

Verduin, J. R. (1967) *Conceptual models in teacher education*. Washington, D.C.: American Association of Colleges for Teacher Education.

Vickery, T. R. and Brown, B. B. (1967) *Descriptive profiles of beliefs of teachers*. Paper presented to the annual conference of the American Educational Research Association (mimeo).

Voth, J. A. (1968) *Effect of video tape recording feedback on teaching behavior of student teachers*. Paper presented to the annual conference of the American Educational Research Association (mimeo).

Waddington, M. (1952) *An investigation of the effects of contact with children in play centres or junior clubs in relation to the training of teachers*. Unpublished M.A. thesis, University of London.

Walberg, H. J. (1968) 'Personality role conflict and self-conception in urban teachers'. *The school review*, 76, 1, 41–9.

Walberg, H. J., Metzner, S., Todd, R. M. and Henry, P. M. (1968) 'Effects of tutoring and practice teaching on self-concept and attitudes in education students'. *Journal of teacher education*, 19, 3, 283–91.

Wallen, N. E. and Travers, R. M. W. (1963) 'Analysis and

investigation of teaching methods'. In Gage, N. L. (ed.) *Handbook of research on teaching*. Chicago: Rand McNally. 448–505.

Walton, J. (1962) 'The study and practice of teaching'. In Smith, E. R. (ed.) *Teacher education: a re-appraisal*. New York: Harper & Row. 125–39.

Warburton, F. W., Butcher, H. J. and Forrest, G. M. (1963) 'Predicting student performance in a university department of education'. *British journal of educational psychology*, 33, 1, 68–79.

Ward, B. E. (1970) *A survey of microteaching in N.C.A.T.E accredited secondary education programs*. Stanford Centre for Research and Development in Teaching, Research and Development Memorandum No. 70.

Ward, W. T. (1970) 'Increasing teacher effectiveness through better use of scientific knowledge'. Address to the National Federation for Improvement of Rural Education 1969. Reviewed in *Journal of teacher education*, 21, 3, 449–50.

Washburne, C. and Heil, L. M. (1960) 'What characteristics of teachers affect children's growth?' *School review*, 68, 4, 420–8.

Weaver, D. C. (1970) *The effect of the first year of teaching on teachers' attitudes to the professional element in their initial training course*. Unpublished M.Ed. thesis, Manchester University.

Webb, C., Belt, D. and Baird, H. (1968) *Description of a large-scale microteaching programme*. Brigham Young University (mimeo).

Webb, J. N. and Brown, B. B. (1968) *The effects of training observers of classroom behaviour*. Paper presented to the annual conference of the American Educational Research Association (mimeo).

Webb, W. B. and Nolan, C. Y. (1955) 'Student, supervisor and self-ratings of instructor proficiency'. *Journal of educational psychology*, 46, 1, 42–6.

Westwood, L. J. (1967) 'The role of the teacher I', *Educational research*, 9, 2, 122–34. 'The role of the teacher II', *Educational research*, 10, 1, 21–37.

Wilk, R. E. and Edson, W. H. (1963) 'Predictions and performance: an experimental study of student teachers'. *Journal of teacher education*, 14, 3, 308–17.

Williams, J. D. (1966) 'Method reversion: the problem of sustaining change in teacher behaviour'. *Educational research*, 8, 2, 128–33.

Williams, R. H. (1963) 'Professional studies in teacher training'. *Education for teaching*, 61, 29–33.

Wilson, B. R. (1962) 'The teacher's role – a sociological analysis'. *British journal of sociology*, 13, 1, 15–32.

Wing, H. (1961) 'The theory and practice of education'. *Research and studies* (Leeds), 22, 56–62.

Wiseman, S. and Start, K. B. (1965) 'A follow-up of teachers five years after completing their training'. *British journal of educational psychology*, 35, 3, 342–61.

Withall, J. (1949) 'The development of a technique for the measurement of socio-emotional climate in classrooms'. *Journal of experimental education*, 17, 3, 347–61.

Withall, J. (1951) 'The development of a climate index'. *Journal of educational research*, 45, 2, 93–9.

Woodring, P. (1962) 'The need for a unifying theory of teacher education'. In Smith, E. R. (ed.) *Teacher education: a reappraisal*. New York: Harper & Row. 140–63.

Woodruff, A. D. (1968) 'The rationale' (of an accepted model of learning). *Theory into practice*, 7, 5, 197–202.

Woollard, K. (1970) 'Group teaching as a part of teaching practice'. *Use of English*, 21, 3, 224–7.

Wosley, E. and Smith, R. L. (1962) 'Studio teaching before student teaching'. *Journal of teacher education*, 13, 1, 333–9.

Wragg, E. C. (1970) 'Interaction analysis as a feedback system for student teachers'. *Education for teaching*, 81, 38–47.

Wragg, E. C. (1971) 'The influence of feedback on teachers' performance'. *Educational research*, 13, 3, 218–21.

Wyatt, J. F. (1966) 'The attitude of students to a piece of educational research'. *Education for teaching*, 71, 55–9.

Young, D. A. (1970) *A preliminary report on the effectiveness of colleague supervision on the acquisition of selected teaching behaviours in a microteaching series.* Paper presented to the annual conference of the American Educational Research Association (mimeo).

Young, D. A. and Young, D. B. (1969) *The effectiveness of individually prescribed microteaching training modules on an intern's subsequent classroom performance.* Paper presented to the annual conference of the American Educational Research Association (mimeo).

Young, D. B. (1968) *The effectiveness of self-instruction in teacher education using modelling and video-tape feedback.* Paper presented to the annual conference of the American Educational Research Association (mimeo).

Young, D. B. (1969) *The effectiveness of microteaching and self instructional models in the acquisition of two teaching behaviours simultaneously.* Paper presented to the annual conference of the American Educational Research Association (mimeo).

Author Index

Subject Index

abstraction, in concept formation, 189

activities, division of teaching into, 53–4, 57, 58, 65

adaptability (resourcefulness): opportunity to develop, as objective in teaching practice, 19, 23, 31

administrators, microteaching in training of, 208

algorithms, 169

apprenticeship, teaching practice in terms of, 7, 8, 24, 134

assessment of teaching practice, 26–30, 145–6, 160–3
assessors, 147, 152
criteria used for, 21–2, 29, 147–8, 153–8; students not informed of, 30, 59, 162; unwillingness to divulge, 28, 29, 161
distinctions and failures in, 148, 149, 157–8
evidence used in, 147, 150–1
feedback to students from, 30, 148, 159, 162
form of, 146–7, 147–50
percentage of total mark contributed by, 159–60
possible elimination of, 30, 130, 137

audio tape, recordings on: for interaction analysis, 110, 137, 141; of microteaching, 82, 83, 137; of teaching practice, 50, 68

behavioural science, teaching as a part of, 12–14

Bellack analysis of verbal behaviour, 111–15

Birmingham, study of objectives of teaching practice made at, 21–2

Birmingham Area Training Organization, sets of behavioural objectives obtained by, 126

Brigham Young University, microteaching at, 75, 126–7, 128

Bristol, study of objectives of teaching practice at, 15–21

categorizing, in concept formation, 66, 188–9, 192, 193, 194, 195

certification of students, 46, 133
after course at teacher education centre, 251
rewards different behaviours in different areas, 162

child-centred orientation, 31, 34, 36

cognitive growth, Taba's teaching strategies for, 10, 11, 13, 54, 58, 116, 187–8, 193–7
implications of, for teacher training, 197–9

cognitive memory, 116
questions involving, 201, 203

cognitive skills, 67, 128–9, 228

colleges of education: effects of microteaching on, 93; interchange of ideas and methods between schools and, as objective of teaching practice, 20, 24; relations between schools and, 6, 24, 42, 138; teaching practice in prospectuses of,